The Social Foundations of
Industrial Power

The Social Foundations of Industrial Power

A Comparison of France and Germany

Marc Maurice, François Sellier,
and Jean-Jacques Silvestre

Translated by
Arthur Goldhammer

The MIT Press
Cambridge, Massachusetts
London, England

Library of Congress Cataloging-in-Publication Data
Maurice, Marc.
    The social foundations of industrial power.
    Translation of: Politique d'éducation et organisation industrielle en France et en Allemagne
    Bibliography: p.
    Includes index.
    1. Labor and laboring classes—France.   2. Labor and laboring classes—Germany (West)   3. Wages—France.   4. Wages—Germany (West)   5. Labor mobility—France.   6. Labor mobility—Germany (West)   7. Industrial management—France.   8. Industrial management—Germany (West)   I. Sellier, François.   II. Silvestre, Jean-Jacques.   III. Title.
HD8431.M3813   1986   331'.0943   85-23894
ISBN 0-262-13213-3

Contents

Introduction

With the publication of *Politiques d'éducation et organisation industrielle en France et en Allemagne* in English, American scholars can now readily learn about and use the research and theories of one of the most important and influential schools of sociological research to emerge in recent years. The authors—sociologist Marc Maurice, and economists Jean-Jacques Silvestre and François Sellier—lead the Laboratoire d'économie et de sociologie du travail (LEST) at the University of Aix-en-Provence, France, from which they conducted their research. This book synthesizes years of field research conducted in French and German business firms and gives a new theory of industrial relations exploring the links among society, the enterprise, and labor-management relations.

In the best tradition of comparative empirical research, the authors uncover astonishing contrasts in the work structures of the two nations studied, and they explain the emergence of these differences. Indeed the authors have gone one step further; their unique contribution is in developing a theory of how a nation's major social institutions decisively coordinate and structure work relations. The authors identify three sets of factors—the educational domain, the business organizational domain, and the industrial relations domain—that determine how work and society are inextricably connected. With public policy implications for educational mobility, training, programs, and industrial relations, their conclusions are important for all economists and sociologists.

The methodology of Maurice, Silvestre, and Sellier is an ambitious attempt to link macrosociological phenomena with microsociological or firm-level behavior. Similar to John Dunlop's theory of an industrial relations system, their societal analysis concretizes the links among the different levels of the social system.

The authors gathered data over seven years on large industrial firms with comparable technologies in France and Germany. Surprisingly their data demonstrate important structural differences in firms in the two countries, especially in the structure of skills and wages. Further, they found no evidence that the two nations were converging to resemble a single model of advanced industrial society as John Dunlop, Clark Kerr, and others had hypothesized with their convergence model. Not only was there no homogenization of work relations, but, the authors argue, the differences between the two nations follow distinct systemic patterns. From school to factory, the national specificities they observed were maintained through relations within what they call the societal domain of each country: education, training, and promotion. More than disproving the theory of convergence through a case analysis of the two countries, by placing the development of the employment relation in its national societal and cultural context, they have proposed an entirely new theory for understanding the development of the employment relation.

If historical convergence was disproved, the existence of a national culture was not; instead the authors gave that notion greater specificity. This book contrasts the overall characteristics of work and society in each nation. Each nation has a unique domain, or overarching structure, within which all other elements of the social system can interact while retaining a considerable degree of autonomy. For example, the German pattern of specialized educational tracking results in close attention to technical training and academic degrees suited to the work hierarchy; consequently skill is the principal criterion for promotion and wage determination. More egalitarian, French general education necessitates more on-the-job training; promotion is therefore obtained by seniority and not by degrees. In this system, wages are determined by job position. Although more bureaucratic, the French system is less focused on the performance of industrial firms than is the German system. The authors' conclusions do not bode well for the future competitiveness of French industry. The German insistence on skill-based qualifications results in a more favorable business culture and seems better suited to the competitive international environment. The comparisons in table 1 drawn from later chapters in the book demonstrate how national characteristics fit together to form a unique cultural pattern.

According to the authors' societal approach, relations between employees and employers are not solely determined by technology, as Joan Woodward and others have argued. Instead relations are linked to the position of the enterprise in society. The authors write, "Whereas classical theories of organizational behavior often conceptualized technology and the environment as organizational constraints, the societal approach sees organizational behavior, ... along with technology and the environment, as

Table 1
Comparisons of French and German Work Systems

Category	Germany	France
Ratio of managers to workers	More blue collar	More first line supervisors
Type of education	Professional	General
Firm hierarchy set by	Training, degrees	Rules, a track
Promotion	Degrees and technical criteria	Seniority based
Wages	Linked to production	Related to age
Wage differentials	Lower	Higher than German
Location of conflicts	Industry level	Plant and company
Firm-society relations	Industrial culture	Bureaucratic culture

parts of social relations in a given society." In order to understand the genesis of the differences in relations between work and society in a culture, that relation must be broken down into its three component dimensions: the educational system, or training domain; the organizational relations domain, where power and cooperation are forged in the companies; and the industrial relations domain, which builds channels for the regulation of conflict.

The organization of the book follows logically from the authors' methodology. In chapter 1, the authors demonstrate the practical usefulness of their societal analysis for understanding workplace relations. Using national data and their own survey results, they contrast the skill structures of the French and German work forces. They demonstrate that German workers acquire their skills through apprenticeship programs in which workers, holding many different kinds of jobs and coming from widely different social backgrounds, all participate. By contrast, in France skills are acquired at school and on the job. Access to on-the-job training in France is largely determined by employee seniority within the firm. In presenting the culturally determined contrast, the authors demonstrate that skills are not only determined by technology but are also shaped by the nature of the society in which they are acquired. What they have called the skill domain is defined not only by the manner in which skills are acquired but also by the opportunities for employment and job mobility offered to workers already possessing given skills. The importance of understanding and structuring training opportunities for subsequent worker social mobility is convincingly highlighted for management and public policymakers around the world. With this educational factor—the link of the national educational system to work place hierarchies—the authors explain what determines skill development.

In chapter 2, the skill domain introduced in chapter 1 is related to its concrete setting in the business firm. The authors look at the job hierarchy of the firm—the occupational factor—in order to understand what circumstances affect job mobility and wage differentials. Here again they link their observations of factory relations in the two countries to the larger organization of society. Again the comparison of France and Germany is enlightening. In Germany, where promotion was more likely to be determined by professional degrees and technical competence, wages were more closely linked to productivity and thus varied widely from firm to firm. Yet the wage differentials between white- and blue-collar workers were significantly higher in France than in Germany. These conclusions have important implications for the future of French firms when they are faced with more productive German competitors

The third factor—the organizational factor—is raised in chapter 3. In the area of industrial relations, the critical interface of the business and society is obvious. The authors analyze the way in which conflicts are managed, the classification of individuals, and the role of collective bargaining country by country. Beyond the specific differences in legislation between the two countries, which many observers, including myself, have considered decisive in shaping workplace labor-management relations, the authors once again demonstrate the complementary fit between the social organization and firm-level relations. They show how impossible it is to understand the human resources management of the firms without referring to how skills are developed and how the firm is organized. Training and organization determine not only the relationship of human resources management to technical management but also the relationship of productivity to social relations.

In chapter 4 the authors present a synthesis of their argument, which confirms the power of their approach. They abandon a more traditional comparative case analysis in order to focus on the theoretical implications of their empirical observations, integrating all four constituent elements of the wage labor relation: educational, occupational, organizational, and collective action domains.

In the appendix, the authors situate their conclusions in the European and Anglo-Saxon scholarly literatures of labor economics, organizational sociology, and the sociology of work. Although this essay is not essential reading for a complete appreciation of their research methodology or conclusions, it is thoughtful and important reading for scholars in these fields.

It is difficult to render the richness of the contrast between French and German work relations and hierarchies in yet a third language. Several terms for categories of workers are difficult to translate into English. The authors have used the French terms *emploi ouvrier* and *emploi non-ouvrier* to distinguish between production workers and all types of managerial employees. While the French terms correspond roughly to the American categories of *exempt* and *nonexempt* employees, in this translation we have chosen to use the clearer and less labored terms *blue-collar* and *white-collar employees.* The difficulty of finding a common language in which to report the research confirms many of the national specificities the authors have described.

The rigorous fieldwork and careful theorization in this book is impressive. Like an intricate puzzle, each piece of the authors' argument contributes to an impressive overall image. The final product has received significant attention in European scholarly circles. At last the research of Maurice, Silvestre, and Sellier is accessible to English speakers and can make a major contribution to our understanding of the links between work and society.

Janice McCormick
Graduate School of Business Administration, Harvard University

1   Industrial Skills and Worker Mobility: A Comparative Study of Educational Variables

We shall be taking, and sometimes combining, several different approaches to the comparative study of worker skills and work force stratification in France and Germany. For example, we shall be comparing the two societies in certain key areas, such as the relations that exist between manual and nonmanual workers and the interdependence between industry and the educational system. We shall also present detailed analyses of certain professional groups and look at particular levels of the worker training systems in both countries and at particular firms where we have been able to gather original data. With each approach, we will use two different methods of description. First, we shall use synchronic descriptions, or descriptions of selected characteristics at a given moment in time in order to arrive at an overall picture of the set of variables in question as it exists at that moment. Second, we shall use diachronic descriptions, or descriptions that focus on changes over time in the variables being considered. In particular, we shall be interested in changes due to worker mobility over both the short and long term.

The chapter begins with a description of the principal forms of stratification of the industrial work force, emphasizing particularly the differences between blue-collar and white-collar workers and the way these differences are affected by such factors as firm size and sector of the economy. Next, we provide a more detailed examination of hierarchies that develop within given categories of the work force, such as unskilled workers, skilled workers, production supervisors, office supervisors, and management personnel. Using specific data we offer a comparative analysis of the skill structures in France and Germany. Finally, we look at worker mobility, focusing on individual and collective forms fo mobility which vary in both countries according to work force stratification and specific training systems.

1.1 Stratification of the Industrial Work Force and Structures of Production

Empirically we begin by dividing the industrial work force into two broad groups: blue-collar (b-c) and white-collar (w-c) workers.[1] In both France and Germany we find systematic differences between workers depending on which category they are in. The training, both general and job specific, of b-c workers is different from that of w-c workers, whether evaluated in terms of age or in terms of seniority within the firm. They are paid differently and carry different weight within the working population as a whole. Such differences between different occupational groups exist in all industrialized countries, but the specific nature of these differences depends strongly on the country. In one country there might be little difference between socioprofessional categories in regard to education but considerable difference in regard to job experience, while in another country the differences might relate strongly to social origin and relatively little to experience on the job market. Any international comparison of work force stratification will reveal certain relations between worker attributes and job classifications. It is also known, however, that these relations may vary within any one country depending on the sector of the economy or the size of the firm being looked at.

1.1.1 Training of Blue-Collar and White-Collar Workers

In Germany there are significant differences in training between b-c and w-c workers. Sixty-seven percent of the b-c workers possess at least an apprenticeship certificate.[2] More than 90 percent of w-c workers also have such a certificate. Among the latter, however, we also find higher-level certifications almost never found among the b-c workers: 24.9 percent of nonmanual employees in industry have clerical qualifications, and 45.3 percent have intermediate-level certification in some technical skill.[3] Briefly, then, the stratification of the German work force can be summarized as follows: more than 75 percent of all workers have a basic apprenticeship certificate (67 percent of b-c workers and 90 percent w-c workers). White-collar workers frequently also have some clerical or intermediate technical certification.

In France, the types of professional training that are predominant in Germany are much less widely distributed. The basic apprenticeship certificate, known in France as the Certificat d'aptitude professionnelle (CAP) is held by only 31 percent of all workers. The vast majority (69 percent) have either only general schooling for which they have received no diploma (41 percent) or a diploma from the public schools certifying that they have completed their elementary education (CEP) or the first level of secondary education (BEPC). The figures are comparable for w-c workers. Thus more than 40 percent of the total work force have at best a general, non-work-related diploma, and barely 20 percent of the w-c workers hold any kind of intermediate professional certification.[4]

Table 1.1 summarizes the results for the two countries.

In other words, only a minority of French workers hold a training certificate. There is little tendency to identify the two groups being studied with a specific type of job training. By contrast, German workers are more likely to be identified according to the type of certificate they hold. We can thus define two essential trends, closely related in both systems: the quantitative significance of the holders of job-related training certificates (40 percent of the workers in France and 75 percent in Germany) and the fact that job training is used by both groups (b-c and w-c workers) to establish an identity and a sense of group homogeneity. We have defined this latter phenomenon as the capacity to structure inherent in job-related training. Thus the capacity to structure is strong in Germany, where many holders of training certificates are to be found, and weak in France, where the opposite prevails.

The relationship between a quantitative factor, the number of certificates held, and a qualitative factor, the capacity to structure of job-related training, could be explained as a mechanical consequence of the system of worker training: only a system that turns out large numbers of certified workers can rely on certification for the purpose of differentiation and identification. We believe, however, that the situation is more complex and deserves further attention.[5]

In France the fact that training has a relatively weak influence on placement does not mean that there are no important differences in educational achievement between b-c and w-c workers. Rather the differences we find have to do not with job-related training but with the level of general education. Thus nearly 50 percent of the b-c workers hold no degree, whereas the comparable figure for w-c workers is only 15 percent.[6] Forty percent of w-c workers have a secondary degree, compared with only 5 percent of the b-c workers. The latter difference is probably understated, moreover, because many w-c workers holding primary diplomas (line 1a of table) have also received intermediate to advanced secondary education (but no secondary diploma). The available statistical information does not allow us to be more precise.[7]

Table 1.1
Education and training of industrial workers, 1970

	France				Germany			
	Type of credential held	B-C	W-C	All workers	Type of credential held	B-C	W-C	All workers
1	None	41.0	9.4	30.4 (23.0)a	Hauptschule	32.3	4.2	25.0 (20.9)
1a	CEP	23.5	19.6	22.2 (22.9)				
2	BEPC, baccalaureate	2.2	12.0	5.6 (12.1)	Abitur, Mittle Reife	1.0	4.2	1.1 (3.9)
3	CAP	31.2	27.2		Worker apprenticeship certification	59.0	14.4	45.5 (28.7)
					Clerical apprenticeship certification	1.0	25.4	8.0 22.6
4	Intermediate-level certification	1.9	20.1	8.7 (11.7)	Intermediate-level certification	6.6	45.3	17.7a 20.4b
5	College degree or equivalent	0.0	11.6	3.9 (4.4)	College degree or equivalent	0.0	6.5	2.0 (5.0)
Total		100	100	100 (100)		100	100	100 (100)
	Secondary school diploma	5	40	17 (30)	Secondary school diploma	5	29	12 (37)

Note: Figures in parentheses give the corresponding percentage for workers in the tertiary sector, to which we shall have occasion to refer below.

a. 6.6 percent foreman's certificates, 5.6 percent technicians and graduate engineers.

b. 3.0 percent technicians and graduate engineers.

In Germany, too, there are significant differences in the general educational level of b-c and w-c workers. Twenty-nine percent of w-c workers in industry have attended secondary school, compared with only 5 percent of b-c workers.[8] The fact that the percentage of w-c workers holding secondary degrees is lower in Germany than it is in France is largely a consequence of the fact that, in Germany, there is a less systematic relationship between the holding of such a degree and access to intermediate-level occupational training than there is in France. Thus, for example, 70 percent of all French workers holding intermediate-level technical certification also hold a secondary degree, compared with 30 percent in Germany. Similarly, 32 percent of all w-c workers in Germany with intermediate-level occupational training have never attended secondary school, compared with only 8 percent in France. Thus the social and professional status of the w-c worker in Germany is directly related to professional training, since the workers general education does not go beyond the elementary level. Workers whose position in the hierarchy depends solely on the level they have achieved in the system of professional training are practically nonexistent in France.

Studies of individual firms confirm the general tendencies described. In French chemical and machinery plants, for instance, we found that 53 percent and 63 percent, respectively, of supervisory staff personnel had essentially completed their secondary education.[9] The comparable figures for Germany were 27 percent and 28 percent, respectively. (source: LEST study 2).

In summary, worker placement in Germany is strongly influenced by job-related training and has relatively little to do with general education. In France, the situation is the reverse. General education appears to have an independent effect on social status in France, and workers who hold professional credentials seem to be the ones who have done well in their general schooling.

1.1.2 Professional Experience[10]

On-the-job experience is another area in which b-c workers and w-c workers differ. Long experience is more likely to be associated with w-c status in France than it is in Germany. As a first index of experience, let us consider age. In both countries, the average w-c worker is older than the average b-c worker. The difference is considerably greater in France, however, as shown in table 1.2.

The table reveals a number of patterns. First, industrial workers are

Table 1.2
Age structure of the industrial work force, 1972 study

Index	France			Germany			
	1 B-C	2 W-C	3 W-C/B-C	4 B-C	5 W-C	6 W-C/B-C	7 Col. 3/col. 6
Average age	36.5	40.5	1.11	38.5	40.0	1.4	1.07
Percent of young workers[a]	col. 1/col. 2			col. 4/col. 5			col. 3/col. 6
All industry	29%	22%	1.32	22%	19%	1.16	1.14
Large firms[b]	39%	23%	1.70	24%	18%	1.33	1.28

a. Workers under thirty years of age.
b. Firms employing more than 1000 workers.

younger on the average in France than in Germany. The greatest difference occurs in the b-c worker category. Thus age seems to be relatively unimportant in discriminating between manual and nonmanual workers in Germany, whereas the gap between the two categories is considerably wider in France. The difference between the two countries is at its widest in large firms. Large German firms employ a relatively old work force, particularly in the case of w-c workers, though the gap between b-c and w-c is not very significant. Large French firms, on the other hand, exhibit a much more striking contrast between the age of b-c workers, nearly 40 percent of whom are young, and w-c workers, only 23 percent of whom are classified in the young group.[11]

It is obvious that age is not a direct measure of general professional experience. To be quite rigorous about it, one should no doubt correct the figures to reflect time actually spent on the job market, which itself is influenced by the duration of training, both in general education and job-related instruction. But we have already seen that w-c workers in Germany generally have some professional certification; therefore they have spent more time in training than their French counterparts and for equal age have less professional experience. Taking the training factor into account, then, would most likely increase the disparity between the two countries.

No such bias is to be found if we look at seniority within the firm, and the differences, shown in table 1.3, are even more striking.

The table shows that seniority within the firm is a variable that offers sharper discrimination between b-c and w-c workers than age does. The differences between the two groups are greater than 25 percent in all cases, whereas they were a good deal less than 20 percent when the age variable was used. The seniority variable accentuates the differences between the two countries. This is especially true of the percentage of senior workers versus workers with little seniority; the difference between b-c and w-c workers in France being more than 40 percent greater in France than in Germany. The significance of these differences is qualitative as well.

In Germany, the group of very senior employees is larger than the group of recently recruited employees in both the b-c and w-c categories, though the size of the difference varies. The French situation is strikingly different. Very senior workers make up a large majority of the w-c category, whereas most b-c workers are recent recruits. Thus there is a tendency in France to identify b-c workers as being relatively young and mobile and w-c workers as being older and more highly integrated, just as there was a tendency in Germany for both categories to be identified on the basis of professional training. Doubtless this sort of identification can be interpreted in more

Table 1.3
Worker seniority, 1972 study

	France			Germany			
Index	1 B-C	2 W-C	3 Col. 2/col. 1	4 B-C	5 W-C	6 Col. 5/col. 4	7 Col. 6/col. 3
Average seniority	8.0	12.3	1.54	8.8	11.3	1.28	1.20
Percent of senior workers[b]	28.0	51.0	1.82	36	48	1.33	1.37
Percent of workers with little seniority[b]	38.0	19.0	0.50	33.0	23.0	0.70	1.4[a]

a. This ratio corresponds to column 3 over column 6.

b. Senior workers are those with more than 10 years' seniority; workers with little seniority have fewer than 3 years on the job.

than one way. It seems likely that it has important consequences for the social and professional significance attached in each country to such characteristics as experience and integration into the firm, structure of the labor market, professional training, and so forth.

The importance of seniority in France holds true in all sectors of the economy and in all firms, regardless of size. It is affected by secondary factors of two types, however. First, the differences between Germany and France summarized in table 1.3 are greater in those sectors of the economy in which the work force is, on the average, the most unstable. By contrast, the gap in seniority between b-c and w-c workers, though still wider in France than in Germany, is more or less comparable in those sectors where the average seniority is highest—that is, where the work force is most stable.[12] Furthermore the difference between the two countries is higher for small firms than it is for large firms. This second tendency is consistent with the first, moreover, in that the average seniority in large firms is markedly higher than the average seniority in small firms.

These secondary effects have to do with the sensitivity of the ratios being considered here to the structures of the firms. Two kinds of sensitivity are worthy of note. In Germany the seniority gaps between b-c and w-c workers for a variety of firms are both lower on the average and less widely dispersed around the mean than in France. In France the seniority indicator depends strongly on the structural characteristics of the firm being considered (size of firm, type of product, degree of capital intensity), which affect the relative stability or instability of the work force.[13] In French industries in which the average stability of the work force is greatest, w-c workers are almost entirely exempt from the effects of instability, the brunt of which must be borne by the manual workers. Thus the gap in seniority between b-c and w-c workers is greatest in these industries. When the structural conditions favor the stability of the work force, on the other hand, the position of the b-c workers is strengthened more than that of nonmanual workers, so that the seniority gap is considerably smaller. In Germany the effects of instability on b-c and w-c workers seem to be more independent of other variables, such as type of product and union organization. Thus in Germany the gap in average seniority separating the two categories of the work force probably reflects a norm that German firms feel called upon to try to meet, whereas in France, the gap varies widely from firm to firm, reflecting a certain autonomy in the range of variability of work force stratification within different firms.

The results obtained thus far show that we are looking at two different ways of internally structuring the industrial work force. In each country the differences between manual and nonmanual workers manifest themselves in certain specific characteristics. In Germany the key variable is occupational training; in France it is seniority within the firm, and, less prominently, general educational level and age. These contrasting structures of the industrial work force in the two countries cannot be explained solely in terms of factors internal to French and German industry. Indeed, it can be shown that the results obtained for industrial wage earners extend to other wage earners in the private sector. In doing so we shall again have occasion to stress the importance of training. The first step is to introduce a new variable: wages. We then explain how the average industrial wage in each country is determined and examine the factors that influence deviation from the mean. This will lead to the identification of further differences between b-c and w-c workers revolving around the proportion of w-c workers in the total work force within a given firm or industry.

1.1.3 Specific Aspects of the Industrial Work Force and Laws Governing the Average Wage

The situation in the tertiary sector is comparable to that of the industrial work force.[14] In particular, in Germany the type of occupational training received is still the key variable. In industry in the area of basic- to intermediate-level training (level 3 of table 1.1 and lower-grade certificates of level 4), basic apprenticeship and foreman's certificates predominate: 51.9 percent of all workers have one of these credentials, whereas only 13.7 percent have a clerical training certificate or a technical school diploma. Higher-level technician's diplomas and nonuniversity engineer certificates are held by 5.6 percent of workers, nearly three times the number who have college degrees (2 percent). In the tertiary sector basic- and intermediate-level training is much less specialized. We can distinguish between two almost equal groups: 34.6 percent of workers have a basic apprenticeship or foreman's certificate, whereas 32.1 percent have a basic clerical training certificate or an intermediate technical school degree. The picture is also quite different from that for industry with respect to advanced and university-level training: 5 percent of tertiary sector workers have college diplomas and 3 percent have technician or graduate engineer degrees.

In France there are no major differences between the secondary and tertiary sectors with respect to occupational training. Nearly 60 percent of workers in both sectors have no occupational certification (compared with around 25 percent in Germany). In each sector there are roughly equal proportions of workers holding basic apprenticeship certificates, intermediate-level certification, and college degrees. A significant difference does emerge, however, when comparing the percentage of workers with general secondary schooling (whether or not they have any kind of professional certification). Thirty percent of workers in the tertiary sector have attended secondary school, compared with only seventeen percent in industry.[15] Another characteristic of French industry is the relatively large number of workers who have neither a high school diploma nor a professional certification (30.4 percent compared with 23 percent for the tertiary sector).

Thus a sector-by-sector comparison of the two countries shows that the relationship between type of occupational training and the structural categories used to classify the work force is the same for the tertiary as for the secondary sector in both France and Germany. In Germany, the main structural categories tend to be associated with specific types of professional training.[16] The close correspondence between work force structure and the structure of occupational training suggests that further investigation of the relationship between job category and type of training would be fruitful; a symbiotic relationship seems to be at work. By contrast, in France the work force seems to be structured in a different way. The hierarchy seems to be based largely on the level of general education. In other words, there is no connection between the educational characteristics of workers and the productive structures within which they work.

The rather close relationship in France between job categories and general educational level goes hand in hand with the existence of continuity between different groups of industrial workers. The socialization process is fundamentally *homogeneous* in France: all workers attend the same kinds of schools, and the level attained determines the place of an individual worker in the hierarchy. There are essentially four rungs on the educational ladder (CEP, BEPC, baccalauréat, diploma from a grande école), corresponding to four levels of success in a system of selection conceived, and to some extent actually perceived, as being open, democratic, and unified (even those who fail totally and leave school without any kind of diploma are defined as failures with respect to this system).[17] The result is continuity determined by success within an inherently homogeneous system. The system also produces certain types of discontinuity. Those fortunate enough to make it to a grande école tend to accede to a qualitatively higher status than those who do not, and they are quite likely to obtain the higher-level supervisory positions in industry; those who leave school without a diploma tend to be relegated to unskilled jobs. These discontinu-

Table 1.4
Comparison of average wages in industry and in the private tertiary sector, for male workers, 1974

Index	France	Germany
Average wage in industry/ average wage in private tertiary sector	0.88	0.94
Average wage of w-c workers in industry/ average wage in private tertiary sector	1.25	1.14
Average wage of b-c workers in industry/ average wage in private tertiary sector	0.72	0.86

Sources: 1974 study of wage structure in retail and service sectors and 1972 study of industrial wage structure, updated in 1974.

ities are all the more rigid and powerful in that they are the result of performance in a school system thought of as being independent of the workaday world.

The different import of the firms' structure on work force stratification in the two countries is confirmed by looking at the relative wage levels of the worker categories. Table 1.4 compares the wages of industrial workers with those of workers in the tertiary sector.

Two points are worthy of special note. First, although the comprehensive wage patterns in the two countries are roughly comparable, the ratio of wages in the secondary sector to wages in the tertiary sector is somewhat lower in France than in Germany. Second, this ratio is different for b-c and w-c workers in the secondary sector. For w-c workers, in fact, the relative standing of the two countries is reversed: nonmanual workers in France are paid more relative to tertiary workers than are their counterparts in Germany. Thus the reason why the overall relative wage is lower in France is that b-c industrial workers there receive a much lower wage in comparison to tertiary workers than do b-c industrial workers in Germany. This suggests that we need to take a closer look at the specific aspects of the internal structure of the industrial work force in both countries in order to find out what factors influence the general average wage level for all industry and how wages vary from one industrial sector to another and one echelon of the hierarchy to another.

Two factors play a crucial role in determining the average industrial wage: the wage hierarchy separating b-c and w-c workers and the number of jobs in each category. In both respects w-c workers are much better off in France than in Germany. The wage ratio between b-c and w-c workers is

1.75 in France compared with 1.33 in Germany. Yet the relatively high pay of nonmanual workers in France has not kept the number of such workers down. In France there are 42 w-c for every 100 b-c industrial workers, compared with only 36 per 100 in Germany. Other indicators tend to confirm this general pattern. A French foreman directs the work of 16 workers on average, compared with 25 for a German foreman. For every 100 b-c workers in France, there are 27 nonmanagement administrative and technical staff personnel (not including foremen) but only 22 in Germany. By and large these results are supported by LEST study 1, which was carried out in the 1970s. The study compared seven pairs of firms and revealed an average of 33 w-c workers per 100 b-c workers in the French firms compared with only 20 per 100 b-c workers in the German firms.[18] The typical French shop foreman or shift leader directed the work of 11 workers, compared with 20 workers laboring under his German counterpart. The part of the work force in France that is most bloated by comparison with Germany is that made up of white-collar nonmanagement staff. Study 1 also revealed significant differences in the ratio of b-c to w-c worker wages: 1.7 in France and 1.35 in Germany on the average.

Thus there are proportionately more w-c workers in France than in Germany, and they typically make more money than their German counterparts. The combined effect of these two differences is that the wages of w-c workers account for 41 percent of the total wages bill in France, compared with only 32 percent in Germany. These factors also influence the wage structure within particular industries: the correlation between the average wage in each of the two-digit industries (under the Standard Industrial Code) and the share of w-c worker wages in the total wage bill is 0.86 in France compared with only 0.19 in Germany.[18] The fact that the patterns of wage setting are different in the two countries goes along with the fact that the differences between wage structures in different industries also reveal significant international contrasts. The coefficient of average wage variation for two-digit manufacturing industries is 27.1 percent in France compared with 11.1 percent in Germany. Thus there is much wider variation from the average wage in France than in Germany because of the combined effects of all the tendencies brought to light thus far: greater inequality between b-c and w-c workers, a larger number of more highly paid workers, and wider differences between sectors of the economy in France than in Germany. The coefficient of variation of individual wages for male workers in 1972 was 55 percent in France and only 33 percent in Germany. The effects of the dispersion of individual wages are felt not only in aggregate but also within individual firms. In the firms compared in our first study, the coefficient of variation of individual wages averaged 42 percent compared with 24 percent in Germany.

The significance of quantitative disparities in wages is not the same in the two countries, however. In France these disparities are influenced by the interrelationship of productive structures with specifically French ways of differentiating between b-c and w-c workers (where the wider wage gap is associated with a proportionately larger number of the more highly paid jobs). In Germany these interactive effects are much less important, and the factors that tend to speed up the increase of w-c salaries in the total wage bill are more tightly controlled. The attributes (education and experience) whereby w-c workers are differentiated from b-c workers are not the same in the two countries. In short, we have identified two related types of structural determination. One is based on the attributes and/or capacities of the workers. How are these characteristics produced, and how are they used to discriminate among different types of worker? The other relates to the determination of the relative number of w-c as opposed to b-c tasks and to the setting of relative wage levels. How do firms make these decisions? Our next task is to describe how these two different types of structural determination are related.

1.2 Work Force Hierarchy

How do the various factors differentiating b-c from w-c workers discussed in the preceding section affect stratification and the internal hierarchy of each group? What tentative conclusions can we draw with regard to skill definition and to the way in which the stratification of the work force is legitimated?

1.2.1 Nature and Legitimacy of Worker Skills

A relatively large number of German workers hold some from of professional certification; German workers are thus defined in a positive way as the certified possessors of certain skills. By contrast, b-c workers in France are defined largely in negative terms: they have relatively little experience and only general educational backgrounds, usually at a low level. It is against the background of these general characteristics that the internal hierarchy of each group is established.

Almost all skilled workers in Germany possess some kind of basic apprenticeship certificate; indeed, only 10 percent of German skilled workers are without such certification. Thus certification is a necessary prerequisite for access to the most desirable jobs within the b-c hierarchy, but it is not sufficient: 23 percent of those who hold a basic apprenticeship certificate accept jobs as unskilled workers and therefore lose their rating under German industrial rules.[19] Nevertheless, professional certification of workers is the crucial element in determining the internal structure of the work force; those who have received a certification of some sort are clearly and permanently set off from those whose training has not been sanctioned by a diploma.

This explains why on-the-job experience is of relatively little importance in Germany in distinguishing between skilled and unskilled workers. In fact the relation between age and experience is the reverse of what one might expect. The average unskilled worker is thirty-nine years of age, compared with thirty-eight for the average skilled worker. The difference is even more striking for semiskilled workers, whose average age is forty. Twenty-five percent of skilled workers are under thirty, compared with only 22 percent of semiskilled workers. The highest proportion of workers at the end of their career is also found in the semiskilled category, 33 percent of whom are over forty-five. This reversal of the relationship between job experience and the skill ratings recognized by industry supports the hypothesis that the system of occupational training has a powerful autonomous influence on work force stratification. The proportion of young workers with professional certification is relatively high, and this fact is taken into account by firms when hiring skilled workers. The other side of the coin is that many older workers without basic certification are limited to unskilled jobs and have no hope of using their experience to rise to higher positions. Moreover experience may even have a negative effect when it is coupled with an obsolete certification (where it is up to the firm to determine what training it regards as obsolete).

If we now consider seniority, we find even greater disparities in qualification. Skilled workers have an average of 10 years of seniority, compared with 6 years for unskilled and 7.6 years for semiskilled workers. The percentage of very senior workers (more than 10 years of seniority) among unskilled and semiskilled w-c workers is high, however: 30 percent across all industries. It would appear that seniority has a modest influence on work force stratification based on calculation of a simple index of the sensitivity of wages to seniority: the ratio of the average wage of workers with more than 10 years of seniority to the average wage of workers with less than 2 years of seniority is only 1.12, which is low both in absolute terms and in comparison with France.

The internal hierarchy of the French b-c work force is based on an entirely different system. More than half of skilled workers have no professional certification. Thus skilled status is not equivalent, as in Germany, to the possession of certification, and skilled workers have a wide variety of educational backgrounds: 48 percent have professional certification, 26 percent have a primary or secondary school degree, and 26 percent have no diploma or certification. This last figure is important because 56 percent of unskilled workers have no diploma or certification, a much higher figure than the 26 percent of skilled workers in this category. Having professional certification increases the likelihood that a worker will be classed as skilled—only 20 percent of unskilled workers have a basic apprenticeship certificate—but the vast majority (80 percent) of skilled workers who do have such a certificate also have a primary or secondary school degree. Thus occupational training has a weak and relatively indeterminate influence on skill rating, and this influence cannot be separated from the discriminatory influence exercised by the level reached by the worker within the system of general education.

Since professional qualification does not have a determinate effect on skill rating, there is room for other factors to play a role, in particular *on-the-job experience*. To a large extent unskilled workers in France are characterized by their youth and relatively low seniority; 40 percent are under thirty compared with only 27 percent in Germany. Skilled workers are on the average more than a year older than semiskilled workers in France, whereas the situation in Germany is the reverse. The positive correlation in France between age and skilled status is all the more paradoxical in that, though proportionately fewer French workers in general are professionally certified compared with German workers, the rate of certification drops off rapidly with increasing age: 44 percent of industrial workers under thirty-five have basic occupational certification, compared with only 22 percent of workers over thirty-five.[20] Workers over forty-five, who account for more than a third of all skilled workers, are unlikely to hold professional certification. On the other hand, it is estimated that nearly 25 percent of workers under thirty in unskilled positions do hold professional certification (compared with less than 20 percent in Germany).

We find similar differences between the two countries with respect to the relative seniority of skilled and unskilled workers. The ratio of the average seniority of skilled to unskilled workers is 1.7 in Germany (10 years as against 6 years) but 2.4 in France (10.5 years as against 4.5 years). Whereas nearly one-third of unskilled German workers have more than 10 years seniority, only 20 percent of unskilled French workers are in this position. Finally, using the index of sensitivity of wages to seniority, which yielded a value of 1.12 for Germany, we find that the corresponding figure for France is 1.32. In other words, the variation in average wage in France is nearly three times greater for a comparable difference in seniority. The aggregate tendency reflected in these differences is reproduced in each sector of the economy, as revealed by our investigation of particular firms.

For example, the difference in the value attached to seniority for b-c workers emerges in all of our studies of individual sectors. The sensitivity index, however, varies from sector to sector. We find particularly large gaps between the two countries in the highly concentrated modern sectors of the economy and, in some cases, in sectors using technologies or manufacturing products that are strongly embedded in quite open systems of international trade. This is the case, for example, in the petroleum industry[21] (index of 1.46 for France versus 1.11 for Germany), cement (1.27 versus 1.06), aircraft construction (1.35 versus 1.06), paper (1.39 versus 1.13), and also, less dramatically, electrical equipment, automobiles, and plastics (1.35 versus 1.12 on the average). Similar figures emerge from our studies of pairs of individual firms, especially in our comparison of two steel plants in study 1, where the index was 1.32 for France and 1.05 for Germany. This difference, which pertains to all b-c workers in the firm, holds true if one treats maintenance workers separately from production workers. We find similar differences in the large chemical and machinery firms studied in the second investigation. There the relevant indexes were 1.45 versus 1.22 and 1.30 versus 1.07, respectively.

Thus the observed differences between the two countries are not a consequence of the difference in relative importance of the modern as compared with the traditional sectors of the two economies, nor are they due to types of firm behavior peculiar to protected industries or industries using very specific production techniques.[22] Rather they correspond to significant contrasts between the two systems of work force hierarchy and, beyond that, between the underlying concepts of worker skill on which the legitimacy of the entire hierarchy is based. The influence of seniority is not limited to a single firm or sector of the economy. Seniority also has nation-specific effects on differentiation outside the firm—that is, on the variation in average wage as between firms or sectors of the economy. A statistical analysis carried out in 1966 showed, for example, that the interindustrial variation in average wages for French b-c workers could be explained fairly well by using a multiple correlation model with an average seniority index and a wage-seniority sensitivity index as independent variables.[23] In the German case, by contrast, such a model did not account for the observed variation. More recent research using 1972 statistics confirms this result.[24]

This research shows that intersectoral b-c wage inequalities are comparable in France and Germany for recently recruited workers, but the wage inequalities increase rapidly in France for the manual workers who remain on the job in a particular firm the longest, whereas the effects of seniority in Germany are not as sensitive to the conditions under which job experience is acquired. In Germany, the intersectoral inequalities remain the same regardless of seniority grade. These miscellaneous results yield a fairly satisfactory explanation of why intersectoral inequalities in average b-c worker wages are markedly higher in France than in Germany, resulting in a high degree of structural segmentation of the work force for which there is no equivalent in Germany.[25] The higher age and seniority gaps between skilled and unskilled workers found in France might also seem to provide a fairly good explanation of why the ratio of skilled to unskilled pay is higher threre (1.29) than in Germany (1.15). But these factors do not explain why this ratio is not higher in Germany on account of the more pronounced differences in occupational training of skilled as opposed to unskilled workers found there in comparison to the French case.

These results suggest a rather close connection between the nature of the hierarchy and skill system of the b-c work force in each country and the *intensity of disparities* within the working population in the industrial sector. The structure of the German work force is largely determined by the professional training acquired by German workers. Workers are trained young and acquire the credentials they will carry with them throughout their careers. Work force stratification in Germany is therefore largely autonomous with respect to the labor market, firms, and the industrial job structure. By contrast, work force stratification in France seems to depend on how individual workers fit into and progress, or find a stable position within the industrial structure, this being the relationship that determines the likelihood of layoff and promotion. Training does influence the hierarchy of manual workers but not in the same way as in Germany. In France, general education seems to be just as important a criterion as job-related training; it is impossible to say with certainty that professional credentials have any independent effect on the stratification of the French working class. Training affects status only if it results in the worker's obtaining a favorable position in the heterogeneous job structure so that he may stay with a firm long enough to acquire and make good use of seniority. In France job-related training does not yield generally valid worker credentials to which all firms refer, as it does in Germany. Training-related credentials therefore cannot mitigate the effects of the division of labor within the firm or between branches of industry or sectors of the economy. Instead differences in training are magnified by production-related differences, with the result that disparities between b-c workers are accentuated and the labor market is segmented to a much greater extent in France than in Germany.

1.2.2 Management Skills and White-Collar Hierarchy

The criteria on which the stratification of w-c workers is based are rather different from those relating to b-c workers. For example, w-c workers in France are more likely than b-c workers to have some sort of general educational diploma but no job-related training, and many have a college degree. These two categories are important. In Germany, on the other hand, almost all w-c workers have some kind of professional credential, whereas not all b-c workers do.[26]

1.2.2.1 Distribution of Credentials
Blue-collar workers in Germany fall into two groups: those with professional credentials and those without. By contrast, the w-c category is much more homogeneous. Almost all w-c workers have professional credentials. This becomes quite clear when one compares two groups of w-c workers, each with its own distinctive place in the organization of the firm: clerical workers and supporting staff personnel (called office personnel in the table) on one hand and upper-level staff personnel and managers on the other.[27] Table 1.5 records data for foremen, who are not included in the managers category and who will be, except for a few specific cases, included in the office personnel column. Two points can be made about the data in table 1.5.

The number of workers with no professional training in each of the three categories of the German work force listed in the table is small. It is true that the percentage of untrained managerial personnel is half that of untrained office personnel, but both are under 10 percent. Second, although there is a difference with respect to the level of professional training between managerial and office personnel, *there is no sharp separation of the two categories,* and the same kinds of certification are found in both. For example, about 30 percent of both groups have basic clerical certification. The percentages of those holding intermediate-level professional certification are also comparable: 42.4 percent of management personnel and 46.3 percent of office personnel. Although there is a marked difference between the two groups in regard to the percentage holding college degrees (16.5 percent of the managers compared with 2.3 percent of office personnel),

Table 1.5
Training of white-collar workers, 1970

	France				Germany		
		Category				Category	
	Credential	Management	Office personnel[a]	Foreman[b]	Credential	Management	Office personnel[a]	Foreman[b]
1.	No professional certification	24.6	46.3 (45.5)	49.2 (51.0)	No professional certification	4.5	10.0 (10.0)	10.0 (10.7)
2.					Apprenticeship	36.3		
1.2	No school diploma	2.3	11.6 (10.3)	15.3 (25.4)	2.1 Worker	8.6	17.1 (17.0)	17.0 (78.0)
1.3	CEP	8.3	23.0 (21.0)	29.1 (23.5)	2.2 Office personnel	27.7	23.7 (31.1)	2.5 (0.0)
1.4	BEPC, baccalaureate	14.0	11.7 (14.1)	4.8 (2.1)	3. Intermediate credential	42.4	46.3 (39.0)	70.2 (9.6)
2.	CAP	9.8	32.6 (30.0)	40.0 (45.3)				
3.	Intermediate credential	20.5	19.9 (22.8)	10.9 (3.2)	Nonuniversity professional degrees[c]	78.7	87.1 (87.1)	89.7 (87.6)
	Nonuniversity professional degrees[c]	30.3	52.5 (52.8)	50.9 (48.5)				
4.	University degrees	45.9	1.2 (1.2)	0 (0)	University degrees	16.5	2.3 (3.0)	0.3 (0)

a. Figures in parentheses are for office workers excluding foremen.

b. Figures in parentheses are for skilled workers.

c. Sum of lines 2 and 3.

these are low figures, even for management, compared with the number of people holding diplomas from nonuniversity professional schools (graduate engineers, higher-level technicians, and technical school graduates). The final point to be made is the high level of professional training among foremen. Only 17 percent of the foremen have just a basic apprenticeship certificate, whereas 70 percent have intermediate-level professional certification. Of these 70 percent, 45 percent are certified specifically as foremen, but 25 percent have technical or professional school degrees or are rated as nonuniversity graduate engineers.

Two conclusions may be drawn about the training of w-c workers in Germany: the skill hierarchy is influenced by a gradation of professional certifications, but the vast majority of these certifications are similar in that they sanction nonuniversity professional instruction.

The situation in France is quite different in that there is a much sharper break between management and office personnel. Two points can be made about this discontinuity. First, it has to do with the large number of college-trained people in management. More than 45 percent of all management personnel have a college degree, compared with only 21 percent holding intermediate-level professional certification. In other words, less than half as many managers are professionally certified rather than college trained, and the percentage of professionally certified managers is actually slightly lower than the percentage (22.3 percent) of managers having no more than some sort of secondary degree. Thus the management ranks of French industry are shared predominantly by two groups: those with college degrees (46 percent), among whom graduates of the grandes écoles occupy a very important position, and those who have either no professional certification or basic certification of the CAP type (24.6 percent and 9.8 percent, respectively, for a total of 34.4 percent). This latter group consists of autodidacts: workers who were named to positions of responsibility (of a technical or managerial kind) without possessing a corresponding certification of their skills.[28]

Another difference between the office and management personnel emerges when we look at what percentage of individuals with nonuniversity professional credentials have intermediate-level professional training. In France the figure for management personnel is 68 percent (20.5 percent out of 30.3 percent) compared with only 38 percent for office personnel (19.9 percent out of 52.5 percent). In Germany the corresponding figures are 54 percent and 55 percent, respectively. The point is that management and office personnel are sharply differentiated in France in this regard: the vast majority of managers have either a college degree or professional credentials (frequently of very high level), whereas no distinctive feature characterizes the training of office personnel, among whom we find all sorts of diplomas and basic professional credentials, as well as intermediate professional credentials. But even of those who have intermediate-level credentials, more than a third have not received the baccalaureate degree.

In the French case it is hard to avoid comparing the training of office personnel and that of skilled workers; 46.3 percent of the former and 51 percent of the latter have had no job-related training. The figures for those with basic professional credentials (CAP) are similar: 45.3 percent of the skilled workers and 32.6 percent of the office personnel. It is true that 19.9 percent of office personnel have had intermediate-level professional training, compared with only 3.2 percent of skilled workers. It is worth noting, however, that the figure of 19.9 percent is too low to establish a significant difference between the two groups (the corresponding percentage in Germany is 46.3 percent). Also there is very little difference between the foremen and the skilled workers with regard to the structure of the degrees and certifications they hold. The percentage of those with some professional training is practically the same for both groups (50.9 percent of the foremen and 48.5 percent of the skilled workers). The distribution of degrees follows a similar pattern, with a slightly higher percentage of foremen holding certifications above the CAP: 10.9 percent versus only 3.2 percent of the skilled workers. The difference between this and the German case should be noted: in Germany 70 percent of the foremen have professional certification above the apprentice level, as do 42 percent of other office personnel, compared with about 6 percent of the skilled workers.[29]

What we find once again in France is that the two groups are distinguished by general educational achievement: 33.5 percent of skilled workers have no general diploma, compared with only 21.8 percent of the foremen and 16.8 percent of other w-c workers (these figures take into account the percentages of workers without any diploma—category 1.2 in table 1.5— as well as those who have no general diploma but do have professional certification—parts of categories 2 and 3 in tab.e 1.5).

The fact that in France the training of skilled workers is comparable to that of office personnel is related to another point: the social origins of these two groups of workers. Table 1.6 will enable us to compare the situations in France and Germany in the early 1970s.

The data show that the gap between skilled workers and workers in the other two categories, as measured by the percentage of workers who come from non–b-c families, is considerably wider in Germany than in France. The same is true when we look at the proportion of workers who come

Table 1.6
Social origins of skilled workers, foremen, and office personnel (categories in 1970)

Social origin	France			Germany		
	Skilled	Foremen	Office personnel[a]	Skilled	Foremen	Office personnel[a]
B-C workers	46.7	41.3	31.8	61.2	45.0	35.4
W-C workers	30.0	39.0	53.0	28.4	46.5	57.5
Nonwage workers[b]	23.3	19.7	15.2	10.4	8.5	8.1
Total	100	100	100	100	100	100

a. Office personnel without foremen. According to our previous classification, managers are not included.

b. Including farmers.

from b-c families: there is a 16 percent difference in Germany between skilled workers and foremen (61.2 percent versus 45 percent) and a 26 percent difference between skilled workers and office personnel. The corresponding figures for France are 5.5 percent and 14.9 percent.

1.2.2.2 Job Experience and Skills
Differences between the two countries with regard to the link between distribution of diplomas and certificates and the hierarchy of w-c jobs will naturally have an impact on the influence of other factors, such as job experience and seniority within a given firm. W-c workers benefited much more than b-c workers from working for firms capable of stabilizing their labor force in France, whereas in Germany the benefits of stability were much more equitably distributed. We are now in a position to take a more detailed look at the situation in France in order to show how the closer tie that exists is related to the continuities and discontinuities in the pattern of training described in the previous section. We find employees with high seniority among two groups of w-c workers: upper-level and supervisory office personnel and management personnel. The supervisory staff personnel fill both technical and administrative positions.[30] Their principal qualification consists of skills acquired with a particular firm. Since so many management personnel are college educated, it is unlikely that these supervisors will ever be promoted into the ranks of management. By contrast,

Table 1.7
Relative seniority of upper-level and supervisory office personnel value of indicator
calculated (x)

| Reference category | Firms in study 2 | | | | 1972 industry study | |
| | Chemicals | | Metals | | | |
	France	Germany	France	Germany	France	Germany
All workers	1.40	1.25	1.27	0.98	1.30	1.00
Managers	1.07	0.88	1.08	0.87	1.04	0.78
Foremen	0.85	0.70	0.86	0.62	0.75	0.57
Unskilled workers	2.95	1.74	2.12	1.17	2.20	1.38

Note: The index (x) is calculated as follows: x = average seniority of top supervisory
personnel/average seniority of workers in the reference category.

the relative, seniority of German supervisory staff is not so pronounced as
that of French supervisors. Table 1.7 summarizes these results.

On this point the aggregate figures are remarkably similar to the figures
obtained for individual firms. Three items are worthy of special note. First,
upper-level and supervisory office personnel have considerably more seniority than managers in France, whereas the situation in Germany is the
reverse. Second, one can draw a parallel in the French case between the
situation of this category of office personnel staff and that of the formen, in
that the skills and hence the positions of both are closely related to their
strong integration within a particular firm. Finally, there are marked differences between the two countries with respect to the relative seniority of
upper-level and supervisory office personnel as compared with unskilled
workers; these large differences are due to the convergent effects of several
of the tendencies already discussed.

Seniority exerts another kind of influence in French firms within the
group of management personnel. Many managers have college degrees,
which means that their qualifications are fairly general.[31] The value of these
qualifications to the firm therefore depends heavily on their work experience and seniority within the company. Table 1.8 records differences in
this regard between France and Germany, using the same index of the
value placed on seniority as was used in previously.

These figures show two important differences between the two countries. First, they point to an opposition between the process of stratification

Table 1.8
Indexes of value attached to seniority for managers, office personnel, and white-collar workers, all industries, 1972

Index	France	Germany
Average seniority of top management/average seniority of other management personnel[a]	1.38	1.12
Average salary of managers with more than 20 years' seniority/ average salary of managers with less than two years' seniority	1.29	1.04
Average salary of office personnel with more than 20 years' seniority/average salary of office personnel with less than 2 years' seniority	1.41	1.03
Average pay of w-c workers with more than 20 years' seniority/ average pay of w-c workers with less than 2 years' seniority	1.37	1.14

a. Here the top management category corresponds to category 1 of the European Common Market study that we are using "Other management" corresponds to category 2; "management" includes all of categories 1 and 2; "upper-level and supervisory office personnel" category 3, and "office personnel" categories 3 and 4 combined. White-collar workers comprise all of categories 1 through 5 (foremen).

within the managerial category and the office personnel category (technical and administrative positions). In France seniority is an important status criterion: the seniority indexes are 1.29 and 1.4, respectively. In Germany seniority has almost no effect on this status indicator (the same indexes for Germany are 1.04 and 1.03, respectively). Second, where seniority does play a role in Germany is in differentiating management from office personnel. When all w-c workers are considered as a group, the gap between the two countries, measured by the same index, is considerably smaller (1.27 for France compared with 1.14 for Germany).

It should be noted, however, that the results in the German case cannot be interpreted, as in the French case, as showing the importance of special skills acquired within the firm. The majority of w-c workers in Germany have professional training whose general value is widely recognized. Because of this generally accepted training, these workers can move readily from one firm to another, and their skill certifications largely determine their place within the hierarchy of w-c workers. Thus in Germany the effects of seniority relate to the homogeneous nature of the qualifications of w-c workers and to the absence of any sharp discontinuity in qualification between office and management personnel because of the extensive use of nonacademic professional certification to cover a wide range of job statuses. In France, by contrast, where there are few intermediate-level certifications (between the level of the college diploma and that of the certification of a skilled worker), the situation encourages the development of isolated groups with different special skills—isolated both by being associated with particular firms and by being associated with particular productive or administrative tasks.

The heterogeneous nature of the w-c work force in France results in wide disparities in pay. The ratio of the average manager's pay to the average office employee's pay is 1.8 in France and 1.34 in Germany. It should be noted, however, that whereas office employees in France are by and large paid much less than managers, they nevertheless make much more than b-c workers; the ratio between the pay of these two groups is 1.53 in France compared with 1.24 in Germany.[32] It is in the office personnel category that the nonmanual work force in France is most bloated in comparison with that of Germany. The proportion of the work force occupying management positions is comparable in the two countries (8.5 percent), whereas other types of w-c worker account for 21 percent of the French work force but for only 17 percent of the German work force.

1.3 Worker Mobility and Work Force Stratification

In the first two sections of this chapter, we have described certain contrasts between France and Germany that may at first sight appear to be the result of different choices in the organization of the educational system or of industrial firms. Briefly summarized, the central differences are these. In Germany the system of training is organized around professional training, whereas general education is more important in France. In addition, firms seem to rely on different criteria for skill and job classification. Depending on the country, a greater or lesser importance is attached to experience or to education, as is also the case within each country depending on the type of job or category of worker. Finally, the influence of these various factors varies widely depending on the sector of the economy or the size of the firm being looked at, beyond differences between the two countries in aggregate.

There are always two aspects to the kinds of worker attributes that we have placed at the center of our analysis. At a given time these characteristics may be regarded as given as used to distinguish different groups of workers. Thus we may distinguish between workers with respect to type of education, level of education, social background, or on-the-job experience, as well as type of job and nature of the job environment, in both economic and noneconomic respects. But these distinctive features do not exhaustively describe a group of workers. Each group has a history: How was it produced over time? In one respect the history of a group of workers is just a mechanical record of changes in its nature and composition: such and such an individual improves his training from level A to level B; the average seniority of the group rises or falls between time t and time t_1; a particular type of bonus is extended from one industrial situation to another; and so on.

But this is not the only kind of history that a group has. These kinds of changes affect the individual and collective trajectories of the group and its members. For the purpose of making international comparisons, there is no special need to take account of such trajectories, so we shall defer more extensive discussion of this important point until later, when we discuss the theory that we have been led by our empirical work to formulate. But some enlargement of our empirical framework does seem called for at the present comparative stage of our work. If we were to limit our comparisons to the kinds of observations made in the previous two sections, we would inevitably be taking one of two equally unsatisfactory attitudes toward certain trends of special significance that have emerged from our work. Either we would work from the observed differences to construct an explanation in terms of a ready-made analytical framework—for example, by looking at worker attributes as accumulated human capital invested in particular work situations—or we would focus exclusively on the social and cultural determinants of the observed differences, which would mean neglecting the conditions under which those differences were produced and imparting a particular slant to the results obtained. This would be the case, for example, if we regarded the difference in educational choices as resulting solely from cultural or historical differences between the two nations. In either case, the comparative data gathered thus far would merely be used as a pretext for a type of investigation in which the differences actually observed would not play a central role. In one case we would be relying on a predetermined model; in the other we would be assuming the existence of national differentia of an institutional, cultural, or historical order.

We can sidestep this criticism, however, by focusing further research on the two specific types of work force stratification that emerge from our preliminary results and by expanding our collection of data in what we might call an endogenous manner, suggested by the structural differences and interdependencies brought to light in the previous two sections. We propose to expand our comparison to take systematic account of the educational, professional, and social mobility of workers. It is on these mobilities that the various distinguishing characteristics of the groups studied thus far are based, with each country exhibiting its own specific pattern. We are thus exploring a new dimension of comparative research, worker mobility. By this we mean both individual and collective forms of mobility. We shall look first at mobility within the system of education and training and second at mobility between jobs. We then conclude with a preliminary analysis of the interrelationships between the different kinds of mobility that we find and raise questions to be answered by subsequent research.

1.3.1 The Tracking System and Educational Stratification

The first two sections of this chapter contain information pertaining to the educational background of the working population in France and Germany in the early 1970s. To understand the origins of the distribution of qualifications, we must look at how the educational systems of the two countries were structured earlier and what kind of guidance was offered to pupils in the choice of courses and careers. The period we are interested in includes the years following World War II and even, for some workers, extends back into the post–World War I era. We cannot undertake a systematic study of so long a period here and therefore will concentrate on the period 1950–1976. We are assuming that we can determine in this way the general tendencies of the two educational systems, leaving aside the considerable changes made not only in the more distant past but also in very recent years (1970–1980).

In Germany the child's education begins with elementary school (Grundschule), which lasts four years and which the average pupil leaves at age ten. At this point students enter one of three educational tracks: track 1, the primary (or basic) school, or Hauptschule; track 2, the middle school, or Realschule; or track 3, the Gymnasium. Students normally spend five or six years in either of the first two tracks and ten years in the third. In France elementary school lasts for five years. Thus the average student is eleven when he enters one of the three possible subsequent tracks: track 1, a direct extension of elementary school, which we shall call the advanced elementary track, from which students normally graduate at age fourteen; track 2, the so-called first cycle of secondary school or its equivalent, the cours complémentaires (secondary modern school); and track 3, which normally leads to the examination for the baccalaureate after seven years of study.

This description raises a problem that we have encountered before. The problem is one of definitions: thus we have had occasion to compare groups of workers, such as b-c and w-c workers or skilled workers and management personnel, in two different countries because the groups were identified by the same name, but we found that these groups were actually made up of workers with quite different characteristics and shaped, internally and externally, by sharply contrasted structural criteria. The same problem crops up when we attempt to analyze the different tracks in the two educational systems. It is true that we find comparable orientations of the similarly numbered tracks in the two countries, at least up to a certain point. But each orientation makes sense only in relation to the underlying realities in each country. It is therefore misleading to regard the tracks as comparable components in comparing the educational structures of the two countries. At this stage of the analysis, we cannot get around this difficultly, but it would be wrong to pass over it without explicit mention of our awareness of the problem. We shall be returning to this methodological problem at several points in the course of our argument and hope to work toward resolving it as we gain greater clarity about the theoretical underpinnings of our approach.[33]

France and Germany differ in the way in which students are assigned to one of the three tracks upon completing elementary school. The vast majority of German students go into track 1 (Hauptschule). Using data available for various age groups, it is possible to estimate that during the period 1950–1970 from 70 to 85 percent of the students between the ages of ten and thirteen were in the Hauptschule (the larger figure applies to the beginning of the period in question, the smaller to the end). Results consistent with these figures are obtained if we count up the number of male workers active in the early 1970s who received a track 1 education. In 1970 83 percent of male workers of all ages fell into this category.

Because so many students go into the primary school, or Hauptschule, the other two tracks are quite selective. In the early 1950s only 10 percent of students aged ten to eleven entered the Gymnasium (track 3), and by 1959 this figure had risen to only 15 percent. Track 2 did not come into being until 1950. In the immediate postwar years the only alternative was between the Hauptschule and the Gymnasium. Track 2 has developed rapidly since 1950, but as late as 1960 only 9 percent of the students leaving elementary school were choosing this course.

For the period in question a good basis of comparison exists for the French and German cases.[34] 1962 nearly 55 percent of students between the ages of ten and twelve were following either track 2 or track 3 (27 percent in track 2 and 28 percent in track 3). Only 45 percent were continuing their primary education (track 1) rather than choosing one of the secondary options. This contrasts with the 75 percent of young Germans in primary school.

These differences are reflected in figures characterizing the active work force at various times. Only 17 percent of male German workers in 1970 had received a secondary education, for example, compared with 36 percent of male workers in France.

The differences between the two countries, already considerable, are accentuated further when we look at how the two secondary tracks are related. In Germany the short and long secondary tracks, tracks 2 and 3, respectively, are completely separate. In theory it is possible to transfer from the senior level of the middle school, or Realschule, to the senior level of the Gymnasium. Such transfers rarely occur, however: only 1 percent of the pupils in track 2 switch to track 3. By contrast, in France pupils in track 2 are far less likely than pupils in track 3 to enter a prebaccalaureate class (classe terminale) and take the baccaulaureate examination. Still, 40 percent of the pupils in track 2 do take the baccalaureate, compared with 80 percent of those in track 3, so that the possibility of making the switch is far greater than in Germany. In France, then, secondary education (tracks 2 and 3) is highly structured and yet relatively open, allowing for continuing competition up to the final years before the baccalaureate among a majority of the 55 percent of any age group who choose one of the secondary tracks.[35] This contrasts sharply with the situation in Germany, where only a small minority of pupils are accepted for secondary education and where the two secondary tracks are strictly separate and do not allow for student mobility.

By now it should be clear how we have begun to describe the two educational structures and to measure the degree of student mobility in each: we look first at the number of students entering each track and then at the possibility of transferring from one track to another. We next turn to a second set of educational indexes, intended to relate student mobility, types of selection, and the socioprofessional background of the students.

If we restrict attention to tracks 1 and 3, the German case is fairly easy to describe. Track 3 is virtually closed to the children of parents engaged in manual trades (industrial and agricultural workers). At most 5 percent of the pupils in this category enter the Gymnasium, and fewer than 2 percent actually finish. This stringent selectivity also has an impact on other social strata and not just on manual workers. Many children of industrial employers, retail storekeepers, office and supervisory personnel, and even managers in the private sector do not make it to the Gymnasium. The only category to send large numbers of its children into track 3 is that of intermediate- to higher-level civil servants. Children of parents in this group occupy a disproportionate share of Gymnasium places. Because of the high academic and social selectivity of the Gymnasium, there are few failures, and the number of students finishing secondary school but not receiving a baccalaureate degree is reduced to a bare minimum.

If the Gymnasium is highly selective academically and socially, the Hauptschule is quite open. Of course, the children of workers and farmers have virtually no other choice. But at the same time 60 percent of the children of office personnel (of all levels) and of low- to medium-level civil servants attend the Hauptschule to prepare for their future schooling and careers. Thus all strata of society are included in the Hauptschule, where the degree of competition and rate of failure are moderate, though not for the same reason as in the case of the Gymnasium. Since tracks 1 and 3 account for the education of most German students, the system has clearly segregative effects but at the same time minimizes the degree of competition among students of widely different social status and academic level. This in turn reduces the degree to which a system of elimination by failure must be relied upon.

The relations between social class and educational tracking in France are quite different. Tracks 2 and 3 constitute a relatively uniform program of secondary education for more than half the pupils between the ages of ten and thirteen. Because of the openness of the system of secondary schooling in France, a high proportion of children of the middle to upper strata of society are accepted; as many as 95 percent of the children of upper management personnel and professionals enter track 2 or 3. But at the same time nearly 50 percent of working-class children aged twelve to thirteen also enter track 2 or 3, compared with only 20 percent in Germany. During the 1960s, working-class children accounted for 40 percent of those entering the lycées (track 3), compared with only 15 percent of those entering the Gymnasium (though the proportion of workers in the active population is higher in Germany than in France).

The openness of secondary education in France to children of all social strata applies mainly to the first few years after elementary school and decreases considerably as pupils move toward the baccalaureate. The probability of a child of an agricultural or industrial worker obtaining the baccalaureate is only 11 percent, compared with 60 percent for a child of an upper-level manager. This wide disparity of outcomes does not alter the fact that many children of all social classes attend secondary school to a relatively advanced stage. Even if they do not obtain a diploma, they take part in an academic and social competition from which the majority emerge as losers. This combination of initial openness and final selectivity accounts for the large number of washouts at various levels of French secondary education. In Germany only 10 percent of students who reach the second cycle of secondary school do not obtain the baccalaureate, whereas the figure for France is 45 percent. In both countries a high proportion of the washouts come from the lower and middle strata of society. But these classes are involved to a much greater degree in France in a system of socialization that relies on high-level instruction followed by selection based on failure.

Track 1 in France resembles track 3 in Germany in that it is academically and socially quite uniform, but the significance of this uniformity is quite different. Eighty percent of the pupils in track 1 in France are children of agricultural or industrial workers. Children of higher-level managers account for only 2.3 percent of the total, and children of nonmanual workers account for only 14 percent. Socially track 1 can be defined by the fact that only 6 percent of the children of higher-level managers and only 24 percent of nonmanual workers enter it. The latter figure is particularly significant since 60 percent of the children of nonmanual workers in Germany aged twelve to thirteen enter track 1.

These results show that Germany and France have two markedly different systems of academic and social competition and selection. Rather than take a narrowly statistical approach, we shall try in the remainder of this book to take a more comprehensive view and to integrate these differences into a broad theoretical schema. At this point, however, we must broach an important question of methodology: the statistical differences that have turned up thus far can be analyzed in two different ways. One might argue, first, that these differences show how each social class stands with respect to the system of selection, particularly by referring to the probability of a child from a given class succeeding in each track. One could then argue that statistical differences between the two countries tell us about the size of the gaps between different social groups, the nature of competition among these groups for access to educational capital, and the results of that competition. One might equally well argue, however, that these same statistical differences tell us about the social composition of the various tracks in the educational system, the nature of academic, social, and cultural competition in the schools, and individual and collective mobility between tracks. By this view the gaps between the two countries would tell us about the different ways in which the tracks themselves *come to be structured* as avenues of social mobility and of access to various kinds of capabilities. In this case, the focus of research would be on class relations *outside* the educational system rather than on the relation of each class *to* the educational system.

With a preliminary analysis of the statistics in hand, we are ready to

move toward a more qualitative analysis and to interpret national differences in terms of combinations of variables generally defined as independent.

A similar problem arises when one attempts to look at how the systems
of professional training in the two countries are constituted and how
students are selected to receive various kinds of training. These systems
appear at first to be extensions of the general elementary and secondary
educational systems.

In the German case there is a close relationship between the Hauptschule
and the basic occupational training course that leads to certification as a
skilled worker or qualified office employee. This course combines classroom
work (compulsory for all pupils up to the age of eighteen) one day a week
with on-the-job training for pupils able to obtain a two to three year
contract with an industrial or commercial firm or craft shop.[36] During the
1960s 70 percent of pupils graduating from the Hauptschule obtained such
contracts (60 percent were as apprentice b-c workers and 10 percent as
apprentice office workers). Only 23 percent[37] of Hauptschule graduates
failed to obtain an apprenticeship contract and left the educational system
without a full course of occupational training.[38] The close connection
between the Hauptschule and apprenticeship is reflected in the fact that 92
percent of those in worker apprenticeship programs attended the Hauptschule (track 1), whereas only 8 percent received secondary education (track
2 or 3). The connection is not as close for office personnel apprenticeships,
where 40 percent of the young apprentices come from secondary schools.

The analysis of apprenticeship in Germany cannot, however, be limited
to its function as an occupational extension of primary schooling, for
apprenticeship is not only an element of the educational system but also an
integral part of the world of small business, retail trade, and industry. We
cannot give a detailed analysis of the institutional structure, economic
function, and educational methods of German apprenticeship and must
therefore limit ourselves to indicating some of what seem to us the most
important features of the system.[39]

While a majority of worker apprenticeships were in craft shops, 40
percent of apprenticeship certificates were awarded by large industrial
firms.[40] The average duration of apprenticeship is three years, generally
spent in a special shop under the guidance of certified foremen rather than
in a production shop, at least in large firms. The training of large numbers
of apprentices is very costly, particularly for firms that train more apprentices than they need to supply their short- and long-term requirements for
skilled workers, as is the case with many middle-sized companies. Finally,
although apprenticeship is organized and administered in a highly decen-

tralized way, it is nevertheless subject to strict regulation by both government (state and national) and by craft councils and chambers of commerce and industry.

Apprenticeship in Germany is a dynamic institution and one whose autonomy is widely recognized, as is attested by two sorts of figures. During the 1960s, 68 percent of the pupils in a given age group went into an apprenticeship program (blue collar or office worker), and 53 percent were certified as skilled workers. Seventy-two percent of the pupils who entered secondary education but did not go on to college went into an apprenticeship program: 42 percent into office personnel programs and 30 percent into b-c programs. Thus apprenticeship is not limited to pupils who did not make it to secondary school. It is also taken up by many youngsters who not only attended secondary school but also achieved some success as students (60 percent of those who receive the Abitur but do not go on to college complement their general education with on-the-job apprenticeship).

The relationship between general education and occupational training is very different in France. Track 1 is much less important in France than in Germany, and insofar as track 1 tends to feed in to occupational training programs, this partly explains why fewer youngsters follow such a path in France. This partial explanation is inadequate for several reasons, however. First, only 29 percent of the students in track 1 in France take up occupational training, compared with 70 percent in Germany. The remaining 71 percent either quit school and gradually work their way into the job market (61 percent) or transfer into track 2 or 3 (10 percent). Thus occupational training *is less favored than direct job seeking* by pupils who have completed track 1. This preference is even more pronounced among pupils who attend secondary school. Only 25 percent of those in track 2 take up occupational training when they reach age fifteen to sixteen. For track 3 the figure is even less: 11 percent. Leaving aside those youngsters who are successful in secondary school and who are therefore in a position to entertain hopes of receiving the baccalaureate (about one-third of those who enter tracks 2 and 3), a large majority of the remaining students choose either to repeat a year, common in the secondary schools, or go to work.[41] Adding up the various figures pertaining to the relation between general schooling and the first level of occupational training, we find that only 18 percent of youths aged to fifteen to sixteen took up occupational training during the 1960s.

The French student's decision whether to continue general schooling, get a job, or take up occupational training cannot be analyzed, as in the case of the German student, simply in terms of the relationships among the various tracks or in terms of the effect that following a given track has on a student's plans because of the content of the teaching or the behavior of the teachers. Account must also be taken of the special characteristics and structure of occupational training itself. In France the system of training for basic occupational certification (CAP) is divided into two quite different parts. About 50 percent of the certificates are awarded after three years of full-time study at a technical high school (collège d'enseignement technique, or CET). The other 50 percent are obtained after a period of on-the-job training with a firm.

One basic difference between the French and German systems is that in France large firms do not play a direct role in providing basic occupational training, which is acquired either in public or private schools or on the job, 98 percent of the time in small craft shops. Thus basic occupational training, particularly in the case of industrial workers, is completely cut off from the world of big business and has not benefited either from the prestige of the large firms or from the dynamism that might have been imparted to on-the-job training programs by the industrial expansion of the 1960s.[42] While it is true that a few large companies have set up programs to train their workers, these programs have not been integrated into national or regional efforts to train new workers. Rather they have been designed to train workers to fill the needs of a particular firm: to fill certain jobs and to meet the requirements of particular organizations. We shall have more to say later about the contrast between company-centered job training in France and industry-wide training in Germany.[43]

The differences between the two systems are not only institutional. They also have to do with the contrasting ways in which homogeneity is combined with heterogeneity. In the French system there is a great deal of social homogeneity: more than half of all workers holding the CAP are children of farmers or unskilled industrial workers. Practically none are children of fathers in intellectual professions. There is not much difference in the social background of those with low-level educational credentials and those with basic occupational certification: for example, 50 percent of those with a CEP (elementary school certificate) are children of farmers or unskilled workers, compared with 48.5 percent of those with a CAP (basic apprenticeship certificate). Thus acceptance in a job-training program does not constitute social selection but is rather one path that may be chosen by students whose social and academic position has already been determined as inferior.

This social homogeneity goes along with certain kinds of heterogeneity. We have already pointed out the institutional heterogeneity of the French system (full-time technical schools, apprenticeship under contract, and apprenticeship without contract). Another source of heterogeneity is the existence of a large number of specialized forms of training, to which widely varying values are attached by families and employers. Finally, students working for their CAP have quite heterogeneous educational backgrounds: a majority (55 percent) come from track 1, but a large minority (45 percent) are pupils eliminated from one of the secondary tracks (2 or 3).[44] Thus basic occupational training in France suffers from a social homogeneity whose connotations are negative, disparity of institutional support, and divergence in the educational background of entering trainees. These factors in large part account for the failure of the system to respond to social change or to develop new methods of teaching, and they tend to limit its social and educational importance. In turn the system's unresponsiveness tends to discourage trainees and reduce the effectiveness of teaching. Many drop out, and the failure rate on examinations is extremely high. The total attrition rate (ratio of number of trainees not awarded certificates to total number entering training) is nearly 60 percent in France compared with 10 percent in Germany.

Basic professional training in Germany combines these diverse characteristics in a very different way. Access to apprenticeship is more socially selective than in France. Only 28 percent of German apprentices are children of farmers or unskilled industrial workers (compared with 48 percent in France). This same group accounts for 59 percent of the pupils who leave the Hauptschule without an apprenticeship contract. Thus there is genuine social competition in Germany over access to apprenticeship programs. This competition eliminates most children from social groups whose position with regard to industry is marginal and favors the children of skilled employees (including skilled b-c workers, technicians, foremen, and engineers). There is also competition within the group of apprentices, whose social composition is a fairly accurate reflection of the working population minus the highest and lowest groups (senior civil servants and unskilled laborers). Competition is further encouraged by the diversity of sites at which apprenticeship programs are offered, ranging from small craft shops to specialized shops in large industrial plants equipped with most modern technology.

Along with this diversity, however, the system of apprenticeship *has an underlying unity*. Among the factors contributing to this unity is the fact that 92 percent of apprentice workers are graduates of the Hauptschule (track 1). Furthermore the same basic teaching principles are widely accepted. Teaching is subject to effective institutional supervision and is carried out largely by qualified foremen. The teaching combines classroom and on-the-job experience and emphasizes learning under actual production conditions or at least in close proximity to actual production. Hence apprenticeship involves not so much instruction in particular kinds of know-how as training for work in industry. Although apprenticeship programs are offered in 500 different crafts, 70 percent of all apprentices are concentrated in just 36 of these, which reinforces the point that the training is conceived as generalized preparation for skilled industrial work.

These differences between the systems of basic occupational training in France and Germany become crucial when we consider intermediate-level occupational training, the importance of which varies considerably between France and Germany.[45] There has been much proliferation of intermediate certifications in Germany because of the dynamism of the basic apprenticeship program. In 1970 28 percent of those who acquired a basic apprenticeship certificate went on to obtain intermediate-level certification as well. The importance of worker apprenticeship programs as a means of access to higher qualification is attested by the fact that 63 percent of those certified as graduate engineers, 73 percent of those certified as technicians, and 100 percent of those certified as foremen had first qualified as skilled workers. The link between the intermediate and basic programs is not a mere mechanical consequence of the number of apprentices. Rather, it has to do with the social diversity intrinsic to apprenticeship in Germany, a diversity that is crucial to the dynamism of the system. Access to the higher levels of training and qualification is determined by the competition that this diversity promotes. The probability that the holder of a basic apprenticeship certificate will go on to obtain credentials as a technician or graduate engineer ranges from 25 percent for the son of a management employee to 2 percent for the son of a farmer or unskilled worker. It is only 4 percent for the son of a skilled worker but 12 percent for the son of a foreman or nonmanagement office employee. The existence of intermediate-level qualifications thus offers a real chance for upward mobility to those who have participated in worker apprenticeship programs. These programs therefore serve as centers of social competition in which employees belonging to the middle class do best. The existence of such opportunities for upward mobility is closely related to the role of apprenticeship in stabilizing the working class: the vast majority of workers, with working-class or peasant backgrounds, cannot rise in this system and are obliged to remain to one side of the wide social and professional gap separating b-c from w-c workers.

The relative dearth of intermediate-level training in France is not, as one might assume, directly related to the comparatively small proportion of workers who obtain the CAP. The situation actually differs from that of Germany in that only a small proportion of those who obtain intermediate certification have previously obtained basic certification as skilled b-c or office workers (of the CAP type). Rather certain students who repeatedly fail the examinations for the second cycle of secondary instruction are sent directly into intermediate-level training programs. Other writers have shown that in the mid-1960s only 10 percent of those students working toward intermediate professional certification had graduated from basic professional training programs.[46] Other sources indicate that 70 percent of students in an age group who obtained intermediate certification in the late 1960s had previously reached the second cycle of secondary school.[47]

Thus the upper level of the nonuniversity occupational training system in France is autonomous with respect to the lower level. And yet there is very little difference between the two levels regarding the social compositions of their student bodies. Consider the percentage of children of nonmanual workers in the group of intermediate-level certified workers, and take the ratio of that percentage to the percentage of children of nonmanual workers in the group of elementary-level certified workers: the figure is 1.7 for France and 2.7 for Germany.[48] This result is important because it shows that in Germany, the dynamism of the entire nonuniversity professional training system results from the interdependence between the two levels as training programs and the relative segregation of the social groups that gain access to each level. In France, on the other hand, the weakness of the training system as a whole goes along with strict compartmentalization with respect to level of training but fairly similar social composition, with students on both levels being drawn mainly from the lower and middle strata of society. The fact that these two structural features coexist in France is not an accident. It has to do with the fact that the students funneled into professional training programs are those who fail at one level or another of the general educational system. Although these failures occur at different levels, the social characteristics of the students involved are similar though not strictly identical.

This information provides a fairly complete picture of the nonuniversity systems of professional training in the two countries and of the types of social mobility to which they give rise. We shall add only a little more information concerning higher education in the two countries, since a full-blown comparison would require a separate study. In the French case it is important to note that in regard to the problem that concerns us here—the training of industrial workers—the importance of the so-called grandes écoles, relatively selective institutions offering scientific and business training, outweighs that of the universities proper. Both the number and quality of regular university graduates in industry are low. We also think it is important to stress the dual nature of the grandes écoles. In the first place they stand incontestably at the summit of a general educational system that effectively implements the functions of social and academic selection. At the same time they also stand at the summit of a system of professional training from whose lower levels they are completely cut off. These characteristics of the grandes écoles are consistent with the principles on which the entire social, intellectual, and educational structure of the French educational system is based. German higher education is organized around the university, and admission is regulated by the stringent social and academic selectivity associated with the Gymnasium, track 3. Thus German higher education is also separate from the nonuniversity professional training system, but the structure of the German system is better than that of the French and its autonomy is greater.[49]

We do, however, see two crucial differences between German and French higher education.[50] In Germany college graduates are not the only group in the work force with high-level technical training. The so-called graduate engineers, who are not college graduates, have top-level technical know-how, though its academic basis is different from that of college graduates. In other words, in Germany there are two types of engineers—graduate engineers and college-trained engineers—whereas in France there are only the engineers of the grandes écoles. Furthermore a university degree in Germany is the culmination of an elite education that begins in the Gymnasium and remains completely separate from the mass educational system (tracks 1 and 2). In other words, a university degree is not the final outcome of the entire educational system but rather of one elite track within that system. The relative isolation of this track (due to its prestige and selectivity) has made it possible for a parallel hierarchy to develop. This second hierarchy culminates not in a university degree but in a high-level professional qualification. The uniqueness and worth of this latter sort of qualification are widely recognized in industry. Nothing of the kind exists in France, where grande école graduates are the ultimate product of the only truly organized and accepted system of mass education that there is: the general secondary educational system.[51] These graduates thus derive both legitimacy and prestige from two facts: not only do they occupy the top rung of the academic hierarchy, but they are also the winners in a competition that is intended to be open to all members of society. The relation between grande école graduates and other members of the work force may be said, therefore, to be marked by both continuity and discontinuity: continuity by dint of the democratic competition from which they emerge victorious and discontinuity by dint of their exalted social status. There can be no doubt that there is a wide gap between those receiving the sanction of higher education and other members of the work force in France and Germany. But the significance of the gap is not the same in the two countries, for the underlying social and academic systems differ.

At this point in the argument we are ready to draw two preliminary conclusions with regard to the professional and social stratification of the work force and the nature of worker mobility.

First, it would be misleading to study the dynamics of the two educational systems by looking at the chronology of student career choices. In Germany, for example, the vitality and central importance of the apprenticeship system have a crucial influence on the choice that most students make to attend the Hauptschule. A particular value is attached to this choice, even by children of the higher strata of society, because of the social, professional, and educational status associated with apprenticeship training, its principal outlet. It is wrong to think that track 1 is somehow intrinsically equipped to accept a certain number of students and that this explains why so many children from fairly high social strata choose to enter it. In fact track 1 is rather well integrated into the overall training system and therefore exercises a certain power of attraction (a power amplified by the high selectivity of the secondary tracks) over all strata of society, thereby increasing the number of students it is prepared to accept. Carrying this reasoning one step further, it can be argued that the importance of intermediate-level occupational training has a decisive impact on the value attached to basic apprenticeship training, which is directly linked to it, and thus also on the willingness of ten-year-old pupils to enter track 1, which leads ultimately to the desired goal. The same point can be made about France, where the intense social and academic competition intrinsic to the second cycle of secondary education influences the decisions made by pupils as early as the end of elementary school.

Our second remark relates to the use and interpretation of the available information concerning the distribution of academic and professional qualifications in the work force at a given time. In supply-demand terms, this information describes the supply of qualifications on the labor market at a specific time. This supply schedule is certainly an important item when comparing two countries and analyzing the possible forms of work-force stratification. But the discussion shows that knowledge of the stocks of qualifications at one moment must be related to knowledge of the flows—what we have been calling mobilities—that influence their formation. We cannot understand the quantitative differences revealed by statistical analysis without understanding the flow processes. Knowledge of these flows is even more vital for understanding how differences in supply are related to the way in which social, professional, and educational differences are produced, something about which it is hard to make direct international comparisons. As we shall see in the second part of this section, the kind of analysis we have in mind goes beyond supply to consider demand as well—and in doing so calls into question the terms in which most current analyses of the labor market are conducted.

1.3.2 Job Mobility and Stratification of the Labor Market

The study of job mobility involves methodological problems similar to those encountered in comparing the French and German educational systems. In particular, we shall be led to consider the chronology of transfer decisions and to ask what relations there may be between chronology and causality. In most cases educational mobility—the formalized acquisition of knowledge and certified qualifications—precedes entry into the job market and a fortiori decisions about whether to change jobs that a worker may face at various points in his career. Job mobility may thus be seen as complementary to earlier training or at least as based on that training. The chronological approach that we shall be taking in this section tends to justify this way of looking at the question, moreover. But we make two caveats.

First, a fairly trivial point, some workers do acquire training after they have embarked on their professional careers. Thus job mobility may in fact precede the acquisition of training, or the two may occur simultaneously.[52] The second point is of a more theoretical and methodological order. Like educational mobility, job mobility is both an individual and a collective phenomenon. Decisions by individual workers to change jobs can be described as consequences of the acquisition of new certification or of certain supplementary qualifications to fill gaps in previous training. The phenomenon of collective job mobility is logically prior to such individual decisions to acquire additional training. Thus collective patterns of job mobility can influence collective shifts in the pattern of choices in regard to education and training, which are the macrosocial outcome of the kinds of individual decision in question.

The theoretical problems implicit in this general remark cannot be treated in full detail in this chapter; we shall return to them in another context in chapters 4 and 5. But the methodological choice made at this stage has some influence on the way we handle the empirical data, particularly in regard to job mobility. Two approaches will be used. First we shall look at the relationship between job mobility and stratification of the work force, and second we shall see how the stability over time of the mobility process helps to produce and to crystallize the collective relations that are logically prior to individual educational and professional choices in each country.

1.3.2.1 Job Mobility and Structure of the Industrial Sector

In the first two sections of this chapter we described some of the special features of the French and German industrial sectors. Wage differentials among different branches of industry were more uniform in Germany than in France, and the industrial sector as a whole contrasted more sharply with the tertiary sector. We shall now find that these differences are complemented and extended by other contrasts that become apparent when we look at certain index of job mobility.

To begin, let us compare the distribution of workers who have already held a job in industry for at least one year and who take up a newly created or recently vacated position.[53] This can happen in two different ways: the worker may either take a new job in the same branch of industry or move to a new branch (from, say, a corrugated paper plant to an automobile plant). In France changes within the same branch account for 30 percent of all changes, compared with only 20 percent in Germany. Thus German industry would seem to be less compartmentalized than French industry as far as barriers between different branches are concerned. Other index amplify this point. For instance, in Germany available industrial jobs are most frequently filled by workers already holding another industrial job, whereas in France a considerable proportion of available jobs are filled by workers who have previously been either inactive or working in the tertiary sector or employed in nonwage jobs (farming or crafts).[54] Thus not only is German industry less compartmentalized, it is also more autonomous with respect to the nonindustrial world in regard to satisfying its own worker mobility needs.

Other indexes record the same kind of difference. We can bring qualifications into the picture by defining a new index, the industry-specificity index for certification of type i, as follows:

$$R_i = I_i/T_i,$$

Table 1.9
Rates of identification of various diplomas and professional credentials with the industrial sector, 1970

France		Germany	
Certificate		Certificate	
1. None	R1 = 1.45	1. No occupational training	R1 = 1.50
2. CAP	R2 = 1.42	2. Worker apprenticeship	R2 = 1.68
	R1/R2 = 1.29		R1/R2 = 0.90
3. Intermediate professional certification	R3 = 0.89	3. Intermediate professional certification[a]	R3 = 1.70
4. College degree	R4 = 0.55	4. College degree	R4 = 0.23
	R3/R4 = 1.62		R3/R4 = 7.40

a. Technicians and graduate engineers only.

where R_i is the index in question, I_i is the number of people holding certification of type i in industry, and T_i is the number of people holding certification of type i in the tertiary sector. Table 1.9 tabulates the values of R_i for four types of certification and for France and Germany.

The absolute values of these indexes cannot be compared directly between the two countries because they are influenced by the highly unequal proportion of industrial workers in the work force as a whole. But this influence is eliminated when we compare the ratios R_1/R_2 and R_3/R_4 for the two countries and discover that they are quite different. Thus the relative proportion of industrial workers with some sort of general educational diploma is much higher in France than in Germany (R_1/R_2 is 1.29 in France compared with 0.9 in Germany). Professionally certified workers tend to remain in German industry, whereas there is a significant tendency in France for such workers to move out of industry into the tertiary sector (R_2 and R_3 are both close to 1.7 in Germany compared with only 1.12 and 0.89, respectively, in France).[55] These differences cannot be accounted for by the varying proportion of industrial workers in the total work force. In France, then, not only is the number of technical certifications offered small, but workers who have them are more likely than their German counterparts to take jobs in the tertiary sector. Qualified French workers thus do not remain in the industrial work force, even if their initial skills correspond to the needs of industry.[56] This tendency has the effect of increasing the gap between the two countries in regard to the supply of qualified labor. In our view it also contributes to the differences in the status attached to various types of professional certification in the two countries, thereby exerting an influence on their respective educational systems, particularly in regard to the balance that comes to be established between occupational training and general instruction.

To this general information we may add what we have found out about the mobility of workers holding basic apprenticeship certification in Germany. Figures compiled in 1970 show that 55 percent of this group leave the company that trained them within one year after obtaining their credentials. By five years after completion of training, this figure rises to 80 percent. Departures are particularly frequent in craft shops (87 percent) but run as high as 70 percent in industrial firms, many of them of large size. These aggregate results are confirmed by our detailed studies of machinery and petrochemical plants (study 2). Eighty-eight percent of the supervisory and management personnel in these plants who had apprenticeship certification had been certified in a plant other than the one in which they were working at the time of the study. These results are important because they show that in Germany, the company-centered training system does not mean that workers, once trained, are automatically integrated in large numbers into the firms that trained them. Their skills are not limited to the particular types of technology and organizational structure they trained with. Rather the high departure rate shows that both workers and employers look upon apprenticeship as providing general skills, useful outside the firm in which they were acquired. This result is not incompatible with our earlier finding that workers with apprenticeship credentials tend to remain in industry rather than look for work in the tertiary sector. Worker-type apprenticeship provides skills of general value within industry but not especially useful in the tertiary sector. This dualism in the occupational training of German workers confirms our earlier hypothesis that industrial apprenticeship not only teaches certain useful skills but also represents a form of socialization that identifies the worker with the industrial world.[57]

The situation in France is quite different. French workers trained directly by a firm tend to be integrated into that firm. This is the case not only for small companies that train the skilled workers they need but also for large firms whose training programs, often conducted on a large scale, lead to the award of in-house credentials.[58] The training offered is often first rate, but it is unrelated to any broad national system of worker training. Thus different industrial skills are not subsumed under any common system of classification generally recognized by both employers and employees, and this fact tends to limit job mobility.

Using the statistical information recorded above, we can begin to describe the differences between the two countries with respect to the relationship between worker mobility and skill acquisition. There are basically two ways to describe mobility. One is to look at the magnitude and direction of actual flows. The other is to try to capture the most prominent characteristics of the social, professional, and psychological environment within which these flows occur. In Germany, for example, we have stressed the fact that for skilled workers, job mobility is influenced by the way employers and employees look at the apprenticeship system in its social, professional, and technical aspects, and at the skills that it teaches.

The economic theory of the labor market, on the other hand, generally emphasizes the first way of looking at the question: economists are interested in the magnitude and direction of worker flows, in terms of which they attempt to explain wage equalization tendencies in the economy, as well as the effects of job mobility on overall productive efficiency. To us, however, it is the *structure of the environment within which mobility takes place* that seems to be the crucial factor for treating questions of inequality and efficiency. This sort of analysis is, we think, the only way to understand the economic consequences of worker mobility. In this chapter, predominantly empirical in character, we cannot develop this point further. We shall return to it in more systematic fashion in the theoretical portion of the book, chapters 4 and 5.

At the present stage in the argument, though, related methodological problems remain to be answered. We shall deal with them again in the next section, where we consider movement between occupational categories. What general laws can we discover governing the relationship between job structures and this kind of worker mobility?

1.3.2.2 Mobility between Socioprofessional Categories and Stratification of the Industrial Work Force

The key difference between France and Germany relates to the ways in which b-c workers move to the w-c category, particularly in regard to differences in the role played by education and the firm. This section will develop this point. At the same time we shall also consider two other important points. To begin we shall look at statistics concerning the rate of mobility between major job classifications. In concluding we shall also consider the impact of general patterns of mobility on worker movements within the b-c and w-c groups.

Before looking at different types of b-c to w-c mobility, it is worth comparing the rates of such mobility in France and Germany. Two sources

Table 1.10
Access to job categories by starting position, 1965–1970

Starting position, 1965	Probability of position in 1970[a]					
	Blue collar		White collar		Nonwage	
	France	Germany	France	Germany	France	Germany
Unskilled			6.2	3.9	2.1	1.4
Skilled			12.1	8.7	5.0	2.4
B-C worker			9.0	6.5	3.4	1.8
Nonwage worker	9.5	5.9	3.5	4.2		
W-C worker	4.2	2.7			2.9	3.1

a. For example, in France, 12.1 percent of the workers who were skilled workers in 1965 had become w-c workers by 1970.

of statistical data are available. One is the 1973 work force study, which yields a figure for the probability that a b-c worker will move to w-c status during a one-year period. The other is the 1970 training, skill, and mobility study, which yields information about movement among three important categories in the work force (b-c workers, w-c wage earners, and nonwage earners, or self-employed) over a five-year period, 1965–1970. The two sources yield comparable results. We find that the probability that a b-c worker in industry would become a w-c worker during the course of the year 1973 was 2.35 percent in France, compared with only 1.75 percent in Germany. The difference is even more marked if we compare the probability of a b-c worker in industry becoming a w-c worker in industry: 1.7 percent in France compared with 1.2 percent in Germany.[59] Bear in mind, however, that these are very tentative results because of the low mobility rates and the shortness of the observation period. Still, the tendencies they indicate are confirmed by the structural data summarized in table 1.10.

The table not only confirms the previous result concerning the rate of passage from b-c to w-c status in industry but also adds the further result that industrial workers in France are more likely than their German counterparts to move out of the wage-earning work force altogether (3.4 percent in France compared with 1.8 percent in Germany; most of this mobility involves industrial workers moving out of industry to become independent craftsmen). The gap between the two countries is particularly wide for skilled workers who leave industry to become self-employed (5.0 percent for France compared with 2.4 percent for Germany).

Two general tendencies emerge from these results. First, mobility in almost all categories is higher in France than in Germany. The only exception is the transfer of self-employed workers into the ranks of nonmanual labor within industry, for which we find a slightly higher rate in Germany.[60] The French situation stands out by virtue of the markedly higher rate that we find there for mobility of unskilled and especially skilled industrial workers who leave manual labor jobs in industry to become either w-c workers in industry or self-employed.[61] This characteristic feature of the French labor market reflects the forces that structure the market. Individual mobility in France is favored by the relatively low level of industrial wages. There is a broad general tendency toward greater fluidity in France than in Germany, not only in the work force but also in the educational system. The consequences of this are important, and they are not all as positive as they might seem at first. From a macrosociological standpoint, it is clear that the working class is a relatively unstable group. The possibility of individual mobility tends to impede the development of a strong sense of collective identity.[62] The significance of these quantitative differences becomes clearer when we consider the concrete ways in which worker mobility takes place.

The points made earlier in this chapter about the importance of professional credentials in Germany versus the crucial role of seniority in France are important in this respect as well. Bringing in the job mobility factor adds another dimension to our description of work force stratification in the two countries and makes it possible to take a more comprehensive approach to the problem of international comparison.

Consider, for example, the role of occupational training in the two countries. In Germany, the existence of a large number of intermediate-level training programs is closely related to worker mobility: workers are able to acquire high-quality intermediate credentials after they have embarked on their careers. The aggregate differences between the two countries in this respect are important. In Germany 18.2 percent of male workers had acquired their highest-level professional certification after entering the work force, compared with only 10.2 percent in France.[63] We find even greater differences when we look at the nature and level of credentials acquired while working. For most German workers these are credentials above the level of apprenticeship certification (such as certification as foremen, technicians, or graduate engineers). In France, only 3 percent of the total of 10 percent obtain credentials on this level, compared with 7 percent who train simply to acquire the CAP. Thus in France occupational training for those already in the work force is directed mainly at filling in gaps in the worker's basic qualification. By contrast, in Germany such training is an effective and widely utilized means of extending a worker's initial qualification, particularly for workers already holding apprenticeship certification.

These differences are confirmed by individual company studies, where we were able to ascertain the educational history of middle- and upper-level managers. In French chemical and metallurgical firms an average of 17 percent of the employees in this group had obtained their highest professional credential after entering the work force (in nearly half of the cases before the age of twenty-five). In the comparable German firms the equivalent figure was 53 percent (and 75 percent of these credentials had been acquired after the age of twenty-five). The differences were least for sales and administrative personnel, for whom the rate in France was 13 percent and in Germany 20 percent. They were greatest for technicians, 70 percent of whom had acquired their highest rating while on the job in Germany, compared with only 15 percent in France.

The considerable variation between the two countries undoubtedly reflects institutional differences that affect the possibility of obtaining the kinds of credentials in question (such as number of schools, availability of courses for workers, and the relationship between training schools and industry). But such institutional differences do not explain all of the variation, and we would even argue that they are merely the systematic consequence of more fundamental differences involving the interrelationship of job mobility, occupational training, company policies in regard to worker qualification, and related, more broadly conceived issues of professional autonomy and social control.

To give a more concrete example, consider the fact that if German companies are willing to accept workers for w-c technical jobs on the basis of intermediate-level technical certification, the other side of the coin is that they severely limit the promotion of skilled workers whose only credential is apprenticeship certification to positions of foreman or technician. Thus in 1970 of all workers possessing basic apprenticeship certification but no other credential and still employed by the firm that had trained them, only 6 percent had moved up to nonmanual jobs (but 93 percent were classified as skilled workers). Seniority within the firm and training by that firm are insufficient by themselves to give a worker much chance of rising to a higher position. For all intents and purposes, a credential of higher level than apprenticeship certification is a prerequisite for promotion.[64]

These statistics reflect a deliberate policy of German employers: to recognize professional credentials as guarantees of skill and to impose strict controls over any change of qualification or status not defined by such credentials. This policy is bolstered by the fact that workers who enter training courses beyond apprenticeship do so on their own initiative and pay a substantial share of the cost themselves, in the absence of any guarantee from the firm they work for that their upgraded qualifications will result in promotion.[65]

Thus the relationship between occupational training and change of job category in Germany cannot be understood without bringing in company policies with regard to access to the most highly skilled positions, policies based on underlying notions of qualification or of the hierarchy of authority. At the same time, though, individual firms have little direct institutional involvement in worker mobility, since this is based on the acquisition of credentials that have a general value in the economy as a whole.

By contrast, in France firms are directly involved in both individual and collective processes of job mobility, and this involvement explains certain characteristic features of the French system, in particular the absence of any widespread utilization of a system of professional certifications. Firms are involved in worker mobility in an indirect way: the more time a worker has spent in the work force, the more likely he is to be promoted, independent of any credentials he may possess. Thus whereas only 22 percent of French workers under the age of thirty-five who have no credential higher than an elementary school diploma hold w-c jobs, this figure rises to 35 percent for workers over thirty-five. In Germany the figure is 12 percent for both age groups. For those who possess basic apprenticeship certification, the gap is still considerable. In France 28 percent of workers under thirty-five and holding the CAP are in w-c jobs, compared with 45 percent of those over thirty-five and holding the CAP; in Germany the comparable figures are 15 percent and 23 percent, respectively.[66]

The fact that employers and company officials have direct power over worker promotion thus emerges indirectly from these figures, which show that the length of a worker's career influences his position in ways not affected by his educational achievement. Because of this, workers are naturally little inclined to obtain higher-level professional credentials or to exert collective pressure to bring about institutional changes that would lead to a more credential-oriented system. Beyond this, the firm's influence can be seen directly when we look at the effects on promotion of training courses taken by workers after they have entered the work force. Between 1965 and 1970 56 percent of workers who participated in training courses

Table 1.11
Probability of holding a white-collar job by seniority industry, 1972

Seniority class	Job category					
	Manager		Foreman		Other	
	France	Germany	France	Germany	France	Germany
Under 2 years	4.2	4.9	1.4	1.5	11.1	12.8
2–4 years	6.2	7.1	2.7	2.0	13.9	13.3
5–9 years	8.0	8.0	5.2	3.0	15.4	13.5
10–20 years[a]	9.9	10.6	9.0	5.3	17.2	12.4
More than 20 years	12.6	12.6	14.3	10.4	17.1	12.9

a. Example: of French workers with 10 to 20 years' seniority, 9.9 percent are managers, 9 percent are foremen, and 17,2 percent occupy other w-c positions; 73.9 percent are workers.

initiated by their employers were promoted, whereas only 34 percent of those who took courses on their own initiative were rewarded with promotion. This suggests that in France training acquired during the course of a worker's career yields dividends only if it parallels or even follows the employer's decision to promote that particular individual.

Even more direct evidence for the firm's influence on worker mobility comes from studying the effects of seniority on the likelihood of gaining access to the most skilled jobs, especially nonmanagement w-c positions. Table 1.11 records data for both countries.

The table yields two significant results. First, the greater the seniority, the greater the likelihood of occupying a management position, with more or less equal probabilities for France and Germany. On the other hand, the effect of seniority on access to the position of foreman or member of the technical or administrative staff varies considerably from one country to the other. Recently hired workers have a slightly higher chance of obtaining such jobs in Germany, but after five years' seniority, the French worker takes the lead and by ten years' seniority is far out in front of his German counterpart. Among the latter group the percentage of French workers in foreman or office posts is 9 percent greater than the percentage of German workers.[67]

These variations cannot be directly interpreted as reflecting differences in worker mobility and in the nature of the job market between the two countries. At least two different interpretations of the results are possible.

They may indicate that French office employees tend to remain for long periods with the same firm. In this case their greater seniority would not necessarily correspond to upward mobility but might indicate only long tenure in the same position. But another hypothesis is also possible: that a fairly significant number of w-c workers with considerable seniority were promoted to their current jobs from b-c positions. If this is true, then the tabulated figures would suggest the existence of promotion channels internal to specific firms, whose purpose would be to fill w-c jobs and to shape the qualifications of workers to meet the firm's internal needs.

To us the second interpretation seems the more likely, for several reasons. First, it is consistent with our earlier observations concerning the higher frequency of b-c-to-w-c transfers in France, though not all these transfers occur within a given firm. Furthermore the second hypothesis is consistent with the results of empirical studies on access to w-c positions in French firms. This work shows not only that internal promotion is important for filling foremen's jobs, as is well known, but also that it plays an important role in turning out technicians and even nonuniversity-trained managers.[68]

Finally, the second hypothesis enables us to suggest an explanation of why the proportion of w-c workers (and especially office personnel) is higher in France than in Germany. It is as though these intermediate ranks are being swelled as the result of constant pressure to reward seniority with promotion. This kind of reward is the traditional or institutionally established way of embodying the principles that govern the production of w-c skills in the structure of the work force. The pressure to promote senior employees is all the more likely to bring results because of the fact that little use is made of professional training credentials as a way of controlling upward mobility. This in turn is a consequence of the way individual and collective mobility is regulated in France, where much of the responsibility for regulation is shouldered by individual firms.

A closer look at the data turns up variations among different branches of industry and different sizes of firm. The processes described do not always work the same way but are modified by the productive structures within which they unfold. German and French job structures differ most in the largest firms and the most concentrated branches (where the average seniority is highest in both countries).[69] The figures seem to show that, in France, the more stable the work force, and thus the greater the power of the workers, both organized and unorganized, the greater the increase in the number of highly prized jobs, particularly jobs involving nonmanual labor. By contrast, German industry seems to be much more capable of keeping the number of such jobs under control. Thus in Germany, the collective strength of the work force, which results from large concentrations of manual labor and/or a monopolistic position in the market for a firm's products, encourages the development of forms of social and technical management that effectively counter any tendency toward uncontrolled growth in the number of command and control jobs. The capability of controlling the number of w-c jobs is undoubtedly related to organizational practices that can be analyzed at the level of the firm; systematic study of these practices will be deferred until the next chapter. This capability is also affected by the impact of certain macrosocial phenomena on individual firms; foremost among these are forms of working-class organization and skill identification.

If we turn now to the various subgroups within the broad categories of b-c and w-c workers, we find that mobility can be described in terms of the same structural characteristics that we have just spelled out in detail in attempting to describe mobility between the two categories. Thus in France, for example, seniority has the same kind of effect on mobility within the b-c worker category. In the French firms we studied closely, fewer than 25 percent of the b-c workers with more than ten years' seniority occupied unskilled positions. In Germany the comparable figure was more than 50 percent in all the firms we looked at. The aggregate figures reflect the same phenomenon: the proportion of senior or older workers in unskilled positions is much higher in Germany than in France.

The limited available information also suggests that, as for the move from b-c to w-c jobs, the rate of mobility from unskilled to skilled positions is much higher in France than in Germany. Fifteen percent of French workers who held unskilled jobs in 1965 held skilled jobs by 1970. The comparable figure for Germany is only 9 percent. Furthermore, downward mobility is more likely in Germany: the probability of going from a skilled to an unskilled position there was 9.5 percent, compared with only 7.2 percent in France. Thus the net mobility between skilled and unskilled positions was significantly upward (15 percent upward versus 7.2 percent downward), whereas the situation in Germany was ambiguous (9.5 percent downward versus 9 percent upward).[70]

These results should be considered along with others mentioned previously. For instance, we saw earlier that 17 percent of skilled workers in France in 1965 had become independent craftsmen or w-c workers by 1970, compared with only 11 percent in Germany. We also know that the flow of workers from self-employed or from w-c positions into skilled jobs was twice as high in France as in Germany. Thus there is much more change in the ranks of skilled workers in France than in Germany. The stock of skill is in constant flux because of the high rates of mobility in the relatively open French system; the result is that the ability of the system to define and control skills in an autonomous way is constantly being undermined. In Germany, on the other hand, two types of flow are important: a large number of older workers in skilled jobs move down into unskilled jobs, and young workers with professional certification move directly into skilled positions upon entering the work force. Thus worker mobility is directly affected by the strong link between skilled status and training, which serves young workers with up-to-date training well but disserves older workers whose qualifications have become obsolete (often forcing those who leave one firm for another to move down to an unskilled position).

Different factors affect mobility within the w-c category. Office and management personnel have quite similar qualifications in Germany. Because of this there is considerable mobility between the two kinds of jobs. In the chemical and metallurgical firms we looked at in study 2, more than 70 percent of the managers had previously held office jobs in the same firms. This figure was only 20 percent in the French chemical firms we looked at and 40 percent in the metallurgical firms. We found that the reason for this difference was the wide disparity between the two countries of the proportion of college graduates among the managers.[71] This disparity was undoubtedly accentuated by the fact that we were looking at large firms, which in France tend to have a very high proportion of grande école graduates among their management personnel. Such aggregate data as we have been able to collect, however, tend to confirm the finding that upward mobility from office jobs to management positions is greater in Germany than in France.

Here as in all our other comparisons, it is worth pointing out that the differences revealed by the indicators suggest that the categories on which the statistical data are based are not comparable. In the present instance, for example, it would seem that the significance of access to a management position in France is not the same as the significance of access to a salaried position in Germany. We are dealing not only with two different patterns of mobility but also with two different systems of job stratification underlying those patterns. Because of this difficulty, we shall have occasion to give another empirical description of the situation in chapters 2 and 3, and in chapters 4 and 5 we shall take up the implicit methodological and theoretical problem.

Summary

It is difficult to give a brief summary of the results obtained thus far. We shall therefore limit ourselves to a few comprehensive remarks.

One fundamental tendency emerges from the data presented: in each country there is a tendency for a close relationship to develop between the organization of general education and occupational training and the behavior of firms. The results convince us that it is impossible to analyze either the educational system (in terms of number and type of degrees offered, nature of competition, tracking and selection, and so forth) or the job hierarchy (in terms of the relation between training and qualification, variation between branches of industry, or direction of job mobility, for example) in isolation. In both countries we find particular kinds of interaction between education and stratification, certain specific national patterns.[72]

The German system of occupational training is both autonomous and very firmly established, and its key position is closely related to the power of industry in Germany and the forms of qualification and stratification favored by German firms. At the same time the position of industry in the German economy as a whole is predicated on the existence of a powerful system of occupational training. We must insist on the fundamental importance of this crucial relationship between industry and the system of occupational training. The existence of a highly developed system of professional training certainly helps to ensure a steady supply of properly trained industrial workers. Correspondingly there is a constant demand for new workers coming from German industry, which encourages further development of industrial training. But this close relationship between training and industrial demand can also be looked at on a different level. The existence of a powerful, autonomous system of training in Germany determines the way skills are defined, while at the same time the prerequisites of industrial employment determine the structure of occupational training. The adjustment of supply to demand thus takes place within a framework determined by the relationship between industry and the educational system in the broad sense, and this relationship fundamentally defines the German labor market.

Analogous remarks can be made about France. The fact that occupational training is not widely relied upon in France reflects the skill structure of industry in a country where firms structure the job market in a direct and quasi-institutional way.[73] Qualifications in the broad sense are thus the result of individual and collective behavior in relation to both the educational system and the job market, behavior that responds to more than just the policies of particular firms and that integrates those policies into the overall pattern we have described.

The full extent of the relationship between industry and training cannot be appreciated without taking account of the many forms of mediation that stand between firms and opportunities for training. Too often this relationship is treated in a purely mechanical way. But in fact it embraces many kinds of mediation, expressed particularly through the various forms of worker mobility: social, occupational, and educational mobility, as well as mobility between firms. These different forms of mobility bridge the gap between institutions, individuals, and collectivities, a point to which we shall return.

Not all the results of this chapter were concerned with horizontal relations between industry and the educational system. We also found certain vertical discontinuities between different categories of worker, particularly between b-c and w-c workers. It is worth stressing that the nature of continuities and discontinuities between these two categories is different in France and Germany.

In Germany the discontinuities are based almost entirely on two characteristics of the workers: occupational training and social origin. These characteristics distinguish skilled from unskilled workers and skilled workers from w-c workers. Differences in these respects are much less clear-cut within the w-c category (between office and management personnel) in that most college degrees in Germany are found among senior civil servants and management personnel in the private tertiary sector, to a far greater extent at any rate than in France.[74] This peculiarity of the German situation calls for further comment.

These results account fairly well for the fact that occupational training and social origin have similar discriminating effects. Occupational training in Germany reinforces both the identity and professional autonomy of workers, at least within the limits of a fairly strict social and professional hierarchy. Professional credentials are used as an effective means of social control in a system that incorporates sharp discontinuities. The nature of these discontinuities, indeed the existence of a dual system of occupational training, emerges clearly from the results of our studies of worker mobility. We will encounter this same duality when we look at the links between hierarchical authority and professional authority in chapter 2. Note, however, that occupational training cannot be analyzed solely in terms of the discontinuities that result from the high degree of coincidence between type of credential and category of job held. We have already pointed out the importance of the fact that the system of occupational training is vertically integrated, in the sense that the great majority of w-c workers who hold intermediate-level professional credentials (as foremen, technicians, or graduate engineers) also have a basic apprenticeship certificate. Thus the highest level nonuniversity credentials can be viewed as an extension of the basic training of industrial workers. As a result the workers who possess such credentials and who occupy middle- to upper-level positions in the job hierarchy in many respects can be regarded as belonging to the same skill domain or span of qualification as the ordinary worker.[75] The basic apprenticeship certificate is both the fundamental credential and the center of gravity of the entire system. It should be noted too that the relative lack of discriminatory power of such other variables as general or specific job experience or general educational achievement is not to be understood merely in negative terms—that is, in terms of an ostensible lack of influence on a worker's position.[76] Rather the unimportance of these variables is what defines the German skill domain (span of qualification) just as much as the importance of certain other variables. Thus the lack of importance of general educational achievement, for example, is the result of the emphasis on worker apprenticeship and influences the way the overall educational system operates.

We can also describe the stratification of the French industrial work force in terms of continuities and discontinuities; however, these are combined in a very different way in France in comparison to Germany. Two types of variables are important: job experience, both general and specific, and general educational achievement. Why these two variables should have similar effects is probably harder to explain in the French case than in the German case. In our view, however, the place to look for an explanation is in the importance of the role played by the firm in determining the stratification of the industrial work force in France. In many respects it seems that this stratification is the result of a process whereby workers at first little differentiated from one another are classified, selected, and oriented by their employers. The statistical analysis shows that, the way general educational achievement defines a potential, which firms then use to make their selections and at the same time the way a worker's relationship with his employer over the course of his working life is used to construct a hierarchy within each firm and, more broadly, within the productive system as a whole.

As in the case of Germany, the characteristics that determine discontinuities within the work force and thus influence patterns of worker mobility also show elements of continuity. But in France it is not the existence of a homogeneous system of professional credentials that unifies the work force but rather the use of universalistic and a priori neutral principles, experience and general educational achievement, to determine a worker's potential and assign him a place in the hierarchy.[77] The fact that occupational training and social origin are of little importance in France merely reflects the fact that these criteria are not of much use to firms in classifying workers;[78] criteria not directly recognized by individual firms cannot easily be integrated into what we shall later define as the organizational domain or span of organization.

The difference between the skill domain and the organizational domain will prove to be of considerable importance later. The use of the term *domain* and the emphasis on the underlying continuities and discontinuities and complex institutional relations bring up the issue of the worker mobilities in terms of which each domain is defined. This issue has come up before in certain of our detailed empirical discussions. We shall come back to it, first in the context of a more systematic analysis (chapter 4) and then in the course of a theoretical discussion of worker mobility and its place in a general approach to the questions raised here (chapter 5).

The discussion of industrial qualifications has raised the issue of the role of the firm, which has an important influence on work force stratification in both France and Germany. So far, however, our discussion has avoided the issue of relations that develop within the firm. In chapter 2 we shall take up the question of the nature of organizational relationships within the firm and the way they relate to broader social relations.

Finally, we have emphasized that issues of skill and stratification cannot be studied apart from the way they impinge on individual workers, workers who are at the same time social actors. We are therefore obliged to undertake a comparative study of the collective organization of industrial workers in the two countries as a logical extension of the study of skill structures and organizational relations within the firm. Chapter 3 will be devoted to this task.

2

Work Systems, Spans of Qualification, and Hierarchy: Organizational Dynamics within the Firm

In this chapter we set forth both the methods and results of research that was done to resolve what seems to economists a paradox that emerges from a comparison of the French and German job and wage structures.

Working between 1972 and 1976, researchers at the Laboratoire d'Economie et Sociologie du Travail (LEST), not only confirmed (at the microeconomic level) the tendencies revealed by European Economic Community statistics (the fact that wage inequalities, wider in France than in Germany, go together with differences in the pattern of employment, there being a higher proportion of w-c workers in France) but also indicated where the greatest differences were to be found within the hierarchy of the firm and how these differences might be explained.

Social facts of two kinds seemed likely to account for our observations: phenomena having to do with socialization and mobility, which were analyzed in chapter 1, and organizational phenomena, which will be discussed in detail in this chapter. We believe, however, that the real explanation is to be sought at a deeper level. As we shall show in chapter 3, it has to do with the interaction between socialization and organization, with the social relations that are at once the result and the condition of the organization-socialization interaction. But before moving to this level of analysis, we must give an analytical account of socialization and organization independently, so that we can gain a better understanding of the processes that give rise to the socialization and organizational domains within which the social relations develop.

This chapter will give prominence to data gathered about the organization of actual firms. This does not mean, however, that we regard the firm merely as an organization. Although we make no claim here to be developing our own theory of the firm, we believe that our results represent a contribution to such a theory in that they show how the interaction between organization and socialization enters in to the constitution of the firm. In other words, we are trying to describe the relationship between the firm and society, that is, to disclose what we might call the social effect on the organization of the firm. We do this not on the basis of a general, comprehensive approach but rather starting from empirical data that enable us to apprehend what we consider to be the most important processes by means of which industrial firms develop their relationship with society at large. The value of international comparison here is heuristic; not only does comparison reveal the differences between the two countries, but it also enables us to go beyond those differences to identify the key elements on which the relationship of firm to society is based in each country. We do not claim that our limited research has enabled us to achieve this degree of generality. We do think, however, that further comparative work would enable us to move closer to this goal. The logic of our research program, then, is aimed not at constructing a general theory of society but at trying to understand those social processes by means of which contingent national differences, as revealed by studies of socialization and organization, are subsumed under general social regularities.[1] If the approach we take tends to give prominence to such structural regularities, it nevertheless does not ignore the social actors, for the following reason: not only do the structures contribute to forming the collective identity of the actors, but the structures themselves exist only by virtue of the relations that exist among the actors.

We now proceed to the study of the interaction between organization of the firm and socialization of the work force. Space does not permit us to do more than present a summary of the results obtained in detailed monographic studies to which interested readers may refer.[2]

We begin by describing the job structures of French and German firms and ask whether they are comparable and what the significance of each related category of social actor is. We then describe the work system in each country and say something about how firms are organized. Finally, we analyze social and technical management and show how these influence the functional and hierarchical stratification of the firm in conjunction with the underlying authority relations and forms of industrial cooperation.

2.1 Job Structures and Classification of Social Actors

We chose firms for comparison on the basis of technology empolyed, product manufactured, and to some extent firm size (number of employees).[3] In this we followed, like much other recent work in the sociology of organizations, the trail blazed by Joan Woodward's study of English firms

(1965), which attempted to explain the characteristic features of industrial organizations in terms of such factors as technology and size. Inspired by Woodward, we focused on the three major types of technology that she identifies, each of which was associated in her work with a different organizational structure and span of control. With this research program we hoped to be able to test the validity of the results obtained by Woodward and many subsequent investigators in different social contexts. It should be noted that it is unfair to accuse Woodward of technological determinism, since her most recent work (1970) incorporates an intervening variable between technology and organization: the forms of control that mediate the expected effects of technology.[4] We shall defer discussion of the interrelationship of social and technological effects until the next chapter, confining ourselves here to a discussion of the differences between our results and those obtained by Woodward in her first study (1965).[5]

2.1.1 Job Structure and System of Production

Table 2.1 compares the job structures associated with various types of production in France and Germany. Job structure is broken down into three major categories: b-c workers, nonmanagement w-c workers, and management personnel.[6] In France those counted as management personnel include the supervisors (agents de maîtrise), office and technical personnel who exercise authority over other workers, and managers (cadres supérieurs). In Germany this group includes the foremen (Meister), nonrated staff (AT, corresponding to the *cadres moyens* in France or middle managers), and the *Leitende Angestellte*, corresponding to the *cadres supérieurs* in France. The table reveals significant differences in job structure for the same technology. Beyond that, national patterns emerge.

We find a higher proportion of b-c workers in the German firms. Conversely, in the French firms, we find a higher proportion of w-c personnel without managerial authority, as well as management and staff personnel in positions of authority. It is tempting to interpret these figures as showing that German firms employ more directly productive personnel, while French firms use more indirectly productive labor, an interpretation that is, however, open to criticism.

The table also indicates the average number of workers under the authority of a first-level supervisor, what Woodward calls the span of control. This is always higher in Germany.

Given the problem of making direct international comparisons, and indeed the problem of comparing a category of worker in one firm with the

Table 2.1
Job structure and supervisory ratios by type of production

Type of production	Metals				Petrochemicals	
	Unit[a]		Batch or line[b]		Continuous process	
	France	Germany	France	Germany	France	Germany
Number of workers	2086	1695	920	656	2635	2642
Job category						
Blue-collar worker	48%	61%	75%	82%	54%	65%
White-collar worker (nonsupervisory)	30	21	12	11	20	10
Supervisory management[b]	22	18	13	7	26	25
Span of control	1 : 10	1 : 25	1 : 10	1 : 25	1	1 : 6

a. The unit production facility manufactured heavy machinery. The batch production facility manufactured metal tubing.

b. Supervisory personnel include production and maintenance foremen, technicians and other w-c employees with supervisory functions, and higher-level management.

Source: LEST, 1977.

same-named category in another firm even in the same country, it is the general pattern rather than the specific figures in the table that should be noted. This pattern reflects both national regularities and differences between one type of production and another and suggests a connection between the regularities and the differences. The effect of technology seems more marked in Germany, for example, though both countries reflect Woodward's main results: that the span of control is greatest in firms using batch or line technology, smaller in firms engaged in unit production, and smaller still in continuous process production. Therefore it would seem that the effect of technology is mediated by a social effect or that there are two interrelated effects. Assuming that the technologies used in the two countries are more or less comparable, what varies is the social use made of the technology.

Let us return, however, to the national regularities that are our main subject of inquiry. We regard the observed differences between the two countries not as a result but as a problem calling for further investigation.[7] In other words, for us the question is why (and how) French firms have

Table 2.2
Supervisory structure by type of production

| Type of production | Metals | | | | Petrochemicals | |
| | Unit | | Batch or line | | Continuous process | |
	France	Germany	France	Germany	France	Germany
Number of employees	2086	1615	920	656	2635	2642
Supervisory category:						
Production and maintenance foremen	21%	14%	57%	34%	40%	43%
Supervisory technicians	22%	21%	16%	26%	31%	31%
Middle and top managers	48%	53%	15%	26%	19%	25%
Total number of management employees	406	299	124	43	751	671
Percent	22%	18%ʼ	13%	7%	29%	25%

Source: LEST study, 1977.

both more office workers and more people in positions of managerial authority than German firms using comparable technologies. Conversely, why do German firms tend to use more b-c workers and fewer people in positions of menagenal? And why is the span of control greater in Germany?

If we look at the kinds of employees who are in positions of authority in the two countries, we can begin to answer these questions.

Table 2.2 shows that while there are proportionately more managers and supervisors in all the French firms, the distribution of these personnel by subcategory is different in the two countries. Thus the proportion of foremen is consistently higher in France. Conversely there tend to be more higher-level managers in Germany. This suggests that the differences between the two countries in regard to the proportion of management and supervisory personnel reflect mainly the higher proportion of middle management in French firms.

In particular, we find a significant divergence in management structures if we group foremen and supervisory technicians on the one hand and managers and office personnel in positions of authority on the other hand. We

Table 2.3
Supervisory structure and type of production

Supervisory type	Unit		Batch or line		Continuous process	
	France	Germany	France	Germany	France	Germany
Foremen and technical supervisors	43%	35%	73%	60%	71%	64%
Top management and other supervisory personnel	57%	65%	27%	40%	29%	36%
Firms:	A1	A1	B	B	A	A
Total supervisory personnel	406	299	124	43	751	671

Source: LEST study, 1977.

then have two types of supervisory personnel: the technical production supervisors and the administrative-management supervisors.[8] Table 2.3 shows that the proportion of technical-production supervisors is consistently higher in the French firms, whereas administrative-management supervisors predominate in Germany.

These results may come as a surprise since it will be recalled from our previous investigation of occupational training in Germany that supervisory personnel there tend to be more technically qualified than in France. We will give a more satisfactory interpretation of these preliminary findings after we have studied the management function and the training of management personnel more concretely.

The effects of national differences combine with the effects due to the use of different technologies. In this regard we find a sharp contrast between unit production, where the proportion of administrative-management personnel is higher, and batch, line, and continuous process production, where the technical production supervisors predominate. This contrast undoubtedly reflects the importance of client relations in unit production, requiring a large design, sales, and marketing staff, whereas the other two types of production involve a greater division of labor in the operation of a highly mechanized assembly line (line) or automated process control, requiring large maintenance and quality control departments.

One way of accounting for the national differences would be to argue that as each industrial system developed socially and historically, there was a tendency for the division of labor to develop in certain ways, associated with certain types of technology, and thus to stamp both practice and ideology in each country with certain specific traits.[9] This does not mean that technology was the sole determinant of the hierarchical and functional organization of production. Technology invariably leaves some room for maneuver in this regard, as the national differences summarized indicate. We propose to conceptualize both the determinism and the margin or liberty in terms of what we are calling the social effect. The fact that some technologies are relatively stable while others change rapidly (or fall to new innovations) might be explicable by the state of social relations in a given society or group of societies.

Another possible explanation of the observed differences is that they are related to the categories in which the data are presented. We have collected the data in terms of standard international categories, but this procedure imposes a uniformity on the data that is not present in social reality. The French agent de maîtrise, the German Meister, and the U.S. foreman, for example, do not have the same social identity or technical responsibilities. On the other hand, these terms are not mere statistical invention. They are real social and technical categories. Periodic debates about them in each of the countries exist quite independent of the uses to which they are put in international comparison. And their content and implications for the distribution of income, authority, and responsibility are the subject of intense dispute and conflict within managerial and labor organizations and often the focal point of industrial disputes and labor conflict. It is our contention that their comparative meaning can be understood only by a comparison of the organizations in which they are embedded in the two countries.

2.2 Work System and Cooperation in the Workplace

In our discussion of worker socialization in chapter 1, we discovered two ways in which firms relate to society. In Germany, industry plays a predominant role in designing and organizing the system of occupational training. Compared with the state-run educational system in France, it may appear that German employers lay a heavy hand on the German system, particularly in the light of the frequent protests aroused in France by any attempt to bring occupational training into closer association with industry. But what is remarkable in Germany is that many other social institutions—unions, churches, and towns—have established occupational training programs of their own, which reveals a fairly broad consensus about the value of acquiring professional skill. Indeed this is a central value in German culture. Stated another way, in a society in which industry enjoys a particularly high status, great importance will be attached to the means of acquiring professional skills.[10]

It seems clear that the apprenticeship system itself is an index of the degree to which German industry is integrated into German society. But there is another side of the coin: the apprenticeship system (by and large regarded as legitimate by all segments of society, at least until now) establishes professional norms and hierarchies that industry must recognize.[11] There is indeed a high correlation between training, credentials, and jobs in German industry, no doubt facilitated by the system of codetermination [Mitbestimmung, or joint responsibility for certain aspects of management by workers and employers—Trans.], which embraces this area of personnel management. In this respect French firms seem to have a freer hand in defining jobs and organizing their internal hierarchies in that the existing system of job classification imposes few constraints and rarely relies on formal credentials. The institutional link between French industry and the relatively autonomous educational system is not highly developed; this corresponds to the greater emphasis in France on in-house training.[12]

Thus we see two different relationships between firms on the one hand and society on the other—or, more precisely, between the productive system and the educational system. This shows how organization and socialization can interact. Consequently the organizational factor (the impact of the organized division of labor on the relation of individuals to society) is just another way of looking at the individual in his social context, which complements our earlier investigation of the educational factor.

The way we approach the study of the organizational factor here emphasizes both the social relations produced by the firm itself and social relations that penetrate the firm from the outside. Indeed the firm itself is constituted by certain aspects of these social relations, which develop within and help to produce a certain context of available skills and a certain organizational environment.

This contrast between the skill domain and the organizational domain is a way of talking about the processes that form the collective identity of the social actors and structure the associated social relations. We shall be looking at two aspects of organization: cooperation and hierarchy. These express themselves in the logic of the work system and the organization of the firm.

2.2.1 Job Requirements and Worker Qualifications: Polyvalence

Our research not only takes account of varying technology but also discloses variation in work organization and personnel management policies as well as job structures.[13]

It would seem that organization affects the influence of technology on the organization of the plant. Although dividing up a production process and defining work stations may seem to be purely technical acts, they are in fact choices based on socially defined criteria. They are not merely contingent but also "true decisions, based on assumptions about the worker's psychology, capabilities, interests, and reasons for working."[14] These decisions, moreover, reflect the social conditions in which they are made: the distribution of skills available on the labor market, the distribution of authority within the firm, and the power structure.[15]

The problems of job definition and organization of the productive process therefore cannot be treated independently of the interaction between socialization and organization. What is important is the way the firm conceives of the socialization process and the differentiation of tasks in the workplace. More than that, organizational techniques are themselves related to the state of social relations in the society at large.

Theoretically a firm can organize its work system in one of two ways: it can define jobs according to its own criteria and require workers to adapt or train them to fit the job definition, or it can take account of the existing qualifications of the work force and design jobs around the capabilities of the workers. In the first case, job demands determine the worker's profile. In the second case, the worker's profile exerts an influence on the job definition. In actual firms, of course, the worker-job relationship is never quite so clear-cut, but the situation is usually fairly close to one of the tendencies observed in our study of French and German firms. The process of job definition seems to be governed by a logic similar to the logic we discovered at work in our analyses of worker training and mobility.

The first process, definition of the job by the firm using its own criteria, is more likely to occur where occupational training is not very highly developed and where relatively few workers receive such training.[16] As a result the firm finds it possible to set work organization criteria of its own in such a way that there is a sharp distinction between nonsupervisory positions, which require only a short period of on-the-job training, and positions involving design and organizational responsibility. This type of job definition tends to devalue the former kind of job relative to the latter.[17] Firms following this kind of procedure will pay attention mainly to a worker's potential, that is, to his capacity to adapt to its internally defined work process and norms. The time a worker has spent within the organization (his seniority) then becomes the best index of professional success.

The second type of worker-job relationship is more likely to be found in a country where occupational training is widespread and socially legitimate, in consequence of which firms will tend to organize production around the norms of the training system. In this case the work system will place greater emphasis on the relative autonomy of the workers and reward the productivity associated with their qualifications rather than their adaptation to the organization.

In order to describe the nature of a work system, we shall make use of the notion of polyvalence: the capability of a worker to shift from position to position within a given productive organization. The notion of qualification implicit in a given work system is revealed by the sort of polyvalence it fosters. Polyvalence also contributes to the development of the social relations of production. It is therefore an important characteristic of any work system.

The fact that the industrial labor market in Germany features a limited number of basic occupational types, employed by all industries[18] and based on early apprenticeship training,[19] is favorable to the development of polyvalence since the skill base on which firms may draw tends to be relatively homogeneous. But different firms can use this basic fund of skills in different ways. Consider the example of a German petrochemical firm (which we shall compare later to a similar firm in France).[20] Polyvalence is rather prevalent in the petrochemical industry in both countries. This has to do partly with the nature of continuous process technology and partly with the desire to build into the system a degree of flexibility in skills and tasks in order to ensure the safety of both personnel and installations and to guard against interruptions of production. In practical terms these concerns translate into a fair degree of rotation of workers from one post to another within plants and even between different production units within a large petroleum processing facility.

Take one type of production unit as an example, say a catalytic cracking plant. Such a plant has several types of jobs arranged in a hierarchy. At the top are the control room jobs, where operators control various processes electronically, and below these positions are various equipment operators and mechanics who perform manual tasks outside the control room. Each team is under the authority of a shift leader who has above him a foreman and an engineer in charge of the production unit. The latter two employees work a normal day, whereas the team members work successive shifts (three eight-hour shifts per day).[21] In the French and German firms we studied, it appears that work was organized in reasonably similar ways (although we did find appreciable differences in the authority structure). However, a qualitative analysis of the way tasks were apportioned within each team and the way access to jobs was determined revealed fairly significant differences in the way the two plants functioned.

2.2.1.1 Polyvalence in German Firms

In the German firm the shift leader had more responsibility than his French counterpart. He had the authority, for instance, to assign specific operators to various posts. He also had responsibility for organizing the regular rotation of operators from one post to another in accordance with criteria decided upon by the control group (the term used to describe the group consisting of the foreman, shift leaders, and workers). The control group was allowed considerable autonomy in determining work zones corresponding to various complementary jobs organized by the Meister (foreman) together with the shift leaders. The foreman was given a free hand to do this with an eye to developing the workers' professional capabilities.

Polyvalence, in the sense we are using the term here, is undoubtedly one of the leading characteristics of work organization in German firms.[22] If there are slightly fewer skilled workers in petrochemical plants than in metallurgical plants, the reason is that no credential-accrediting skilled petrochemical workers existed until 1960.[23] But even those workers lacking such a credential are capable of doing most of the jobs in the plant because of skills learned in the course of rotation from job to job under the foreman's supervision. According to the manager of one of the cracking plants we visited, 90 percent of the workers in the plant were qualified to do any job in the plant, and most envisioned studying for certification as skilled chemical workers: "Even those who have mastered the job of panel-operator in the control room continue to rotate two or three months out of the year, so that they stay familiar with all the jobs in the plant." To qualify for all jobs, a worker requires a minimum of two to three years of experience. Not all workers have an equal chance of getting such experience. According to one shift leader, "Of twenty workers in the unit, eight are fully capable of working the control panel (the most highly skilled jobs), and ten, that is half, can work as equipment operators."

The fact that we find such a degree of polyvalence in this German firm, where it serves not only as a method of organizing work but also as a means of training workers, is all the more remarkable in that what might have been expected was a greater division of labor and some degree of deskilling of the nonsupervisory positions in an industry as highly auto-mated as this one and without the craft traditions of the metals trades.[24] This raises the question whether relatively recent developments in technology will not disrupt patterns of work that have persisted in the metallurgical and particularly the machinery industry without major changes from the early days of industrialization up to the present. Where know-how based on manual skills derived from old craft traditions has hitherto dominated, can we not expect to see the development of a more abstract form of the division of labor? Will this not accentuate the distinction between design functions, reserved to engineers and their technical assistants, and routine functions and monitoring tasks requiring no real skill but merely a capacity to adjust psychologically to monotony and risk and even physiologically to eight-hour mass production shift work? Also interesting about the petrochemical plant is the way the technology used leaves the firm and particularly middle management a significant margin of liberty in defining jobs and assigning workers to different positions. As Duncan Gallie remarks in his important recent study of oil refineries in England and France, "One of the factors that makes the level of employment particularly problematic in a continuous process industry is the extreme difficulty of establishing criteria to assure a level technically adequate to run the installation."[25] The difficulty comes from the fact that the labor requirements vary depending on whether the plant is operating normally or has suffered a serious breakdown. In between these two extreme situations it is hard to know what the optimum level of employment is. Hence company policy in this regard is always some sort of compromise, and as Gallie rightly notes, this tends to strain worker-management relations. The question of employment level becomes an issue for both management , and the workers and their unions, whose interests are in conflict.

Should the reserve work force kept on to deal with unforeseeable incidents and to allow for flexibility in production be skilled or unskilled? Gallie's work turns up significant differences in practice between French and English firms, and our own work reveals further differences between French and German firms.[26]

In the German firm, we found that automation did not necessarily limit the workers' acquisition of skills. This apparently paradoxical situation becomes clearer after talking to a number of unit managers. They commonly put forward an argument that goes like this: It would be possible to automate some units further, but optimal operation of the installation requires leaving certain operations under manual control. This is desirable because it keeps workers on their toes and interested in what would otherwise be no more than routine monitoring work in many cases. But beyond that, even if the plant were fully automated, workers would still have to perform certain tasks manually: those that would have to be done manually in case of a technical breakdown requiring a halt in production followed by a fresh start-up of the process. The know-how required to perform these operations is essential and must be part of the worker's professional qualification.

What makes this argument even more convincing is the fact that in this and similar firms, management is always concerned to limit the level of employment while increasing productivity through technological innovation.[27] But this objective can be achieved in different ways. In the plant we looked at, it is reasonable to conclude that reliance on polyvalence not only promoted cooperation within the work team but in so doing enabled management to achieve optimal functioning of the plant with a minimum of manual labor reserve. "A fifteen-man work-team could actually get by with twelve workers," according to one shift leader.[28] This observation is not inconsistent with the fact that the proportion of b-c workers in the German firm is higher than in its French counterpart. As we shall see, this difference reflects a similar difference in the number of workers, technicians, and managers in the two firms. The fact that there are more b-c workers in the German case may indicate that their productivity is greater than that of their French counterparts, partly because polyvalence has given them a more well-rounded qualification that enables them to shoulder part of the burden assumed in the French firm by the white collars.[29] It should also be noted that cooperation develops not only among the b-c workers who rotate from job to job but also, extends to the skilled workers, foremen, and graduate engineers, whose basic professional training was similar to that of the b-c workers under them.

Polyvalence is not confined to the petrochemical industry. In the batch and line metals industries we studied (a steel tube plant and an automobile wheel rim plant), we also found polyvalence in the German firms. Thus in Germany polyvalence cannot be explained by the continuous process technology or the high proportion of skilled labor in the work force. This observation leads to an important point about the differences between skilled and unskilled workers. There are in fact two kinds of apprenticeship in Germany, each corresponding to a particular type of skilled qualification: long apprenticeship is better known, but there is also short apprenticeship.

Long apprenticeship prepares skilled workers, known in Germany as Facharbeiter, who correspond formally to the French professional grades OP2, OP3, and OQ. The short apprenticeship trains semiskilled workers or *angelernte Arbeiter*, equivalent to the French OP1. Short apprenticeship (which is recognized nationally by the chambers of commerce and industry and prepares workers for trades listed in the official catalog of occupations, or Berufsbild) is conducted within the firm. For a period of two years the apprentice (who is not necessarily a young worker) is assigned to various jobs that fall within the province of his future trade (or occupational specialty). One day per week he also receives theoretical instruction, either on the job from his Meister or in a professional school (Berufsschule). Systematic rotation designed in this way to serve as an apprenticeship program for training new workers is another form of polyvalence, which is particularly prevalent in both batch and line production industries, generally said to have low skill requirements. Given this state of affairs, it would be misleading to compare the German semiskilled worker, or angelernte Arbeiter, with the French semiskilled worker, or ouvrier spécialisé (OS). Indeed there is reason to think that many so-called semiskilled workers in Germany are in fact more qualified than many French workers classified as OP1 or OP2 (in skilled categories).[30] This observation casts doubt on comparisons of job structure that use formal classifications to compare different categories of workers.

In the German steel tube and wheel rim plants (both batch and line production, highly mechanized, and partially automated production facilities) the fact that there is a relatively high proportion of semiskilled workers indicates that the potential skill base is fairly high compared with what we find in comparable French plants. We are well aware, however, that the basis for such a comparison is tenuous in that it assumes the existence of a skill standard against which actual skills can be measured, and our research tends to cast doubt on the notion of such a standard. Rather the way in which professional know-how is acquired is different in the two countries. Workers therefore acquire their collective identities in different ways, and this means that the skill potentials in the two countries are not necessarily similar in kind, let alone in degree; thus the productive efficiency of a worker in one country cannot be compared directly with the productive efficiency of a similarly classified worker in the other.

Consider the wheel rim plants. B-C workers account for about 85 percent of the total work force in the German plant (more or less equivalent to the French plant). There is a slightly higher percentage of skilled workers in the German plant: 20 percent versus 17 percent in France. But the proportion of semiskilled workers is far higher in the German plant, accounting for about one-third of all b-c workers. Thus about half of the b-c workers in the

German plant have undergone either the short or the long form of apprenticeship and can therefore lay claim to some degree of polyvalence in their skills. This is all the more remarkable in view of the fact that two-thirds of the workers were at this time (1976) immigrants [guest workers—Trans.] (whereas only half the workers in the French plant were immigrants). One shift leader we interviewed indicated that one-third of the workers on his team could do any job that came up, though none was a certified professional. The Meister in each production unit or production line (of which there are several, corresponding to the various products manufactured by the plant) is responsible for rotating workers from one job to another and for updating each worker's personnel file to record skill level in each area of competence.[31] In this way the company maintains a sort of skill reserve on which it can draw to fill machinist and line operator jobs and to select shift leaders (Vorarbeiter) who play an important role in organizing and monitoring the progress of work.[32]

Similarly, in the German tube plant, which also had a high proportion of b-c workers (88 percent compared with 76 percent in the French plant), nearly two-thirds of whom were not certified skilled workers, the foremen were responsible for rotating workers from one job to another. In the welding shop, for example, the Meister describing the organization of the work stated that the "chief machine operator" (who sets up and controls the automatic welding machinery) was the most qualified worker in the shop "because he had done all the other jobs before being promoted to his present position." Similarly most shift leaders are familiar with all the machines in the shop; at a minimum they have completed the apprenticeship of a semiskilled worker. The company itself runs training programs for shift leaders. After taking one of these courses a worker is added to a roster of skills until a position becomes available. In contrast to what takes place in the French plant, in the German company training precedes promotion. This is standard practice in German companies at all levels of the hierarchy. The foremen encourage workers to participate in these training programs. As one shift leader put it, "They like it around here when you've had any kind of occupational training, and they like it even better when the training is in the metal trades." Here again the emphasis placed by the company on occupational training is all the more remarkable in view of the fact that around 80 percent of the workers are immigrants.

These observations of two line production plants show that polyvalence is found not only in industries with a high proportion of skilled workers in the work force.

2.2.1.2 Polyvalence in French Firms

In the French job classification system, each job is assigned a coefficient and is thus situated along a continuum running from the lowliest worker to the highest manager. Since the coefficient attaches to the job rather than to the worker, the system rates the skill requirement of the position rather than the skill of the worker.[33] The classifications are arrived at by negotiation within each branch of industry, but each firm is free to assign coefficients to previously defined job categories in the light of the job content set forth by the collective bargaining agreement for the branch as a whole.

The rigidity of this system (which a recent reform has attempted to simplify and make more flexible) has a direct influence on personnel management and on the way the work system operates. The situation is in some respects reminiscent of the functioning of the civil service.[34] As Michel Brossard has observed, "The assignment of coefficients to jobs results in attributing considerable importance to the organizational structure of work as a bargaining issue and means that grievances must be treated at a high level of the industrial relations system.[35] We shall have more to say about the significance of this system when we compare it to the German system, where the worker's qualifications and training are given the highest priority. For the present the important point is that the French system (in which the importance of administration outweighs that of professional competence) tends to hamper the development of polyvalence of the sort that exists in German firms.

Although polyvalence does exist in French petrochemical firms, it was first conceived purely as a personnel management technique. The practice was adopted mainly as a way of coping with absenteeism and of ensuring continuity in the production process; also in some cases it was used as a way of overcoming labor problems by integrating manufacturing and maintenance work more than had been done previously.[36] Thus polyvalence was not intended to be used as one component of a program of worker training, though it might incidentally contribute to extending the knowledge and experience of those few workers who were affected by the use of polyvalence for reasons of personnel administration.

In one of the firms we looked at, the production manager, a chemical engineer, described the reasons for first using polyvalent workers: "Those chosen were among the best workers, those most capable of adapting.[37] Because of their special working conditions (they must be on call and change shifts frequently), these workers receive a stress bonus and thus make more money than other workers although their coefficient has not changed." What in fact happened was that gradually the polyvalent workers came to form a higher-status category; conscious of the fact that they represented a sort of worker elite, they demanded a coefficient higher than that of the skilled workers, indeed high enough to place them among the top foreman ranks.[38] But this demand met with opposition from supervisory personnel and management. The head of the general services department of the same firm was quite explicit about his reasons: "A polyvalent worker is someone who is familiar with two, three, or four jobs.... He is not in any way an intermediate supervisor of some sort. He fills in for absent workers but doesn't give orders. You may very well know plenty of jobs and yet not be capable even of being a shift leader if you don't know how to give orders or organize work.... They [the polyvalent workers] are familiar with a number of jobs, but still all that's involved is repeated procedures, handiwork, nothing more. So it's not clear that being a polyvalent is the way to jump up to shift leader."[39] This opinion seems to be rather widely shared among supervisory personnel in the petrochemical industry. The point to notice is that it reveals a way of thinking about polyvalence consistent with the idea that qualification is an attribute of the job rather than the worker. Since job assignment involves nothing more than finding an individual with the right profile (or potential) to fit a specific job (defined as a set of tasks of a certain technical complexity), polyvalence can only be thought of as a capacity for holding several jobs (for taking on new tasks), and the notion of the worker's professional status as such does not even come up.[40] Rather polyvalence tends to mark out a specific category of worker and set them apart from the rest. This explains why polyvalent workers in this particular firm demanded special status, whereas in another petrochemical firm, union representatives opposed such a demand on the grounds that "it would destroy the solidarity of the work teams." Indeed this statement is a succinct formulation of the logic of the work system in use in France and of the logic of polyvalence itself. In other words, whereas polyvalence in the German system helps to broaden a worker's training and contributes to the development of a collective consciousness of professionalism in the work force, in France its purpose is seen as that of establishing a marginal group of elite workers whose skill is to serve the company's interest by ensuring that production will not be interrupted. Union representatives cannot help feeling that polyvalent workers therefore hinder worker solidarity, a solidarity fostered by a system of advancement based largely on seniority and by the practice of attaching coefficients to jobs rather than workers. In a system that is comparatively bureaucratic, any practice perceived as an exception to the rules inevitably hinders group solidarity (which in this case is more a matter of shared status than one of professional community).[41]

The ambiguity of the polyvalent worker's status was described in a clear way by one shop foreman, who said that polyvalence has been confused with multivalence. What is really involved is a contradiction between two ways of conceiving of professional qualification. Polyvalent workers themselves refuse to substitute on the least skilled jobs (on the pretext that their coefficient is too high for such work). The workers who normally do such jobs then point to their indispensability to try to have their own ratings upgraded. It is easy to see that no true polyvalence can develop in such a context. Assuming that the real purpose of polyvalence is skill development, it may be that the practice is incompatible with a system of personnel management based more on administrative management than on professional development.

It is also noteworthy that in French firms using batch and line production technology, polyvalence is not used as a means of upgrading the skill of the work force, whereas it is used for this purpose in Germany. The reason is that polyvalence is in many ways incompatible with the work systems and personnel management procedures employed in such firms.

In the tube plant, for example, which was similar to the German firm in technology and type of product and also employed a high proportion of unskilled workers, professional experience and on-the-job training mainly served to reinforce the hierarchy rather than to develop the collective capabilities of the work force. This was true in particular of the line operators chosen by the foremen from the ranks of the assembly line workers for their capacity to adapt to several different jobs. According to the production manager, this practice represented "nothing resembling a true notion of polyvalence" but rather a way of coping with the high absenteeism in the plant. The best line operators are ranked as acting craftsmen—classed P1 or P2—and given on-the-job training as back-up line operators for a period of nine months to a year.[42] Their function is essentially technical. Although they work in a team with three or four ordinary workers, they do not exercise authority. Until recently shift leaders were selected from this group. Lately, however, a new category of workers has been established: head mechanics, who are "something like technical assistants to the shift leader." Chosen by supervisors in the same way as the line operators, their function is also technical, but they are classified differently. The shop manager explained their role in the new organization as follows: "Their job is to relieve the foremen, who had to spend too much of their time making technical adjustments to the machines. With a head mechanic at each work station, the foremen have enough time to do their real job as shift leaders: supervise the workers, do all the administrative work, and of course handle all the problems with the union representatives." We shall have more to say about the functions of the foremen, but already we can see from this brief look at the line operators and head mechanics how little autonomy is left to the regular assembly line workers.

This example (on the basis of which it would obviously be wrong to generalize) shows that worker qualifications and even worker status are unstable quantities: a small minority or workers who show "an above-average adaptability and motivation" (as one shop manager put it) are co-opted by the hierarchy. These workers receive on-the-job training and are then assigned to jobs more technical than those left to the regular assembly line personnel. The latter are restricted to the purely repetitive tasks for which they were hired, while their fortunate colleagues acquire know-how that enables them to relieve the foremen of the need to perform technical jobs (thus showing that the foreman's role is not essentially technical) while awaiting promotion to a supervisory position of their own. It would seem, then, that the reinforcement of the hierarchy is based on the (long-term) weakening of the collective professional capacity of the work force, since only a minority of workers are chosen to become acting professionals. This is interpreted by some as an attack on worker solidarity, in that workers who are rated above average are put in the position of becoming candidates for supervisory jobs.

This tube plant does not appear to be an exceptional case. We find similar worker promotion procedures in another plant manufacturing rims for automobile wheels. These procedures actually tend to reduce the skill potential of the bulk of the work force. As in the comparable German wheel plant, most of the workers in the French plant were semiskilled. The product, manufactured on a line, is relatively simple. The main production problems are that frequent retooling takes place and that stringent quality control checks must be carried out to ensure road safety. In recent years immigrant workers have been used in this kind of work in France and Germany. Immigrants account for half the work force in the French plant and two-thirds in the German plant. In this respect the industrial logic seems to be the same in both cases.

In the French firm (which, like its German counterpart, is a subsidiary of a major corporation), workers are hired mainly for their physical fitness rather than their skills.[43] The high noise level in the shops rules out hiring anyone with hearing problems. Candidates are given psychotechnical tests to evaluate their dexterity, precision of motion, and speed of reaction. According to the personnel manager, "Adaptation is rapid. After one week we know if a new worker will fit in or not. No skill is required." In his opinion a primary school certificate (CEP) is better than a professional certificate (CAP): "They've got to know how to read and write, and school gives them a certain education which is good for internal promotion.[44] This mainly involves head mechanics and provides advancement for a small number of semiskilled workers. They start out P1 and end up P3 or P4 with seniority if they're good. Head mechanics are never hired off the street. They're men who come up through the ranks. After being spotted by the chief mechanic (P3, P4) and the foreman, they start out as replacements. It's experience that counts. Unfortunately, the fellow the foreman likes is not always the most highly skilled but the one who does him the most favors." If the new head mechanic shows himself adept at assuming responsibility (stopping the line, assigning personnel, giving orders, training new men) he can eventually move up to chief mechanic or even shift leader, "the pivotal position between workers and management." A technical training course— one day a week taken out of work time for a month or two was recently organized for workers who had already been promoted. Thus training in the French firm was offered to complement promotion rather than being, as in the German firm, a prerequisite for promotion. The head mechanics thus form "a breeding ground for future supervisory personnel."[45] In the meantime they constitute a reservoir of technical competence between the ordinary workers and supervisors: the ordinary workers have no need of such know-how ("their jobs don't require it") and neither do the foremen ("for them technical training is no longer necessary—they've acquired work experience in house, and their job is to work as supervisors, not technicians"). The company, because of this specific form of work organization, operates now under a system of "supervisory personnel with technical support (the head mechanics)." We shall see that this work system also relies on the contribution of technical departments whose work precedes actual production; the result is to shift part of the technical burden away from the production line, further reducing the level of technical competence required of the ordinary worker.

We have now looked at two French firms engaged in line production and found many common features, though the type of product is different in each case. What is perhaps more significant is that in many areas of personnel management and work organization, these two firms resemble the petrochemical firm we looked at earlier, even though the latter uses a highly skilled work force and very advanced technology.

Already, then, we see that there are common features shared by firms in a particular country though they use different types of technology. As we shall try to show in the remainder of the book, the explanation of these similarities lies not in the effects of some sort of invisible hand or teleological principle but rather in the systematic structure of social factors influencing both the formation of the actors and the development of the industrial work system, factors that are at once the result of specific social relations and the cause of those relations.

Before we turn to this task, however, we must complete the analysis by looking at other organizational factors affecting the nature of the work system. We can then take an overall view of the system by which work is supervised and the social relations on which that system is based.

2.2.2 Technical Know-How and Task Execution

As our last example, we shall look at German and French firms using unit production technology. The firms in question are large facilities specializing in the manufacture of tanks and pressure vessels of large capacity for conventional and nuclear power plants as well as turbine and generator parts. The companies are subsidiaries of large corporations specialized, in the French case, in electrical and mechanical construction and, in the German case, in metal work and mechanical construction.[46]

In contrast to the metallurgical plants we looked at earlier, these plants have a relatively highly skilled work force, including both ordinary workers and technicians and engineers (whose number is proportionately greater). The specialized nature of the product requires just as much in the way of design studies, production planning, and work preparation as it does machining, folding and bending of thick sheet, and high-quality welding of special steels. The equipment being manufactured has parts that are of large size that nevertheless must be handled with great precision and close control of tolerances.[47] There is all the more reason to compare these two firms in that both face similar social and technical problems.

More than other kinds of production, this type of unit production requires careful planning of the work and close cooperation between the design department, the sales and service departments, and the manufacturing shops. A major concern of supervisors in all departments, apart from the quality of the product, is adherence to deadlines. These deadlines are of great economic significance to the firm because of the need for optimal utilization of very costly machines and facilities and because penalties for failure to meet schedules are written into sales contracts. This crucial ability to meet deadlines cannot be ensured simply by bureaucratic measures. In fact it is closely linked to the characteristics of a firm's organization and particularly to skills in interpersonal relations on which the professional level of the various categories of worker, from skilled craftsman to engineer, has a direct bearing.

Accordingly, in our analysis we treat the deadline problem in terms of qualification and professionalism.[48] We describe the social relations of production in terms of these characteristics. Both in themselves and through their interactions, each category of professionally qualified worker contributes to forming the identity of each actor in the industrial system and to establishing the social relations that define the firm. Such characteristics as differentiation, complementarity, and compartmentalization may be used to describe each category of qualification. Together these constitute the work force or human resources of the firm and determine not only its relational capacities but also the quality of its social relations. This is true even independently of the power relations or strategies that may develop among the various categories of actors in the productive system.[49] Note that relative levels of qualification, while contributing to the stratification of the firm's personnel, are not independent of relations of authority or power. By the same token, relations of cooperation cannot be isolated from the hierarchical relations through which the social relations of production express themselves.

For convenience, we shall refer to the relations that exist between categories of workers with different kinds of qualification as skill relations. We shall have more to say about skill relations when we discuss them in relation to the work domain.[50] For the moment, however, we shall confine ourselves to comparing French and German firms in the light of what we have already found out.

2.2.2.1 Master Workers and Demonstrators in One French Firm

We found the same kind of relations between workers and supervisors in two different kinds of firms in France: the firm using unit technology and the firm using batch and line technology. Notice that there are two lines of control in these firms. One set of supervisors represents the formal line of authority in the firm, embodied in the foremen, but there are also highly skilled workers who constitute a sort of technical hierarchy, forming both a worker elite and a staff providing technical backup to foremen absorbed by their administrative and liaison functions. In the firm using unit production technology, we find the same duality in the case of the master workers and demonstrators.

The master workers (there are two ranks in the official classification) are a minority within the ranks of highly skilled workers. They are capable of assuming broad responsibilities and taking initiative in accomplishing highly complex, precise work.

Although their responsibility is not as great as that of the foremen, they are responsible for on-the-job training and technical supervision of professional workers (OP2 and OP3) engaged in delicate machine work, assembly, and welding. Paid on a monthly basis (well before the agreement concerning monthly pay of production workers signed in 1970), the master workers are comparable to the foremen in terms of level of responsibility and seniority. (At least six years' seniority is required for a man to reach the first echelon, and this requires to recommendation of both foremen and shop supervisor).[51] In reality, though, their function is more that of worker technicians, helping to overcome the gaps in the skill and technical knowledge of the professional workers and the foremen.[52]

Although the number of demonstrators is relatively small compared with the number of master workers, their role is sufficiently important to warrant special attention.[53] They are not classed as workers, although their skills are often quite similar to those of workers. The ambiguity in their professional status is reflected in their organizational classification: "some are classified as technicians, others as supervisors." Their pay is comparable to that of foremen. Established more recently than the master worker category, the demonstrator category provides its members with an avenue of advancement. Skilled workers to begin with, demonstrators can rise to a coefficient of 340 (equal to that of the shop supervisors). Thus they rise above the highest worker echelon, for which the coefficient is 231 (the coefficient of master workers, second echelon). The demonstrators have a direct role in the production process and function to ensure deadlines, intervening to resolve breakdowns, delays, or unforeseen technical problems by supplying machinery, assembly, or welding operators. They are relatively polyvalent: demonstrators must be adept at adjusting machinery, setting up tools, and cutting metal. Advisers and technical experts, they do not hesitate "to turn the crank themselves if they feel it is necessary."

How does an employed become a demonstrator? It is up to management to "select the best men: those who are not only skilled with their hands but also show some gray matter."[54] Their training is essentially on the job, but before they actually go to work in their new jobs, they take company-run professional training courses "so that they won't switch directly from being workers to being demonstrators. . . . The training is not technical but focuses on the rudiments of educational technique." This is not a general rule, however.

The plant manager was quite explicit about the place of the demonstrator in the firm's system of skill relations, between the workers and the supervisors: "on the big machines, which frequently need two people to run them, rather than use a journeyman and a laborer (as is usually done) we preferred using a journeyman and a demonstrator, *who supplies the gray matter.* It's not entirely true to say that the journeyman is reduced to the position of a laborer, but he does follow orders: *the demonstrator is the brains of the operation* [emphasis added]." [55] Although demonstrators are paid as much as supervisors and although there is one demonstrator for every six or seven journeymen in the heavy equipment departments (machine shop, assembly), the plant manager felt that this arrangement was obviously advantageous economically: "We can make the same components ten to fifteen percent faster than other plants." [56]

As for social relations, the demonstrators generally seem to be accepted by the journeymen, "who always respect competence." They are not so well received, however, by the supervisors, who feel that they are gradually losing some of their professional know-how and being reduced to an administrative or disciplinary role. This accounts for a certain malaise among supervisory personnel, whose authority often seems to rest on uncertain ground when it comes to dealing with more competent young professionals and technicians from the design or industrial engineering departments.[57] Company policy is to make the supervisor a "human relations specialist." Moreover, since there is a certain disparity in the quality of life in the shops compared with that in the offices (to which young professionals are attracted), the company has adopted the following rule: "All other things being equal, we pay our shop supervisors and demonstrators 10 percent more than employees working in the front office.[58]

All in all, then, the case of the demonstrators is a good one for making clear the nature of the relationship between skill and social relations. A similar sort of relationship has been found in other French firms, though the details vary from case to case.

2.2.2.2 Work Distributors in a German Firm

In the comparable German firm using unit production technology, we also find a special category of workers who deal with scheduling and deadlines. The nature of this function is not the same as in the French firms, however, in that it is based on a different set of skill relations. In Germany these workers are known as work distributors. They monitor work in progress and play what one shop manager described as the role of "deadline beaters." In fact they perform a liaison function between the technical planning department and the production shops. Their main function is to help bring the time allocated for various jobs (in the planning stage) into line with the time actually required in the shop.[59]

As in the French firm, we find here signs of constant tension rising from the conflicting demands of deadlines, plant utilization, and time allotted for various tasks. The German firm has solved the problem in a different way, however. In the French firm the demonstrators take a direct hand in production, contributing their technical know-how to help solve production problems and keep work on schedule. In the German plant, the work distributors play only an indirect role in production by helping shift leaders and workers figure out how to do a job in the shortest possible time, given the utilization of each machine in the shop, in order to keep to the schedule laid down by the planning department. Thus the role of the work distributors is more to facilitate cooperation between the technical departments and the shops. The time constraints are different in the two cases.

Roughly, one might describe the two situations as follows. In France the demonstrators make up for deficiencies in the technical knowledge of the skilled workers; they overcome delays by bringing their individual technical prowess to bear on knotty problems. By contrast, the work distributors in the German firm improve cooperation between the shop floor and the front office by serving as go-betweens in negotiations over the time needed for certain jobs. It is possible in both countries to correct time allocations in the production schedule. In France, however, production planning is characterized by complicated formal procedures, and any attempt by the shops to get changes made in the production schedule has to be passed on through hierarchical channels.[60] In Germany there is a wider range of cooperation between technical support services and the shop floor, exemplified by the function of the work distributor itself.

What is the basis of this cooperation? Using the observations we made in this and other German plants, we can begin to answer this key question for understanding the German work system. We shall have more to say about this later. For the time being, however, two points need to be stressed: the emphasis placed within the firm on the importance of the production department and the fairly broad consensus on the principle of productivity. In French firms the technical departments generally control the production shops, a situation in keeping with the relatively limited autonomy afforded the production supervisors. In Germany, on the other hand, the technical departments (planning, maintenance, design, quality control, and even sales and purchasing) are in the service of the production department. This gives a relatively exalted status to the official in charge of this department (Produktionsleiter).[61] Accordingly the shop manager can resolve most problems associated with faulty time allocations as a result of the presence in the shop of work distributors and shop monitors reporting to the time allocation section of the planning department.[62] The most important problems are discussed in weekly meetings attended by the shop supervisors and all other supervisors as well as production and technical planning executives.

As far as the quality control department (which is independent of the production department) is concerned, the production manager told us that "cooperation between the quality control department and production is often so close that you might call it support rather than control." Notice, moreover, that, whereas in the French firm the quality control department reports directly to company management, in the German firm it reports to the executive in charge of the product group, which tends to foster a closer relationship between the quality control and production departments.[63]

Doubtless the importance attributed to the production department is related to the fact that there exists a broad consensus concerning productivity. We shall treat this problem more directly in the next chapter, but some aspects of it are worth considering here in the light of the role of the work distributors. Unlike most French firms, where time study experts (reporting to the time and methods department) often meet with hostility on the shop floor, in German firms there is recognition at all levels of the legitimacy of time scheduling allocations. These are established by specialists trained by an independent agency (REFA) and fall within the purview of codetermination. Thus the members of the company council, some of whom were trained by the same agency, participate in the setting of time standards.[64] While in both countries there are tensions and even conflicts concerning time allocations and deadlines, which are of great importance to company and workers alike, the standards set are regarded as the common concern of both, a concern that finds broader expression in the notion of Leistung (meaning both performance and personal commitment), probably one of the key words in the German industrial system. The Leistungsprinzip is in fact an essential ingredient of the system of "joint regulation"[65] (to borrow J.-D. Reynaud's expression) of industry and the market economy in Germany, a principle invoked by unions as well as employers.[64]

2.2.3 Relationship between Maintenance and Production Departments: Subcontracting

Another form of cooperation between production and technical departments that is found in both French and German petrochemical firms has to do with the organization of maintenance work. This is particularly note-worthy because in this industry maintenance workers account for 30 per-cent to 40 percent of the b-c work force. The number of laborers actually varies widely from one firm to another, depending on how much use is made of subcontracting. In the major French petrochemical firm in our study, the proportion of manual workers was as high as 50 percent, much higher than in the comparable German firm.[67] Other studies appear to show not only that maintenance is organized differently in this branch of industry in the two countries[68] but also that there are considerable dif-ferences in the number of workers assigned to maintenance tasks, largely because of differences in the use of subcontracting.[69] We cannot deal with the latter question directly here (no doubt a separate study would be required). We shall confine our attention to the relationship between the maintenance department and the production department and to the effects of this relationship on the cooperative work system.

There are two main ways of organizing maintenance in petrochemical plants: one can have either a central maintenance department separate from the production department or a maintenance section integrated into the production department. Both the French and German firms we looked at chose a central maintenance department.[70] However, although the organi-zational model is the same, the division of labor is rather different.

2.2.3.1 Organization and Maintenance in the German Firm

In the German firm, where there are twice as many workers in the mainte-nance department as in the French firm, some workers are detached to work in the production shops, while others, more numerous, work in the central maintenance department (actually there are two—one for electrical and the other for mechanical repairs). The comparable French firm has the same type of organization, but only a few workers and foremen are permanently assigned to the production department. There are more such workers in the German firm, and they include technicians and engineers. The presence of engineers and technicians reporting to a technical department in the pro-duction facility itself has to do with more than just maintenance. In one of this company's major cracking facilities, for example, we found not only engineers, technicians, and adjusters working for maintenance hut also three graduate engineers attached to quality control and monitoring, two supervisors, and two skilled workers (set-up men) from the same depart-ment. It is not hard to imagine how such an organization, with all its attendant questions of authority, complicates relations between technical and production personnel. For example, foremen in the central maintenance department take their orders from engineers detached to production. But mechanics detached to production take their orders from the production shift leader, although formally they report to maintenance.

The German firm seems to have overcome the difficulties inherent in such a complex form of organization by developing a spirit of generous cooperation at all levels, beginning with management in both the production and technical (including maintenance) departments. We did, however, find that production management tended to take precedence over technical management, as is indicated by the following remark of the personnel manager in regard to one production executive in the cracking facility: "He comes to the regular meetings between the production and technical people and is treated as the first among equals." In the personnel manager's mind, this state of affairs had to do with the special status of production in comparison with the other departments, since in the case in question there was no formal difference of rank involved.[71] The status of the production department is enhanced by another factor: in most chemical firms the production managers are chemical engineers with doctoral degrees, whereas most maintenance engineers are graduate engineers (nonuniversity trained). We shall have more to say about this when we discuss access to various jobs.

The cooperation between production and maintenance is based on a special notion of the maintenance function. Maintenance is not limited to repair or to what is usually called preventive maintenance. In the maintenance department we studied, the manager, a college-trained engineer with the status of Leitende Angestellte and Prokurist, supervised three other engineers of the group, themselves college graduates and Leitende Angestellte.[72] These three engineers in turn supervised a number of graduate engineers and technicians working in the various production facilities. This hierarchical structure is surprising in comparison with the maintenance organization of French firms, where there are fewer supervisors and less formal organization.[73] The reason becomes clear when we look at what the engineers and technicians do. The assistant to the maintenance manager is responsible for both maintenance planning and further training of all maintenance personnel.[74] The maintenance manager not only supervises current maintenance operations (emergency service, repairs) but also plans expanded maintenance operations as the firm grows amd helps to improve the production process. In this latter role, which involves both technological innovation and improvements in chemical processing, he must work to ensure close cooperation between the maintenance engineers and technicians and the chemical engineers in charge of the production facilities.

Periodic meetings are held in the various production facilities involving both maintenance and production engineers. Ways of improving existing technologies are discussed. The aim is to improve the quality of the product, to make the plant more reliable, and to decrease costs and environmental pollution. The maintenance engineers from group headquarters and the engineers attached to particular divisions are assigned to find out what the most common causes of breakdown are and to show how technical operations can be improved. They relay this information to the production engineers. Maintenance engineers are involved in more than just maintenance: they take part in doing the calculations necessary for running various chemical processes and even participate in the preparation of reports required for obtaining financing.

Because maintenance services are incorporated into a broader scheme of production improvement and technological innovation in which both maintenance and production experts take part, the problems inherent in the operation of a complex organization are reduced, thus alleviating the danger, high in such organizations, of conflicts of loyalty or sphere of authority. Cooperation is thus encouraged, and if conflicts are not eliminated, at least they are more easily dealt with than a glance at the formal organization chart might suggest.[75] Furthermore the existence of this kind of cooperation tends to despecialize technical capabilities and makes them available to the production facilities. This reduces the need to resort to outside subcontractors to perform maintenance tasks. If, on the other hand, maintenance is conceived in a narrower sense, limited to making repairs and coping with emergency breakdowns, it no doubt makes sense to rely on subcontractors. Cooperation of this sort can only magnify the effects of the professional socialization process already begun by training and education and by job selection procedures. Cooperative forms of work organization further tend to promote unity among empolyees based on commonly shared skills or professional backgrounds and thus to overcome the inevitable divisions inherent in any organization.

2.2.3.2 Maintenance Organization in the French Firm

Turning now to one of the comparable French firms, it is all the more surprising to find how differently it operates, given how similar its formal structure is to that of the German firm. This being the case, we can dispense with the description of the firm's formal structure and go directly to a discussion of how it differs from its German counterpart—in regard to the relationship of maintenance to production. To be sure, this firm, like all others in the petrochemical business, was forced to try to reduce costs by limiting the number of employees directly or indirectly associated with the production process. This cost reduction campaign began in the 1960s and not, as is often thought, with the recent oil crisis. Because of the nature of the technology used in this industry, firms have a certain degree of freedom in the use of workers. Hence job assignment issues become an important focus of labor-management relations. It is in this context that firms must decide how to organize the relationship of maintenance to production. A widely practiced system, much in favor with management consulting firms, is to subcontract for maintenance services and thus reduce its in-house maintenance staff to a bare minimum.[76] For reasons that deserve further study, French firms seem to have utilized this system more often than firms in other countries.[77]

By studying the history of changes in the organization of maintenance in one French firm, we can better understand the inner logic of the firm's organization. During the 1950s and 1960s the primary concern of petrochemical firms was to maximize output in every way possible, consistent with the need to ensure continuous operations. In this period maintenance was conceived of as a way, in fact the most important way, of achieving this goal. This required the most direct possible relationship between the maintenance and production departments. The effectiveness and quality of maintenance were seen as being more important than its direct cost. The objective was at all costs to avoid production stoppages.[78]

In the early 1970s, however, a radical reorganization was undertaken after a study by a management consulting firm. As the price of the product rose (leading to a new emphasis on quality rather than quantity of production and to redoubled efforts to develop new marketable by-products), the need arose for greater reliability of the installations and greater flexibility in their operation (especially as production became more diversified). Maintenance became more autonomous than it had been, and its contribution to the overall profit picture became a crucial concern. Corporate headquarters decided that fixed costs had to be reduced as much as possible. The maintenance department was attached to the general services department, and the maintenance manager now reported directly to top corporate management, just as the production manager did.[79] Among the new corporate goals was that of cutting back the number of maintenance personnel employed by the firm and using subcontractors to do both emergency and regular maintenance work instead. The new maintenance manager (who had previous experience in maintenance in an oil refinery) chose to set up a central maintenance shop and to locate smaller shops in each production facility. The aim was not so much to match maintenance skills to production skills as to meet an economic requirement: to load up a minimum number of personnel with a maximum amount of work, while carefully planning what maintenance work to subcontract out.[80] From this point on maintenance policy was dictated by economic considerations. Closely monitored by corporate headquarters, the maintenance manager in turn carefully supervises the work of engineers and supervisors reporting to him. These employees are constantly caught between two conflicting demands: to perform maintenance work as cheaply as possible while being useful to the production people with whom they must work closely. A commonly heard complaint is that "we are caught between two systems. Frequently we would be happy to oblige production by replacing a defective piece of equipment, but the maintenance manager says, 'No, that would cost too much, figure out some other way to do it.'" Having little autonomy to make decisions on their own, maintenance engineers are forced to invoke procedural rules that define when, where, and what they may do in order to avoid conflicts with their colleagues in production.[81] Maintenance jobs of any size must be approved through both maintenance and production hierarchical channels. As the maintenance manager told us with considerable pride, "Those decisions come to me." His relations with the engineers and foremen under him are thus much the same as his own relations with his superiors, particularly his superiors at corporate headquarters.

This form of maintenance organization, with an autonomous and centralized maintenance department, is probably not as conducive to the development of cooperative work relations as the system in the German firm we examined earlier. Worse, the fact that maintenance operations are governed by criteria of cost defined internally by the maintenance department itself, which also determines its own functions rather narrowly and independently of the production facilities and other technical support departments, means that maintenance is inevitably compartmentalized and cut off from the rest of the firm's activities. This economism, to coin a term to describe this style of management, may make sense from an accounting standpoint (and, indeed, stringent accounting techniques are employed in the firm in question), but it works against efficient management of the firm as a whole, management that would foster technological innovation and constant improvement in the production process, which is what the German firm seems to have achieved. But is the only difference between the two firms a matter of organization? Formally the two structures are very close. The original problems with which both firms were confronted were quite similar. The real difference seems to lie in the logic of the two systems and their attendant social relations.

It does no good to compare the two organizations directly. What matters is the actors, viewed not so much in terms of their strategies (in one case based on codified rules, in the other case on joint regulation revolving around the values of Leistung and Bildung) as in terms of the processes that shape their collective identities, as well as the work space within which they establish social relations among themselves.

We shall accordingly turn to an analysis of these processes. In particular, we shall be looking at how people are selected for various functions within the firm and at how hierarchies of authority and systems of social control are established in each country.

2.3 Hierarchical Structures and System of Supervision

The organizational hierarchy or supervisory structure of the firm has often been studied by sociologists. Paradoxically, though, most of these studies, while telling a good deal about how organizations work, add little to our knowledge of how an organizational hierarchy is constituted. Organization theorists generally regard the structure of the hierarchy as a functional requirement made necessary either by the size of an organization or the type of technology employed. Specialists in management take the view that hierarchy is an inevitable concomitant of all rational and efficient industrial management; to be sure, management is not always optimum, but its defects (destined always to be eliminated) are, by this view, reflections of cultural deficiencies or economic backwardness.[82] The ideal management model is supposed to be universal, and any nation whose management structures vary from the ideal merely makes manifest some defect in its conception of the management function. Some Marxist-influenced writers take the view that the industrial hierarchy is a reflection of class domination in the sphere of productive relations, a form of exploitation and extraction of surplus value. We shall have more to say about these interpretations of the role of management later. For the time being it is enough to call attention to what all of them have in common: the claim that the industrial hierarchy is universal in character. The hierarchy is seen as a response to functional requirements due to the size of the firm, the technology used, or the need to maximize profit or surplus value. The social characteristics of the actors involved in the hierarchy are unimportant in any of these models, except perhaps in a purely abstract way.

We take a different approach. The questions we want to ask are the following: How are the different groups of actors involved in the hierarchy created in each country? How are they differentiated from one another?

And how is access to specific echelons of the hierarchy determined? We take for granted the fact that some form of domination exists in any society and is reflected in the existence of hierarchies and other phenomena associated with social stratification. But the specific form that social domination takes is not given in nature or predetermined by history; furthermore the social meaning of domination varies from one society to the next. These are the areas for social scientists explore. Consequently we do not assume that the form of the industrial hierarchy is independent of the way in which that hierarchy is produced socially. In other words, the industrial hierarchy stands in dialectical relation to social relations in the society at large, in part both cause and effect of those relations.

Our approach suggests that the way to understand the industrial hierarchy is to look at the interaction between organization and socialization. We cannot hope to understand the hierarchy within the firm unless we have some idea about how its employees are socialized. In particular, we need to know how access to education and professional training are determined and how these relate to the assignment of employees to different career tracks and to the way work is divided within the firm. In any society both the socialization process and the organizational process are shaped by the same social forces, and both therefore play a role in unifying and stabilizing the social structure.

Now that we have looked at some of the key features of the work systems employed in French and German firms, we are ready to look at the ways in which access to different job categories is determined and at the way collective identities are shaped, in particular those collective identities that go into the creation of the industrial hierarchy.[83] We shall also look further into the question of access to b-c jobs, because it is our conviction that the study of management is inseparable from the study of workers, just as the study of the front office is inseparable from the study of the shop floor. The firm—meaning an organization together with the social relations that animate that organization—is thus what is sometimes referred to as a totality but a totality that is neither homogeneous nor hermetically sealed. Comparison of firms in different countries is therefore a useful way of identifying the most important dividing lines in each country's social structure and of determining how open or closed each society is.

2.3.1 Industrial Hierarchy in Germany: Span of Work and Production

In France and Germany access to industrial jobs varies considerably depending on the type of production, which influences the skills required. We have seen, for instance, that the proportion of skilled workers is higher in petrochemical plants and in plants of firms manufacturing heavy equipment with unit production technology than it is in plants manufacturing wheels or tubes with batch and line production techniques. Our observations also revealed that technology does not determine skills required as rigorously as might have been thought. In firms using the same or similar technologies, we found considerable disparities in the number of workers having various kinds of skills when we compared French with German plants. That was not all. We also found that the way skills were acquired, and even the nature of those skills, was different in the two countries. Hence the relations between skilled and unskilled workers and between workers and their direct supervisors (foremen and shift leaders) could be interpreted differently depending on which country we were looking at, because these workplace relations were based on different social relations in the wider society.

2.3.1.1 Blue-Collar Span of Work; Facharbeiter and Vorarbeiter

Rather than review here our previous discussion of worker training in German firms, which is based on the use of polyvalent workers trained in a variety of jobs under the supervision of the Meister (a system that extends down to semiskilled workers in some firms), we shall instead describe the status of workers in German industry and the relation between status and worker mobility. The statistics set forth in the previous chapter suggested that the differences between the two countries in this respect were considerable. In particular, b-c workers tend to remain for longer periods of time with firms in Germany than in France. Furthermore we know that the proportion of b-c workers in the German firms is higher.

These results might be interpreted as showing that the area of production is rated as more important in German companies than in their French counterparts. But even if this is the case, is it not ultimately because of the high status accorded to workers in German firms and in German society as a whole? We shall come back to this point when we discuss the formation of the working class in the two countries. What should be noted here is the basis of the worker's professional status in Germany. The two cornerstones are training (Bildung) and achievement (Leistung, an almost untranslatable term referring both to a worker's productivity and to his general motivation and attitude, his personal commitment to his job).[84] To be more precise, the status of German workers generally is founded on respect for the skilled worker, or Facharbeiter. Skilled labor is extremely important in Germany in both quantitative and qualitative senses, and the whole productive apparatus of German industry is built around the skilled worker.

Apprenticeship is one of the key institutions of the German industrial system. Not only is apprenticeship the only way to become a skilled worker (or Facharbeiter, which is a legally protected status like that of the engineer in France), but it is also a prerequisite for acquiring credentials as a Meister (foreman) and until recently was a prerequisite for becoming a graduate engineer.[85]

About 40 percent of all industrial workers are certified as skilled workers; they hold the license known as a Facharbeiterbrief. This credential is quite widely distributed: almost 30 percent of the entire working population, including many middle- and upper-level managers, hold the Facharbeiterbrief.

The fact that many nonworkers hold the same kind of credential as the Facharbeiter helps to enhance the status of all workers, all the more so because company personnel policies emphasize the value of skill certification and ordinarily allow skilled workers a good deal of professional autonomy.

Accordingly skilled workers enjoy a fairly privileged position in German industry, as several recent German studies seem to indicate.[86] Skilled workers are professionals in the sense that, because of their broad range of skills, they are capable of filling a large number of posts in industry, and also because they play a key role in the structure of the firm, establishing liaison between the technical support personnel and the production personnel. Thus the skilled worker is crucial to the kind of cooperation characteristic of German industry, since not only production foremen but also many technicians, engineers, and managers began their careers with training as skilled workers. This system of socialization establishes a broad professional community and tends to facilitate communication and cooperation between employees occupying different positions in a firm's hierarchy. It represents the central element of the span of work concept.

Still, although this common background facilitates communication and cooperation, it does not necessarily translate into a high rate of mobility from the ranks of the skilled work force into the administrative or technical hierarchy of the firm. Indeed we find that German workers are more likely than not to remain workers and to raise children who also become workers.[87] This may in fact be regarded as a consequence of the relatively high status of workers in Germany: the sharply defined social and professional identity of skilled workers goes along with the fact that the ranks of skilled labor are relatively closed to outsiders.[88] Firms tend to control worker mobility rather strictly, either by requiring certain kinds of diplomas or credentials as prerequisites for access to w-c jobs or by hiring workers whose level of training is no better than average, in order to limit the demand for subsequent promotion.[89]

Two different career strategies are available to the German worker. Because of the high value ascribed to professional training, a relatively large number of workers find it advantageous to acquire some kind of credentials, at least to the extent of signing up for a short apprenticeship course of the sort that opens the way to semiskilled jobs.[90] But even those who choose not to follow this course can still hope for subsequent career advancement (shown by the fact that the gap in wages between workers certified as skilled and those without such certification is relatively small). They may, for example, attend training courses, usually sponsored by their employer, in order to acquire new skills (for example, skills needed to operate a special type of machine). In other words, Leistung (motivation and achievement) may make up for deficiencies in Bildung (education and training); this was the way the personnel manager of one electrical machinery manufacturer put it to us. Thus a German worker's professional progress depends on his ambition and motivation and is not as routine, not as cut and dried, as the use of the word *career* tends to suggest in France, where it is taken over from the terminology of government bureaucracy and suggests automatic promotion awarded by the book.[91]

What promotion there is in German firms tends to involve a change of pay grade rather than a step up from b-c to w-c status. There are generally six such pay grades, and moving from one to another signifies that a worker has mastered some production operation and is capable of working independently with minimal supervision.[92] The most significant step up is to the grade of Facharbeiter (grade 5). Under the terms of collective bargaining agreements, the highest grade, grade 6, is usually restricted to skilled workers who have received additional training or who have broad professional experience by virtue of which they have acquired "special knowledge and capabilities, and who normally perform difficult tasks with minimal supervision." Normally a worker's pay grade is determined by the Meister, but for a worker to be classed in grade 6 requires the approval of the employer and factory council as well. The employer and council together agree on the total number of workers to be admitted into grade 6 under the criteria set forth in the labor contract.[93] A Facharbeiter who has reached grade 6 has three avenues of further advancement open: he can become a technician (Techniker), a foreman (Meister), or a graduate engineer (Graduiert Ingenieur). For each of these, special training is required to obtain the necessary certification. Although the Facharbeiter license is required to obtain any of these certificates, each marks the beginning of a different career pathway. From this point on the worker ceases to be a worker and follows one of three divergent paths into the higher echelons of the industrial hierarchy.

Before we examine the Meister, one of the most important job classifications in German industry, it will be useful to discuss the shift leader, or Vorarbeiter, to shed further light on what is unusual about German industry. Whereas in France the shift leader has supervisory status and is not considered a worker, this is not the case in Germany. Hence there is a sharp dividing line between the shift leader, who is classed among the workers, and the Meister, who is classed as an Angestellte, or w-c employee.[94]

The Vorarbeiter (literally, "one who comes before the worker") is in a paradoxical position. Although he plays a supervisory role in the shop, he is not classed as a supervisor. It is tempting to regard the Vorarbeiter as a sort of Meister second class, but officially his status is that of a worker, not a foreman. This paradoxical situation is indeed characteristic of the system of authority in Germany, which to the French mind seems odd in more than one respect (a typical example of French thinking on the subject of authority and hierarchy may be found in the work of Fayolle).

All of our research in German firms, as well as our interviews with German managers and workers, confirms that the Vorarbeiter enjoys considerable autonomy in his work. He must possess a high level of technical competence and on occasion may take over some of the responsibilities of the Meister. Finally, he exercises (by delegation) considerable authority over other workers (for example, in assigning workers to specific jobs). Taken together, these various qualifications suggest that the Vorarbeiter is a sort of assistant Meister destined one day to become a Meister himself. But in fact nothing of the kind is true. Many Meister have never worked as Vorarbeiter, and, even more important, only those Vorarbeiter who have obtained the appropriate license first may become Meister[95] except for those few individuals whose work experience gives them access not to the legally protected title of Meister but rather to the lesser title of industrie-Meister (equivalent to the so-called in-house foreman in France, a foreman designated by the company and not externally certified).[96] One essential difference between the Vorarbeiter and the Meister is that the former is not ranked among the supervisory personnel, while the latter belongs to the first echelon of supervisors. In particular, this means that the Vorarbeiter assumes no personnel responsibilities. Organizationally the Meister, not the Vorarbeiter, is responsible for all the workers in the group and conveys the orders of the general manager to the ordinary workers. This does not mean that the Meister will not frequently consult with the Vorarbeiter working under him before making decisions concerning raises for individual workers, moving a worker from one pay grade to another, or reporting on a worker's performance. By contrast, the Vorarbeiter is usually closer to the workers on his shift than to his Meister. For example, the Vorarbeiter will help his workers to take steps to increase their output in order to make sure they receive productivity bonuses.[97] Or he may take the initiative in approaching the time-study personnel to have time allocated for a particular task adjusted. Many similar examples could easily be cited. In the tube plant, the Vorarbeiter, who leads a crew of from three to seven workers, does not work directly on the line. His main job is to supervise tool changes and mounting of new tools. He checks the adjustment of the machines and makes corrections on the basis of information supplied by the quality control department. All of these activities are intended to improve productivity. The shift leader shares in any productivity bonus won by his crew. Two Vorarbeiter from the shop floor sit on the factory council of the tube plant as worker representatives. It is not uncommon for Vorarbeiter to join with workers in making certain demands—for example, concerning safety. These last two examples suggest that the first allegiance of the Vorarbeiter is to the workers and not to management; no hierarchical gap separates him from the men under him.

In the petrochemical industry we find not Vorarbeiter but rather what are known as Shiftführer, shift leaders, whose role is similar. They work with minimal supervision, particularly on the night shift, when the Meister is not present. The responsibilities of the Shiftführer include assigning workers to various jobs, dealing with breakdowns and taking necessary safety precautions, and monitoring that everything is operating properly. Generally, however, the Shiftführer has no true supervisory responsibility. Like the Vorarbeiter, his job is to enable the members of his crew to work together as efficiently as possible, while leaving each man to work with a minimum of supervision.

In summary the Vorarbeiter's job is essentially to carry out tasks assigned by the hierarchy (in particular, by the Meister). Using his professional know-how and leadership capabilities, he helps to organize his crew in a manner intended to facilitate the achievement of the assigned goals. But he is not directly in charge of the men on his crew. Ambiguous though his position may seem, it is very common in German industry. Indeed at all levels of the hierarchy, we find employees who act as assistants to those in authority (and not merely in a technical sense). It is wrong, however, to think of these assistants as staff personnel, as opposed to the line personnel occupying the positions of authority (if we may borrow for a moment the

staff-line terminology common in the English-language management literature), because in the German case the assistant may, in certain circumstances, replace the man in the position of authority.[98]

2.3.1.2 Professional and Social Status of the Meister

The position of the Meister is interesting in that it is one point of convergence of the two lines of authority that exist within the German firm: 108
the administrative channel and the technical channel.[99] The Meister is at
once part of corporate management, in his role as Angestellte (w-c employee), and part of the social system of the production shop (in his b-c
role). In Germany, unlike France and other industrialized countries, foremen
do not seem to be suffering from endemic malaise. It would seem that the
relatively high status and prestige of the Meister are related to the fact that
he fits into both the technical and the administrative hierarchies.

The Meister derives his social and professional identity from two things:
first, he has been trained as a Facharbeiter or skilled worker (a prerequisite
to being licensed as a Meister), and second, he represents the first echelon
of management, the level directly in charge of the production process. The
Meister thus exemplifies the incorporation of technical competence into the
line of authority, a phenomenon characteristic of German management.[100]
As a manager of both men and machines, the Meister is in a special position
to mediate between the production, technical support, and personnel departments. Hence his role in the firm, and in society, is strategic. His
training specially prepares him to play this role, and it is worth noting
some of the features of that training. The foreman's training begins with
apprenticeship in some skilled trade. This involves three and a half years of
practical and theoretical training and leads to the award of a Facharbeiterbrief. Then comes an average of six or seven years of work experience in
industry as a skilled worker, followed by two and a half years of study for a
Meisterbrief or foreman's license (the criteria for which are set by law).[101]
The program of study consists of courses organized by the chamber of
commerce and industry (Industrie- und Handelskammer) together with on-
the-job training. In these courses technical subjects and organization theory
take precedence over training in how to deal with the human and social
problems of the workplace. Training in human relations concentrates mainly on questions of teaching technique, since one of the jobs of the future
Meister will be to train new personnel. The Meister not only assigns
individual workers to specific jobs but also helps them to develop their
skills and continue their training on the job, particularly when workers are
being shifted from one industry to another.

Although this specific way of organizing the training of the Meister is relatively recent in some industries, such as petrochemicals (where the training course was first set up in the 1960s), the basic idea is as old as German industry, in which the Meister has always been an important figure. The exalted status of the Meister is in fact the result of the carrying over of craft traditions into industry,[102] traditions of which genuine survivals may be found even today.[103] Because of this long tradition, German industry seems willing to accord a relatively large degree of autonomy to the Meister and to the Meistergruppe, the group comprising all the foremen in a particular plant.[104] We are not, however, interested in the history of the institution of the Meister but rather in such traces of that history as may remain in evidence today, for these may lead to the identification of invariants of the social structure of German industrial firms. To further our understanding of the Meister, we turn to the study of a number of specific cases.

In German plants the Vorarbeiter or shift leader relieves the Meister of many responsibilities that fall to the Meister's counterpart, the contremaître, in France. In the German wheel plant, for example, each line has one shift leader assigned to it (one for each shift, the plant operating two eight-hour shifts per day). The shift leader has no specific job to do in the shop. Instead he decides what he will do each day in accordance with the needs of production. A changeover from one type of production to another requires changes in tooling and reassignment of workers. In all the German plants we looked at, regardless of whether unit, batch, and line or continuous process technology was used, we found that it was the Vorarbeiter who took direct charge of the workers, helping them to set up their machines and to organize their work, and representing the interests of the crew in meetings with technical personnel. Relieved of these immediate concerns, the Meister can take a broader view of the production process and devote himself to such tasks as training workers, distributing the work load in the shop, and dealing with the technical support personnel.

In the wheel manufacturing plant both the shop supervisors and the Meister are constantly on the lookout for workers "worthy of being promoted to supervisory positions," and they encourage the best workers to sign up for courses organized by the firm's training center. Workers who obtain a Meister's license do not necessarily become foremen right away, however. Their names are first marked down on a foreman's eligibility list. In this company, training programs are not directly linked to job vacancies. Rather they serve to create a skill reserve, which no doubt helps to maintain a relatively narrow gap between the pay of workers and the pay of foremen. Even when foreman's training is conducted by the firm, access is highly selective, and only a small minority of workers actually rise to the position of foreman. It has been observed that in most firms, the men who serve as Meister are generally near the end of their career. Becoming a foreman is thus not a stepping-stone to a still higher position, such as shop supervisor, as it is in France. Indeed men who are licensed as Meister tend to remain Meister, just as licensed Facharbeiter tend to remain at that level.

In other words although the position of Meister does designate a place of authority in the hierarchy of the firm, it is really more of a professional status attaching to an individual than a hierarchical status within a particular organization. This is reflected in the fact that the technical aspects of the foreman's job outweigh the administrative and disciplinary aspects; the technical skills required reflect the experience of the man rather than his structural position in the firm's hierarchy.[105]

Hence it is not surprising that we find in some firms Meister who play no direct supervisory role but rather serve as expert advisers or assistants to the production supervisors. In the tube plant, for example, one Meister's main job was to make sure that the equipment in the welding shop was operating properly and yielding the maximum possible output. He was constantly concerned to make improvements in the technology of the operation. Workers and shift leaders turned to him for help with technical problems.

Similarly in the large-scale metal fabrication plant the Meister generally agreed that their function was to "find ways to fix technical problems." For the most difficult problems they could go for help to either the shop supervisor (a graduate engineer) or the head of quality control who employed his own specialists in welding and materials.

Just because the Meister are technically skilled, however, it does not follow that they have no supervisory responsibilities. This is far from being the case. Indeed the Meister works in close contact with the shop supervisor in administering the shop and the men in it. All production supervisors meet weekly to discuss technical problems and questions of personnel. The most important decisions are made jointly. Speaking of the manager of the catalytic cracking unit in the petrochemical plant we looked at, one Meister said that during the weekly production meetings, "He does about half the talking; we do the other half." Meister working in such different departments as production, maintenance, tooling, and quality control cooperate fairly closely. In the petrochemical plant, regular seminars are held for all the Meister to meet and discuss technical and personnel matters; this fosters better relations between the various departments in the plant. "Many problems can be resolved at the foreman level," one personnel manager told us. The foremen are also useful for resolving problems between management and worker representatives elected by the plant's employees.

Finally it is not infrequent for foremen to be consulted during meetings with department managers or sales executives concerning fairly high-level decisions, such as investment planning, machine purchases, or the budget for safety.[106]

Because of their training and the firm's willingness to assign them broad responsibilities, Meister are not limited to the traditional functions of the foremen such as worker assignment and shop discipline. They are capable of taking initiatives and participating in the decision-making process; they get involved in such diverse areas of company policy as quality control, maintenance, and equipment purchasing. In some cases they advise the sales staff or deal directly with customers.[107]

The role of the Meister in effecting liaison between the production department and sales and purchasing brings the latter more directly into the line of authority in the firm, so that sales, purchasing, and engineering departments in German firms should be regarded as line rather than staff. There is cooperation on a wide range of issues between manufacturing personnel and more specialized support personnel, and in some firms decisions are taken jointly. The fact that the line of authority is so clearly defined and so powerful tends to limit the proliferation of specialists and experts that one finds in other countries.[108]

We have seen, then, that the Meister exemplifies many of the distinctive characteristics of the German industrial system, combining the authority of his position with technical competence deriving from his experience. We find this same combination of attributes at the next higher level of the hierarchy, that of the shop or production supervisor (Produktionsleiter).

2.3.1.3 Graduate Engineers and College-Trained Engineers

Moving up to the middle-management level, we come to one of the most distinctively German forms of qualification: the so-called graduate engineer, commonly found at this level of the industrial hierarchy.[109] Space does not allow us to go into detail here about the training of the graduate engineer.[110] It is worth explaining, though, how the graduate engineer is socialized and fits into the organization of the firm. The graduate engineer is a distinctive product of the German educational system, which historically has been able to maintain a fruitful tension between university education in science and technology and training more directly related to the needs of industry. The so-called Ingenieurschule (where graduate engineers are trained) were born at the end of the nineteenth century in reaction against the then dominant trend toward integrating engineering training (which originally was practical in orientation and offered in local technical high schools) into the university system, in what came to be known as Technische Hochschulen, or technological institutes.[111] The reaction came largely from the association of German engineers (the VDI) and of industry, both of which wanted engineering training to be more practically oriented and less selective. The Ingenieurschule offered a way of responding to industry's growing need for polyvalent technicians while protecting the status of college-trained engineers. Recently further reforms of the educational system have once again attempted to raise the level of the Ingenieurschulen nearer to that of the universities by making them over into Fachhochschulen, or "specialized universities," offering more theoretical instruction to a more select student body than the Ingenieurschulen. This recent development has dismayed many employers and even some well-placed observers of the German educational system.[112] In reaction against this development some German Länder (such as Bavaria and Baden-Württemberg) have established industrial training programs (Industriesemester) to complement the training of graduate engineers and make up for the overly theoretical orientation of the new system.

The training of the graduate engineer was well suited to the nature of the work and educational systems in Germany. The qualifications of the graduate engineer extend those of the Facharbeiter and complement those of the Meister. In the technical language of sociological analysis, we describe this situation by saying that the skill domain or span of skill in German industry is relatively homogeneous. This promotes broad cooperation between Facharbeiter, Meister, and engineer, based on their common background of theoretical and practical knowledge. Such cooperation is found not only within production departments but also between production and engineering or other support departments that employ personnel sharing in this common fund of technical knowledge. One important feature of this system is worthy of special mention: individuals tend to be polyvalent in their qualifications (as we have already noted in the case of the Facharbeiter) and capable of working with minimal supervision. These individual characteristics are well adapted to a work system that is highly flexible and requires workers to be able to move easily from one job to another. This kind of system is quite different from one in which jobs are highly standardized or in which the division of labor is carried to an extreme. It is also quite different from an overly hierarchical work system, in which one echelon of supervisors is piled upon another ad infinitum.

In recent years those who have tried to change the training of graduate engineers by integrating it more intimately into the existing system of higher education have pictured themselves as progressives opposed to a system that they regard as too conservative because it is too closely identified with industry. But the work of Lutz and Kammerer, among others, has cast doubt on the wisdom of this kind of reform, which, they argue, risks exacerbating the division of labor by further deskilling this intermediate level of the work force. Clearly Germans, whichever side of the debate they choose, have been facing up to the implications of the fact that socialization and organization are inextricably intertwined, a fact that is not without influence on the possibility of reform.

The frequently negative attitude of businessmen to the recent reforms is most likely related to the fact that until now it has often been possible for a firm to use graduate engineers and university-trained engineers more or less interchangeably in many kinds of jobs. The former are probably found more often in production and production-related engineering departments, whereas the latter are more prevalent in higher-level management posts. Still, our own observations of German firms, recently confirmed by other studies, make it clear that a fairly large number of technical supervisory functions can be carried out equally well by either type of engineer.[113] This suggests that firms are fairly free to set their own standards for engineering qualification, even within the confines of a system of personnel management based on the generally accepted principle that credentials should be matched to job status. It would therefore be a mistake to assume that college-trained engineers are invariably superior to graduate engineers. The professional qualifications of the two kinds of engineer are often interchangeable and generally complementary. The real difference between them has more to do with questions of technical specialty and the way knowledge is organized than with any disparity of status.[114]

By looking now at supervisory personnel in production and engineering departments, we shall be able to gain a clearer understanding of the differences between French and German firms. Consider the production supervisor, for example, a middle-level manager who stands between the direct supervisory personnel and the production manager, himself responsible to top corporate management. The first distinctive mark of the production supervisor is the route by which he arrives at his post. It is extremely rare to find a Produktionsleiter in Germany who was promoted to his job by virtue of seniority, without having obtained some professional certification superior to that of Facharbeiter. In the two line-production plants we looked at (the wheel manufacturer and the tube plant), the production supervisors, who previously had qualified as Facharbeiter, had been certified as engineers before rising to their present positions. The production supervisor in the wheel factory had worked in a drafting department planning for new plants. By contrast, the supervisor of the welding shop in the tube plant, who has eighty men including three Meister working under him, is college trained. He is aware that this is a matter of tradition in this particular firm, which needs the services of specialists in welding technology. But he says that college training is not necessarily the best way to prepare for a job that requires above all "knowledge acquired through practice." Assisted by a graduate engineer who monitors the progress of work through the shop, the supervisor devotes most of his time to improving the welding process and to liaison with quality control and sales. In the large-scale metal fabrication plant, one of the top production managers first obtained his baccalaureate (Abitur) and then entered apprenticeship in a skilled trade (not unusual in Germany, particularly since the reform in the training of graduate engineers) and then took technical training in an industrial school.[115] In his view, a college degree is not the best preparation for the type of work that he does, which requires working to very close tolerances on metal pieces of very large size. His on-the-job experience in the computing department and rigging crew of a company specializing in the processing of boiler plate was more useful to him than his courses in theory. Like the other production supervisors, this man devoted most of his time to technical problems (process improvement, investment planning, and liaison with engineering, quality control, and production planning personnel.[116]

We find more or less the same picture when we look at production supervisors and managers in the catalytic cracking division of the petrochemical firm. The petrochemical industry differs from the metals industry in that it employs many university-trained engineers (most top managers and department heads in fact hold doctorates in chemical engineering).[117] Still we find many graduate engineers in middle management positions and in production-related technical service departments (such as maintenance, quality control and instrumentation, and the computer center where production programs are established).

Most of the engineers in the production area, including the head of the cracking unit and the heads of other shops, are graduate engineers.[118] These men work with minimal supervision and are responsible for seeing that the goals set by the executive in charge of production, a Ph.D. in chemistry, are met. This executive believes that "optimal operation of the plant still depends largely on the know-how and experience of the unit managers." The unit manager in one cracking facility that we looked at, which employs ninety-three people, was a graduate engineer with the status of Leitende Angestellte and was assisted by three other graduate engineers. The assistants were not integrated into the line of authority; rather they formed a kind of staff that stood ready to assist the unit manager whenever he needed help. He assigned them work and occasionally delegated responsibility. This kind of organization is not unusual in Germany. It shows the extent to which, from the top to the bottom of the hierarchy, qualifications are associated with individuals rather than positions in German industry. This allows for a certain flexibility because job descriptions are not rigidly determined by the organizational structure but merely specify fairly broad areas of competence.

2.3.1.4 Relations between Authority and Expertise in the German Management System

In this section we shall give some examples of how supervisory functions are organized in production and production-related departments. In our view the logic underlying this organization is the same as that creating the various categories of actors in the industrial system. In particular the same rationality is at work in the determination of access to specific functions as governs the mode of organization and the administration of labor.

As Peter Lawrence rightly observes in his study of German management, one often has the feeling that in Germany technology (and related questions) takes precedence over hierarchical divisions. This should not be regarded merely as a feature of German culture; rather it is a consequence of the interaction between socialization and organization or between professional qualification and the division of labor. All of our observations suggest that cooperation tends to bridge gaps created by the formal structure of the organization, whether hierarchical or functional.[119] It would seem that the collegiality that exists at the general management level (particularly within the Vorstand, where graduate engineers frequently work together with college-trained engineers) is increasingly regarded as a general organizational norm in dealing with both social and technical management problems.

As a result it has become more common for conferences to be organized with the firm, whether involving just one or a number of different departments. These conferences do more than provide occasions for the exchange of information, since important decisions are often made at these sessions. Their function is to ensure compatibility among decisions taken at various levels of an organization in which there is much overlap, both horizontal and vertical, (something close to a matrix) and very little of the kind of unified command structure that Fayol is so fond of.[120]

To give one example, in the petrochemical firm, where we have already studied the complexity of the relationship between the production and maintenance departments, a personnel conference attended by the personnel manager and all department heads is held once a month. According to one production supervisor, the purpose of this conference is "to reduce the distance between the personnel manager and the guys on the front lines, the production people." In this way it is possible to have some measure of decentralization in personnel administration (in which the foremen play a large role) while ensuring that the decisions taken at various levels of the organization are mutually compatible. The personnel conference also ensures that high-level technical people (in this case Ph.D. chemists, all of whom are classed as Leitende Angestellte and some as Prokurist) become involved in questions of personnel, thus keeping the technical management of the firm in step with personnel management. This has the further consequence of keeping down the size of the personnel department.[121] There is also a monthly sales conference attended by representatives of the purchasing, sales, and production departments. The head of the largest production section meets regularly with the maintenance manager, the unit managers, and the Meister to deal with such matters as the division of responsibility between production and maintenance and technical questions concerning the planning and implementation of manufacturing operations.

Similar if rather less formal meetings are held in the large-scale metal-fabricating plants. Unit production means that customer relations are of particular importance, and the fact that sales and production personnel meet on a regular basis may help to explain why in this German plant there is no counterpart for a type of employee found in large numbers in the equivalent French firm, the sales engineer. It is true that sales representatives are better trained in Germany, where there is a so-called sales apprenticeship program (Kaufmännische Lehre).[122] This serves in some cases as a springboard to more advanced training, some of it fairly sophisticated. As in the case of the engineers, a distinction is made between sales personnel with college degrees (Diplomakaufmann) and graduates of the so-called Fachhochschulen für Wirtschaft (FHW, or business administration schools), which offer the diploma known as the Betriebswirt.[123] Access to the latter is restricted to those who have completed the sales apprenticeship. The 1970 Fachhochschulen reform affected the FHW, which have since been made part of so-called Gesamthochschulen (comprehensive universities), though they still offer degrees distinct from the normal university diploma.[124] Many employers have responded negatively to the reforms on the ground that in their judgment, graduates with the Betriebswirt are better fitted out for work in industry than college-trained Diplomakaufmann. Some chambers of commerce have set up Wirtschafthochschulen (business administration schools one step below the FHW in status) in reaction against the current tendency to make business training more scientific at the expense of practical knowledge better suited to the needs of public and private corporations.

Whatever the ultimate fate of these reforms may be, they indicate the importance attributed in Germany to training in business administration, of which there is a full program of studies ranging from apprenticeship to university training, with particular emphasis on the intermediate-level degree (Betriebswirt, or degree in business economics). The courses emphasize applied economics more than business administration or what in English and American parlance is known as management science.[125] Economists predominate among the faculty of the FHW, though there are also psychologists, jurists, engineers, and mathematicians. Because the training is (or at least has been until recently) applied in orientation, teachers are required to have at least five years of practical experience in addition to a degree in their field, thus distinguishing the faculty of the FHW from their counterparts in the universities. Some teach on a part-time basis and are employed in industry (as managers, government regulators, lawyers, and so on). The result of this system of training is that business specialists are found in industry at all levels, not only in such production-related departments as planning and time study but also in sales and purchasing, which maintain close contact with production personnel.[126]

All of this is not without consequence for the way time and productivity are conceived in German industry. Considerations of both technology and management control are involved. In the metal fabrication plant, where it is frequently difficult to estimate how much time will be needed for a job, one production manager told us that time allocations "are much more important for figuring the price of the product than for computing the workers' pay." Productivity is ordinarily associated with the economic performance of the firm, though the primary objective as far as many technical employees are concerned is to turn out a quality product.[127]

We have previously stressed the importance of the fact that social and technical management are closely associated at all levels of German industry. The category of sales personnel is very broadly defined in Germany, and the sales staff constitutes a second, generally less formal hierarchy parallel to the technical hierarchy.[128] Although there is professional specialization, it does not result in compartmentalization (whether hierarchical or functional) but rather stimulates close cooperation between administrators and technicians.[129]

We are working toward a comparison of French and German supervisory structures. Now that we have described the hierarchical structure of German industry, we must do the same for France before we can compare the two.

2.3.2 The Supervisory Structure of French Firms: Relations between Blue-Collar and White-Collar Workers

As we did in the case of Germany, we shall begin by describing stratification within the working class and tell how this relates to the way the industrial work force is managed in France. It is no exaggeration to say that the whole supervisory structure of industry is a reflection of the way work is divided among workers directly involved in the productive process.

2.3.2.1 The Blue-Collar Span of Work: Mobility and Destabilization

From our previous studies of French firms it is possible to describe a sort of "career model" for a typical industrial worker. Take as an example the line production plants: the automobile wheel factory and the metal tube plant. A semiskilled worker who begins as an OS2 can hope for promotion to the ranks of skilled workers, starting as an OP1 and ending as an OP4 or even chief mechanic, the equivalent of a shift leader. The OP4 classification was described by one personnel manager as a "training ground for future supervisors." The best workers (the most adaptable workers with the greatest leadership capabilities) are identified by management and, as they acquire seniority, promoted to shift leader, foreman, and ultimately perhaps to production supervisor. In the tube plant particularly, the position of head mechanic was created to "relieve the foremen of part of their burden." The head mechanics also free the shift leaders (who in this plant are classed as supervisors rather than workers) from having to devote too much time to technical problems, thus enabling them to do their real job, which is to convey orders to their workers and handle what the plant manager describes as an "extremely heavy" load of administrative work. Would-be shift leaders are selected by the production supervisor in conjunction with the chief engineer and trained by the company for a period of several months.[130] The training emphasizes human relations, leadership, labor law, and principles of management and organization.

Selection and training are similarly the watchwords governing promotion to the ranks of foreman and production supervisor. In other words production supervisors in French firms are socialized within the company for which they work and prepared step by step to move up to higher-level positions within the firm. In the course of their careers they acquire specialized knowledge and learn to accept certain standards imposed by the company. Their status, unlike that of their German counterparts, is not based on possession of nationally recognized credentials certifying acquisition of a certain level of practical and theoretical knowledge.

Small though the number of workers who actually rise through the ranks to become supervisors may be, the possibility of such promotion tends to destabilize the work force by maintaining most industrial workers at a low level of qualification. Under the circumstances it may be asked why firms do not hire workers with a CAP capable of filling positions requiring considerable skill, such as mechanic or line operator. The answer is that although some managers would like to do this, it is difficult in a system where production-related jobs tend to be prized less than technical jobs. The personnel manager in the tube factory told us that "when a worker has a CAP, he would rather work for one of the technical departments, which offer greater possibilities for training." This tendency is accentuated by the fact that it is hard to move from one department to another and particularly hard to move from production into a technical department: "The only way to go here is up—and without training you can go anywhere."[131] But in fact training generally follows promotion in France (where training programs are generally in-house), in contrast to the situation in Germany. Supervisors and personnel managers are concerned to spot worker potential, meaning those qualities that will enable a worker to move up in the hierarchy.[132]

Even in the machinery industry, for example, where production requires a higher proportion of skilled workers, we find the same tendency for the work force to become destabilized, as is shown, for instance, by the CEREQ study that brings to light the tendency for a skill hierarchy to develop on the basis not of credentials but rather of on-the-job experience. The situation in France may thus be described as one of socialization by seniority, with the result that the internal labor market (within the firm) assumes a particular importance and the hierarchy develops in such a way as to give undue emphasis to both supervisory functions and technical support services.[133]

The tendency for rank to correlate with length of experience is shown by the same study to be relatively independent of the type of technology employed. More important than technology is the way workers and jobs are classified in this system. The result is that career strategies and even technologies tend to be modified to suit the organization rather than the reverse.[134] Our own observations support this conclusion.[135] Even in technical departments such as maintenance, foremen "come up through the ranks." One interviewee told us that "in this company a P3 [skilled worker] is considered ready to become a shift leader if he shows leadership potential. Nobody would even think of promoting a worker under the age of thirty-four or thirty-five to the grade of P3. It's not a question of age; it's a question of maturity." In fact both age and seniority are regarded in France as signs that a worker accepts corporate values and has been socialized into his role. Indeed the two are intimately related, since a worker can acquire training only by staying on the job with a particular company.[136] Acceptance of company standards and culture is a prerequisite for promotion to any supervisory position, from foreman on up to top management.

2.3.2.2 Transition from Worker to Foreman

To make the step to foreman is to cross the most important dividing line in the hierarchy. In both French and German firms most foremen started out as workers. But the way in which workers are promoted to foremen is different in the two countries. In France there is no foreman's license and the title of foreman is not legally protected as in Germany.[137] Rather it is awarded by a firm to workers of its own choosing, based on their leadership abilities and know-how related to experience, usually rather lengthy.[138] The main responsibility of the French foreman is not technical, as is shown by foremen's answers to our questions about the use of their time. A majority stated that most of their time was occupied by administrative work and shop floor relations.[139] German Meister also devote time to these activities but integrate them more fully into their technical activities.

Because personnel management is more highly centralized in French firms and because there is a wider gulf between production and technical support departments than in Germany, there is a tendency for foremen to assume greater responsibility for control, coordination, and communication.[140] In the area of social relations, French foremen play a critical role as a countervailing power between management and workers.[141] But the foremen have little autonomy in this sphere; they exercise authority but do not hold power. What authority they do have is delegated from higher levels of management; they are not capable of responding to worker demands on their own. Most demands are in fact passed on through channels to the personnel manager or presented directly to management by the union delegates.[142] The fact that the number of foremen per worker is relatively high in France may indicate that the control function is particularly important in a system in which ordinary workers have little autonomy and labor conflicts can be resolved only at the top management level.[143]

The foreman's lack of power is probably a reflection of the nature of his professional competence. The foreman's competence is not general but specific to a particular firm. Selected by the company according to its own criteria, the foreman's qualifications do not inhere in the individual as much as in the position he occupies within the organization. His authority is legitimated by his place in the hierarchy rather than by his possession of generally recognized credentials. These circumstances have a considerable impact on the relations between foremen and their superiors and subordinates. The company will try to bolster the foreman's authority by putting a certain distance between him and the workers under him. This is why a worker promoted to foreman must undergo a course of training. The point of this training, according to one personnel manager, is to set the prospective foreman apart from his worker colleagues. An effort is also made to smooth the rough spots in a new foreman's manner in order to "facilitate communication with his superiors." By the same token, the fact that the difference, in terms of pay, between foremen and workers is greater in France than in Germany might be interpreted as another way of differentiating the former from the latter.[144] Thus the authority of the French foreman, in contrast to that of the German Meister, is not based on any personal investment in training but more on the role attributed to him by the company. More integrated than the Meister into the company structure, the French foreman tends to identify more with company norms. In consequence his status is dependent on the company and as such is relatively tenuous. Many of our interviewees related the "malaise of the foremen" to a loss of authority in recent years.[145] An employee in one machinery factory told us that "the foremen have lost some of their prerogatives to other levels of management." There is some reason to think that the growth of new categories of worker (such as master workers and production technicians) has weakened the authority of the foreman, who is overwhelmed by his administrative load.[146] The more technical decisions (often based on computerized data) have been transferred from the foremen on the shop floor to technicians in the engineering and design departments.[147] This tends to undermine the authority of the foreman, particularly with young, professionally trained workers who are often more skilled than their superiors (a situation exacerbated by the fact that French foremen tend to have a great deal of seniority). Finally recent efforts in the direction of job enrichment and restructuring of work, while limited, have also tended to diminish the importance of the foreman's role and therefore also his status, which is closely connected with the usual hierarchical forms of work organization.[148] Even the foreman's traditional role in training new employees (inherited from the days of the master craftsman) has been taken away from him of late and turned over to a human resources department, a skilled worker, or a professional (in this regard, see the recent UIMM accords on classification).[149]

The foreman's malaise seems to be a fairly constant feature of French industry, even if it has been exacerbated in recent years by new ways of rationalizing industrial work. As early as 1954, two American management specialists, Harbison and Burgess, pointed out that the ratio of foremen to workers was higher in France than in Germany or England.[150] They stressed the uncomfortable position in which French foremen found themselves, caught between workers and management. Excluded from management by company policy and labor law, the foremen were cut off from their roots in the working class without being able to establish new ties with management and supervisory personnel (Harbison and Burgess were surprised to find foremen underrepresented on company councils).[151] Our research by and large confirms the observations made by these authors in both France and Germany, though we do not subscribe to their interpretation of the facts, which is inspired by liberal management philosophy with a bit of technological determinism thrown in for good measure. In brief their interpretation goes like this: if supervisory structures in France and Germany do not correspond to the model structure of the American firm, the reason is that industry in these two countries is comparatively backward. Industrial development, they argue, goes hand in hand with the development of a participatory form of management. But a look at current conditions in the industrialized countries belies this convergence thesis and with it the theoretical and ideological underpinnings on which much work in economics and sociology in the 1950s and 1960s was based.[152]

The fact that we reject the convergence thesis does not mean that we accept some form of structuralist theory that disregards historical factors altogether. Our aim is rather to emphasize the unintentional consequences of intentional actions, particularly as these impinge on authority structures and the distribution of power in industry.[153] In this light, our descriptive and comparative work should be regarded as a first step toward the development of a more comprehensive theoretical framework. To that end an essential first step is to give an analytical definition of what we mean by a supervisory system. Such a system is composed of what we shall call positions.[154] Each position in the system is defined by its relations to other positions. For example, the position of foreman is defined by its relations with the positions of shift leader, manager, and so forth. The action of the supervisory system is governed by a logic that derives from the nature of the social relations that develop among the various positions in the system. Furthermore the various actors in the system (occupants of its positions) develop identities based on the nature of the system, and the system tends to maintain these identities over time.[155]

The logic of the system determines the characteristic attributes of foremen, for example, and this same logic governs not only the division of labor but also social relations in the firm, not only within management but also between management and workers, both blue and white collar. In fact it is the logic of the system that makes sense of the actions of each category of actors. Not that a hierarchical supervisory system is homogeneous, functional, or linear. The formal neatness of the organization is deceptive in this regard. The apparent continuity of the formal structure conceals sharp dividing lines between those with power and those without. Power relations in the firm are in fact highly asymmetrical. This is true of both France and Germany. But the nature of the asymmetry and the underlying reasons for it are not the same in the two countries. As a result, the identities of the various actors in the two supervisory systems are also quite different. Work and responsibility are divided in different ways, and the status of an actor in one country may in fact be quite different from the status of an actor in another country who seems to occupy a formally similar position.

2.3.2.3 Transition from Foreman to Manager
To return to our description of the French supervisory system, we want to stress that the disparity between manager and foreman is just as great as the disparity between foreman and worker. This can be shown by considering access to management jobs and by investigating how work and responsibility are divided between management and nonmanagement personnel. Note, however, that the nature of the disparity between manager and foreman is not the same in France and Germany. To see this we will have to add a few more details to our discussion of access to supervisory positions in Germany, the better to point out what is different about the situation in France.

One factor that contributes indirectly to differentiating the French from the German system is the following. In Germany workers are relatively stable in their jobs, whereas in France they are not. *Stability* refers both to individual job mobility and to status changes between different generations of the same family. Specifically we have the following statistics: whereas 61 percent of German workers are sons of workers, this is true of only 46.7 percent of French workers.[156] Looking at the entire working population, we find that 75 percent of those whose fathers were workers remain workers in Germany, compared with only 63 percent in France, where 35 percent become self-employed workers (versus only 23 percent in Germany).[157]

As for the social backgrounds of foremen (contremaîtres and Meister), we find that a high percentage of foremen in both countries are children of workers (45 percent in Germany, 41 percent in France). But there are also significant differences. Forty-one percent of French foremen are children of unskilled workers or peasants, compared with only 23.6 percent in Germany.[158] More of the German Meister are children of either Meister or craftsmen (20.5 percent for Germany, 13 percent for France). These figures reflect the apparent instability of the working class in France, to which the mobility of workers of peasant origin is a contributing factor.[159] Against this we have the relative stability in a socio-occupational sense of the German Meister, whose social identity is rooted in craft traditions and indirectly in the professionalism of skilled labor, itself related to craft apprenticeship traditions. Consistent with these remarks is yet another difference between the two countries: the disparity between the skilled worker and the foreman is more marked in Germany than in France. Whereas 20.5 percent of the Meister are children of Meister or skilled craftsmen, only 10 percent of skilled workers are. In France, however, the contrast is much less marked: 13 percent of foremen are children of foremen or skilled craftsmen, compared with 10.4 percent of skilled workers.

The gap between the highest stratum of workers and the lowest stratum of management (where for present purposes we are placing the foremen) relates to a corresponding disparity in occupational training; 70.2 percent of German Meister have received professional training above the skilled worker level (45 percent are licensed Meister; 25.2 percent are licensed technicians). By contrast, nearly 50 percent of French foremen have no professional training, and only 11 percent have training above the level of the CAP (above the level of the skilled worker). In France the most significant educational difference between skilled workers and foremen is related not to occupational training but to general educational achievement: proportionately more foremen than workers have received a primary school certificate (CEP). By contrast, the proportion of skilled workers with a CAP is higher than the proportion of foremen with this certificate.[160] In Germany, 70.2 percent of the Meister have received training above the Facharbeiter level. (It must be remembered that 78 percent of the skilled workers are holders of the Facharbeiter diploma.)

These statistics already show that access to the position of foreman is regulated in different ways in France and Germany. In France upward mobility into the foreman category tends to destabilize the social groups from which foremen are drawn originally: 21.5 percent of French foremen are sons of unskilled workers and 19.8 percent are sons of peasants. Furthermore among the children of unskilled workers, 27 percent are of rural origin on their father's side. Occupational training plays a small part in this social mobility. In fact the mobility in question is not so much vertical as horizontal, involving a break away from the father's occupation and environment. But it does involve a high degree of integration into the firm, which serves as a substitute for worker training.[161] The worker must spend a good deal of time learning the company's standards and values before he can hope to rise in the hierarchy, as is shown by the fact that French supervisory personnel generally have more seniority than their German counterparts. We have already called attention to the fact that in France training usually follows promotion rather than the reverse. In-house training is generally more normative than technical-instrumental. Along with wage differences between workers and supervisors, this kind of training helps to establish distance between the foreman and the men under him.

Thus the kind of social advancement in French industry involves having a worker first break away from his original social group and then integrate himself into the hierarchy of the firm. This applies not only to the case of the worker promoted to foreman but also to the foreman promoted to middle management.

In Germany the situation is somewhat different. Meister differ from skilled workers not only in social background (Meister tend to be children of other Meister or of independent craftsmen) but also in level of occupational training, higher on the average for Meister than for skilled workmen. These factors help to give legitimacy to the Meister's authority; the firm need not intervene to bolster the foreman's power over his men. In fact since the qualifications of the Meister are widely recognized, both on the labor market and in the status hierarchy, his authority tends to be regarded as socially legitimate rather than an artifact of his position within the firm. The Meister's status attaches to him personally and not to his position. This does not mean, however, that the way labor is divided within the firm does not help to shape the professional content of the Meister's status, the professional identity, as it were, of the Meister as a social type.

Thus here again we find evidence of interaction between socialization and organization. Indeed this interaction defines a field of action that is broader than the firm or organization. Our analysis cuts across the usual dividing lines between microanalysis and macroanalysis, whether economic or sociological.[162] By focusing on the interaction of the two social processes, we are able to go beyond the well-known distinction between an organization and its environment. In fact our approach brings to light types of action and social relations (to say nothing of categories of actors) that are neglected in the usual ecological approach, which is generally couched in terms of available resources and interorganizational relations.[163]

To return to the main line of our discussion, in Germany the fact that the Meister is distinguished from skilled workers in two ways (social background and level of training) goes along with a fair degree of homogeneity in the span of work—homogeneity in the sense of the qualifications involved and the type of social relations that develop. To clarify, recall the three main occupational groups that constitute the social system of the German workplace: the Facharbeiter or skilled worker, the Meister or foreman, and the Graduiert Ingenieur or graduate engineer. We call these groups homogeneous because they share (or at least did share until the 1970 reforms) a common professional background based on apprenticeship in a skilled trade, and we say that the social relations that develop among them are homogeneous because they are based on cooperation and polyvalence.

In such a system the firm does play an important role, even if it is mainly one of legitimation. German firms rely on management methods that emphasize the complementary character of professional qualifications sanctioned by credentials and licenses, which are awarded by a training system approved and supported jointly by industry and the state.[164] Accordingly it may seem that German firms are less autonomous than their French counterparts. By accepting the system of professional credentials, they assume a place within a system of social relations in which the main actors are industry as an institution (whose power in Germany we shall have occasion to emphasize later) and the state.[165]

This brings us to the authority relations between management and workers. In the German system the authority of such management personnel as the Meister, the production supervisor, or the chief engineer, who is usually production manager, is legitimated primarily by professional competence rather than by hierarchical position in the firm's chain of command. Position is based on competence and know-how so there is no need to increase the distance between workers and supervisors by means of large pay differentials or status symbolism.[166] Thus it is possible for authority to be exercised without destroying cooperative professional relations among the personnel (as is the case in any professional organization, in which hierarchical relations tend to take on less importance than functional work relations).

In the French system, the authority of the foreman (and more generally of middle management) is legitimated not so much by professional competence as by status and pay differences between supervisors and workers. This is necessary in France because differences with regard to training and social background do not play as great a role as they do in Germany. As a result the nature of authority relations is different in the two countries. In France the role of the supervisor is less professional than it is to maintain work discipline and enforce productivity standards. The French foreman closely monitors both the work of the men under him and the way they relate to one another. Hence it is not surprising that we find a higher ratio of foremen to workers in France than in Germany. This is due to more than just the differences in skill relations between the two countries; it is not merely because French workers are generally less qualified than German workers that a larger number of supervisors is required in France.[167] Skill structures vary from industry to industry, and yet we find a certain persistence in the ratio of supervisors to workmen, as though French firms patterned their hierarchies after a common model of authority. It is reasonable to assume that this model has something to do with the way individuals in various occupations are socialized. It appears that in France the social-normative dimension of socialization is of greater importance than the technical-instrumental dimension.[168] Support for this interpretation is provided by the fact that in-house training is so important in France; furthermore the constantly high proportion of self-taught supervisory personnel also tends to support our view. As we shall see, the stability of this system is enhanced by a process that we call joint regulation,[169] which is bound up with a kind of professional relation unique to France.[170] What we have said thus far applies not just to foremen but to the middle levels of management as well. What can we say about top management?

2.3.3 Top Management in France and Germany

There is in France a fairly sharp distinction between managers and such nonmanagement w-c employees as clerks and technicians.[171] Managers are three times as likely to have college degrees as the latter. This same criterion also distinguishes French managers from German managers (including all noncoefficient managers and Leitende Angestellte): 46 percent of French managers have college degrees, compared with only 16.5 percent of their German counterparts.[172] But the situation is the reverse when we look at intermediate-level professional certifications (*intermediate* refers to the level between apprenticeship and college-level training): 42.4 percent of German managers have such credentials (nearly half of them being certified as graduate engineers), compared with only 20.5 percent of French middle managers.

Social origin, which is not unrelated to college education, is also worth mentioning. We find that the rate of social reproduction of top managers in France is much higher than that of top managers in Germany. By rate of social reproduction we mean the percentage of members of a given social group who are children of members of the same group. Nearly half of French top managers are children of top managers, compared with only a third of their German counterparts (allowing in Germany for those who are children of top civil servants). Top managers in Germany are twice as likely to have working-class parents as their French counterparts.

Another difference between managers in the two countries is that some French managers are autodidacts; that is, they have no college degree and rose to their positions through the ranks. Generally they have a good deal of seniority in the firm. There is no real equivalent in Germany for this type of manager. But in France almost 40 percent of the engineers and managers in the metals and extractive industries belong to this group (a percentage that has held steady for the past twenty years). In the firms we studied, the percentage of such individuals in management ranged from 32 percent to 36 percent, depending on the branch of industry. A substantial proportion of this group had finished secondary school (some with the baccalaureate, some without). Other studies have shown that although the majority of these individuals come originally from the middle classes (including children of middle managers, w-c workers, low-level civil servants, and craftsmen), a small number are children of top managers, professionals, and the self-employed. For them, becoming managers after failing to obtain a college degree is, it has been suggested, "a way of regaining social status."[173] All of these socialization processes are closely related to the way firms are managed. It is common to refer to those we are calling autodidacts as company-trained managers, which perhaps gives a better idea of how dependent these individuals are on internal company policy. In fact some companies have a policy to promote not only managers but also technicians, clerks, and even skilled workers, so that the epithet autodidact can in fact be applied to all occupational categories from worker to top management. Middle managers are distinguished by their relatively high seniority. Whatever educational beggage they carry with them is, according to a number of personnel managers we spoke to, commonly regarded as evidence of their "potential," their "capacity to adapt to the firm's norms." This should perhaps be regarded as proof that the educational system is in some respects well suited to the functional requirements of idustry.[174] But the point is that regardless of the type of training received prior to entering the work force, an individual's real chance to move up begins only after he starts work. The firm then takes a hand in offering further training (sometimes in-house, sometimes in outside institutions). And usually the firm has made up its mind to promote someone before sending him to a training course. It is as if the point of training were to fit the individual into the job slot selected for him. Prospective managerial personnel may, for example, be sent to receive training in new technology, sales methods, or administrative techniques. Training therefore tends to destabilize professional groups by taking individuals and moving them out of one group and into another rather than upgrading skills within a given group.

College graduates (and especially graduates of the grandes écoles) predominate in the top ranks of management in France. It may come as a surprise, however, that even these high-level executives tend to have a good deal of seniority within the firm for which they currently work. In fact their seniority is comparable to that of the autodidacts. This shows how important internal socialization is in France, where it is seen as a way of inculcating company norms.

Social mobility plays a part in access to management positions in Germany as well, but the nature of the mobility is different. Here the role of the firm is less prominent. Social advancement is regulated more by the system of training and professional certification. Mobility rates (from b-c worker to w-c worker and from w-c worker to manager) are therefore lower than in France. But to say this can be misleading. If we ask not how likely it is that a worker will become a manager but rather how likely it is that a manager started out as a worker, we find that the situations of the two countries are reversed. Looking at the group of noncoefficient managers in Germany, we find that 35 percent started out as workers, compared with only 4 percent of their French counterparts (cadres). At the top management level the difference is even more striking: 24 percent of Leitende Angestellte started their careers as workers, but no cadre supérieur in France ever comes up through the ranks.

In the petrochemical industry, three-quarters of French managers (including top executives) were recruited at the management level. This compares with only 14 percent of those classed as "noncoefficient managers" in Germany; only 67 percent of the Leitende Angestellte were recruited at the managerial level, the rest working their way up from below.[175] The comparable figures for the German metals industry are 24 percent and 17 percent, respectively.

The rate of social reproduction of management personnel therefore seems to be higher in France than in Germany. But above all the criteria of selection, the filters, are different in the two countries. In Germany adult education (Weiterbildung) is particularly important. In the firms we studied, nearly half of all managers (noncoefficient managers and Leitende Angestellte) received their highest-level professional credential after entering the work force. In France the comparable figure is only 10 to 18 percent.

Summarizing these results, then, we find, that French management tends to recruit from within the managerial group, while German management is more open. But the underlying social processes are just as important as the rates and amplitudes of mobility in describing the nature of the management system in each country.[176]

For example, the relative closure of the managerial class in France is closely related to a previously mentioned source of instability in the working class: the existence of a third category of individuals who are neither workers nor managers: w-c employees, technicians, administrators, and so forth. Promotion to management status is a significant step up in France, but the selection is no more stringent than in Germany, since a fair number of individuals in this third category move into management after acquiring sufficient seniority, constituting the group we referred to earlier as autodidacts. In this kind of system, seniority tends to be a prerequisite for any kind of mobility, including entry into the top executive ranks; in particular, seniority is essential for anyone who wishes to move into a supervisory position, from shift leader on up to upper-level manager.[177]

If management ranks are relatively more open in Germany, it must be remembered that the German educational system is more selective, even if it does allow for some mobility between categories. The fact that there is a substantial degree of correspondence between diplomas and credentials on the one hand and job categories on the other hand tends to stabilize these categories more than is the case in France (particularly the categories of skilled worker and foreman). At the same time, however, mobility is possible for those who wish to take advantage of a system of adult education that is more highly developed (and apparently more effective) than its French counterpart. Consequently in Germany it is more common than it is in France for those who are neither workers nor managers (mainly w-c personnel) to move into managerial positions (noncoefficient and Leitende

Angestellte). Not only is such a move more likely in Germany, but the criteria on which it is based are different. Professional training, not seniority, is the key. This training is often rather advanced (such as the graduate engineer's course) and can be turned to account anywhere in the labor market. In this respect German technicians and graduate engineers, even before they become noncoefficient or Leitende Angestellte, must be regarded as being a different kind of employee from the autodidactic French manager.

In summary, the management systems in the two countries are quite different. It is impossible to compare them directly except in a general way that tends to ascribe an undue universality to the status and role of management personnel. To be sure, systems of selection are at work in both countries in the educational system as well as in industry. But each system of selection must be studied in itself in terms of its impact on the identity of the various types of actor in the system and thus on the kinds of relations that will develop between any given actor and other actors with whom he must establish functional or hierarchical relations. In other words, by studying socialization and mobility, processes inextricably bound up with the division of labor in industry, we can get a better idea of the way in which each type of actor acquires a specific identity. In short, the differences we have noted between French and German management can be interpreted only in terms of the complex, multifarious interaction between socialization and organization.

3   The Industrial Dynamics of Conflict and Negotiation

Conflict is a salient feature of social relations in any industrial system, and all the developed countries have established means of coping with it. Workers have sought to find ways of protecting themselves against the power of the firm to make unilateral economic and organizational decisions. Firms, obliged to accept limitations on their unilateral powers, have tried to shape the rules and institutions that govern labor relations so as to maintain their authority and protect their competitive position. In this way systems of industrial relations have developed over time. These systems shape the struggles between workers and management, in which the stakes are nothing less than the professional identity, both individual and collective, of industrial workers. Worker identity tends to crystallize around pay and representational issues. Pay is the direct economic expression of the value accorded to a particular category of labor. It is obviously a major object of conflict because the way in which pay issues are resolved is the immediate determinant of how national income is divided between the classes. Less directly, the settlement of the pay issue also determines the system's capacity to sustain investment and to develop future consumption. Representation is the political expression of collective identity, as well as the most effective means for a group of workers to defend their interests against the power of the firm and, more generally, of the economic system, where considerations of profitability must inevitably be paramount.

Whether the issue is pay or representation, the workings of the system of industrial relations depend crucially on the specific identities of each of the various categories of actors. As we saw in the two previous chapters, such attributes as qualification and classification are also related to the way in which specific actors' identities interact with their system. The industrial relations system in part consists of certain institutions and is governed by certain rules, which are themselves products of the interaction among the actors, the organization, and the larger social system. Hence there is always pressure from the actors in the system to change the rules and institutions that define the system.

3.1 How Is Pay Determined?

This work began with the observation of national differences in industrial pay structures that could not be explained in terms of neoclassical theories of the labor market. On the basis of these observations we proposed a hypothesis: differences in pay scales are not determined by any economic mechanism abone but depend also on social factors, such as stratification, work organization, socialization, systems of job classification, and so on. Industrial relations come into the picture under the topic of work organization.

We do not deny that economic factors alone may be decisive in some respects, for example, in determining the share of labor costs in total production costs. In any branch of industry this share remains more or less constant regardless of whether we are looking at France or Germany.[1] But it is impossible to explain pay structure in detail without taking into account the way in which different societies value different kinds of work and resolve social conflict arising from disparate evaluations of different types of labor. Conflict pits one power against another. The balance of power may change over time, but the strategies and procedures of conflict remain stable. The outcome of conflict is generally some temporary form of structurally determined compromise, and this too remains stable over time. Among the important structural factors to be considered are the professional identities of the actors in the system, types of industrial organization, nature of the institutions involved in resolving labor conflicts, and forms of institutional interaction.

3.1.1 Determination of Pay Scales within the Firm

Table 3.1 records the pay structures for paired firms in the metals and chemical branches. The table shows considerable differences between the two countries concerning extracontractual bonuses awarded to b-c and w-c workers. In the German firms these bonuses go mainly to b-c workers (as well as to foremen in one of the two firms), while other categories of workers are paid amounts much closer to the minima fixed by contract. In the metals firm, for example, the three groups of manual workers receive supplements on the order of 40 percent of their contract pay, compared with supplements of around 5 percent for other categories, excluding management personnel, who receive 30 percent. In the corresponding

Table 3.1
Range of actual wages and ratio of actual wage to nominal contract wage in two pairs of firms

	Petrochemical				Metals			
	France		Germany		France		Germany	
	A	R	A	R	A	R	A	R
Unskilled	100	171	100	164	100	145	100	137
Semiskilled	103	155	116	174	110	167	118	144
Skilled	128	162	132	172	138	168	120	136
Supervisory personnel	196	169	168	178	190	168	158	108
Junior technician	131	163	146	157	144	135	89	103
Senior technician	178	161	164	131	197	152	157	105
Junior administrator	118	165	104	117	101	134	93	106
Senior administrator	190	171	145	123	162	136	131	103
Management	435	177	205		305		220	130

Note: A = unskilled worker (= 100); R = ratio.

French firm the gap between contract pay and actual pay is markedly wider for all categories, and the difference between b-c and w-c workers is less pronounced. B-c workers in the German metals firm receive bonuses 25 to 40 percent higher than w-c workers, as against 6 to 20 percent higher in the comparable French firm. (See table 3.2.)

In the chemical firms the difference in supplementary pay by category is even sharper. The difference between actual and contract pay for b-c workers (including supervisory personnel and low-grade technicians) in the German firm ranges from 55 percent to 74 percent whereas for other categories the differences range from 17 percent to 31 percent. In France all categories receive bonuses of the same order of magnitude. Thus the relative bonus of b-c workers in Germany is 12 to 40 percent, compared with a range of −7 percent to +3 percent in France.

These observations call for two comments. In France, the industry-wide contract establishing a minimum wage for each category of worker serves to lay down a pay structure for the industry, a hierarchy of wages and salaries that each firm in the industry reproduces by offering more than the

Table 3.2
Absolute and relative wage supplements, metals industry

		Blue collar	White-collar workers, administration or technical services	Blue-collar supplement relative to white-collar personnel
Unskilled	France	145	134	+8%
	Germany	137	106	+29
Higher class	France	168	136	+24
	Germany	136	103	+32
Semiskilled or nonrated technical	France	167	135	+24
	Germany	144	103	+41

Source: Study 2.

minimum wages for each category. Furthermore the fact that the average increase over the negotiated minimum is high, on the order of 60 percent, indicates that French firms have a relatively free hand when it comes to departing from the minima laid down by the industry contract. In Germany the freedom of the firm to make such variations depends on whether the category is blue or white collar. French firms award bonuses to all categories across the board, treating each similarly. In France a firm is therefore free to set the average level of wages and salaries that it wants, but it cannot modify the industry-wide pay structure laid down by collective agreement.

The foregoing explains in large part why the pay differences between b-c and w-c workers are so much less in Germany than in France. In fact, the figures reflect the importance that is attached in Germany to productivity bonuses. But there are many different types of productivity bonus, and the nature of the system used is more important than the mere existence of a bonus. The significance of productivity bonuses varies widely depending on the professional autonomy of the workers involved and, more generally, on their relation to the personnel foremen who supervise their work. Where productivity depends mainly on the intensity of work, where workers have little freedom to take the initiative, and where the division of labor is such that the computation of productivity norms is easy, productivity bonuses are ultimately a way of exploiting the work force to the greatest possible extent ("sweating system"). But where the results of work are hard to monitor, where jobs are relatively complex and likely to encounter numerous unforeseen problems, and where technical prowess is more important than mere speed, the use of productivity bonuses tends to be advantageous to the worker. Various circumstances may reverse this tendency. In particular, if the relationship of supervisory personnel to workers is one of hierarchical domination, the supervisor may, by adjusting work norms, be able to cancel any advantage that the worker might otherwise have been able to derive. For the bonus to be advantageous to the worker, the worker-supervisor relationship should be one of authority based on professional cooperation rather than one of pure surveillance; that is, the supervisor should be seen as a superior professional, a man whose competence is recognized and who can be called upon for help by the workers—in other words, he should be a primus inter pares rather than a tool of management. In Germany, the supervisor's prestige and social status are widely recognized, so that the foregoing conditions are met, and workers therefore tend to view productivity bonus systems as advantageous to themselves. One worker in a German metals firm put it this way: "Sure, there are always problems with the times allotted. They never figure on enough. But the supervisor sees to it that they're changed or recalculated." The whole production process is under the supervisor's direct supervision. Even the shift leader has a good deal of professional responsibility: "He is expected to cooperate with the workers and help them figure out how to save time." But when it comes to worker evaluation, the supervisor has the last word. He selects men for each crew on the basis of his estimate of their capabilities. As the man in charge of production, he has a good deal of latitude in determining how much the workers under him should be paid. The importance of productivity bonuses in Germany cannot be fully understood unless the relation of supervisor to workers is taken into account. We shall therefore consider the nature of this relationship.

3.1.1.1 The Worker-Supervisor Relationship
Relations between workers and supervisors cannot be fixed by decree. They depend on the worker's professional status, the way work is organized, and the criteria used for evaluating work and workers. These factors are not independent of one another; what is more, they are closely bound up with educational and organizational factors.

We have already treated the worker's professional status in the two previous chapters. Here we want to comment especially on two aspects of status. First, even if, institutionally, the German supervisor is considered a w-c employee, he is both more of a worker and more of a professional than his French counterpart. That he is more of a professional is clear from a glance at table 1.5, which shows the relationship between professional credentials and job classification. As for his being more of a "worker," the reasons for this have to do with both differences between France and Germany in regard to criteria for promotion and the specific nature of the German working class. Having the right credentials is more important in Germany, but it is perhaps the criterion governing access to the training required to obtain those credentials that is the most crucial difference between the two countries. In France access to training in preparation for being a supervisor generally requires a prior decision by the employer to promote the employee in question. Such a decision is usually based on an estimate of a man's leadership capabilities. Professional competence is not irrelevant, and the evaluation of the production supervisor is important, but the final decision is in the hands of the personnel manager, who is also in charge of assigning the individual to a selected training program, in which the central focus is usually leadership techniques. In Germany the whole process is in a sense reversed. An individual must first acquire a supervisor's license before he can be considered for promotion to that position. And it is largely up to him whether he does so. In any case the personnel office seems to play little or no role. A sign of the division of responsibility in this regard between the administrative and technical management teams is provided by the following comment of one of our investigators, who was assigned to study training methods in German firms: "The personnel offices were rarely able to tell us what measures were taken at the corporate level to provide training for workers. In part this is because refresher courses and supplementary training (Fortbildung, Weiterbildung) of production personnel are not within the competence of the personnel manager but are organized by the production department on its own initiative, to some extent in collaboration with the training office."[2] This remark is not specifically concerned with courses to prepare for acquisition of the Meisterbrief. But still the example shows that training in German firms is a responsibility closely associated with production. The production supervisor is responsible for setting in motion the process that will take a worker up the ladder to group leader, shift leader, and finally supervisor. In one firm we visited, training for each of these stages took about 200 hours of course work at the Konzern's training center.

The importance ascribed to training, together with the fact that its character is primarily technical, has two consequences on the relationship between workers and supervisors. First, the skilled worker and the supervisor have a common professional background. The supervisor's training is in many respects merely an extension of the training of the skilled worker. For another, the fact that promotion to supervisor depends on the production supervisor rather than the personnel manager means that the character of the promotion is more professional than administrative or managerial. The German supervisor is thus less a part of management than the French supervisor. This is confirmed by the social image of the supervisor in Germany: unlike w-c workers and managerial personnel, he is considered a worker, a member of the Arbeiterschaft.[3] This is a result of his technical and professional background, as well as the fact that he takes a direct hand in the production process. By the nature of their profession, both Facharbeiter and supervisor belong to the working class, of which they are the most prestigious members.

Productivity bonuses are also awarded to semiskilled workers. Since many of them have not acquired formal credentials, their status must be otherwise determined. Here lies one of the paradoxes in the comparison between France and Germany: the percentage of French semiskilled workers with the CAP is surely higher than the percentage of German Angelernte with the corresponding diploma, the Lehrabschlussprüfung. It is therefore reasonable to ask whether it is valid to compare these two categories. Obviously classifications make sense only in relation to the type of work organization. An organization on the French model, in which work preparation and the job breakdown are of paramount importance, is likely to have just as negative an impact on the professional autonomy of semiskilled as of skilled workers. Therefore there is justification for thinking that the Angelernter cannot be identified with the French ouvriers spécialisés (semiskilled workers). Hence it seems likely that the relation of semiskilled workmen to supervisors and the payment of productivity bonuses to semiskilled workers cannot be directly compared between the two countries.

3.1.1.2 Work Organization and Job Assignment

The organization of work plays a crucial role in structuring social relations within the firm. The standards according to which workers are evaluated and promoted are also basic in determining how a worker's pay will change over time. Somewhat schematically a distinction might be drawn between the way work is organized in Germany, where teams of workers (headed by a group leader or a shift leader under the supervision of the supervisor) are made responsible for specific jobs, and within which one worker can by and large be substituted for another, and the way work is organized in France, where large tasks are broken down into individual job assignments with a fixed content and clearly defined rate of pay. In Germany the pay an individual worker will receive depends in part on his wage group (classification), determined by his training and experience, and in part on the supplements awarded as compensation for his individual productivity or for the productivity of the group, as judged by the supervisor. Thus each man's pay depends on two judgments: one that determines his assignment to a particular pay classification and another that depends on the supervisor's estimate of his work as he rotates from job to job on his work team. In some plants a more formal work arrangement has been adopted: workers are systematically rotated from job to job until they have mastered all the jobs there are to be done in a particular shop, the time required for this varying from individual to individual. A rotation plan worked out by the supervisory for the various shops in conjunction with the engineer lays down the sequence of rotation and the time normally required to learn each job. Each job is related to other jobs in the plant in a specific way, and the sequence of rotation is chosen so as to enable the worker gradually to learn them all. Rotations are sometimes made at regular intervals, for example, in plants working around the clock (three shifts), when workers return from their rest period. In this system a worker's pay classification does not depend on which job he is actually doing but rather on his general level of training and the general aptitude he displays in the course of his rotations.[4]

By contrast, in the French system, the most important element in worker evaluation is the specific job to which he is assigned for a period of time. The classification system is based on the coefficients assigned to each job, without regard to the training or credentials of the person occupying the job. This system is found not only in the government bureaucracy but also, more surprisingly, in private industry. What determines a man's pay is the post to which he is "entitled," allowing for the general employment situation. No doubt low-level jobs are sometimes refused to workers who are "overqualified," mainly in order to avoid having workers protest that their skills are being underutilized and underpaid. But the principle is still that it is the job rather than the worker that is remunerated. Job classifications are established by the technical personnel in the plant, who produce a classification chart for the firm. Each coefficient groups a certain number of jobs, which are regarded as involving work of similar difficulty. The production process is then designed in such a way as to fit in with this scheme of classification, being broken down into a number of work stations, each of which involves specified operations performed at a regular rate. Since wages are associated with coefficients and coefficients with jobs, a worker can be awarded a raise only if he changes jobs and moves into a higher-rated position. This normally requires either that a job be created or, more commonly, that a post be vacated. But unless major technological changes have been made, it is difficult for a firm to make this kind of promotion, for it would establish a precedent. In particular, supervisors and production supervisors are not allowed to make promotions of this sort on their own initiative because to do so would undermine the pay system. Furthermore this kind of promotion is unlikely because of the fairly strict separation of maintenance from production departments, which is common in French firms.

Pay in both countries is related to seniority. In the French system just described, however, the role played by seniority has little in common with the payment of so-called seniority bonuses. Except in cases where a firm increases the number of its employees, promotion depends on job vacancies. In firms where few employees quit and in jobs where there is little turnover (generally the most desirable), promotion will depend on a worker's seniority with the firm. Of course, many companies have a grading system for employees, with grades kept by the supervisors or production supervisors based on a whole range of personal qualities. But because of the coefficient system and the scarcity of job vacancies, changes are the exception and a worker's grades have almost no effect of his pay or chance of promotion.

This analysis makes clear how the system of work organization affects the relations between workers and supervisors. The supervisor is deprived of all professional authority in a system in which the job definition and pay classification, and thus ultimately the attribution of status to the worker, are rigidly determined by the structure of the production process. No better example could be found of the way technical and social management are dependent on administrative management.

It is also clear how the French system affects the status of the worker himself, since his place in the firm and his hopes for promotion depend far more on the rate of job turnover than on his professional skills and motivation. The advantage of such a system resides in its impersonality. The risk of conflict is reduced by the use of objective, uncontestable administrative criteria such as seniority instead of subjective evaluations by the supervisory personnel of workers' professional skills and attitudes. These remarks explain, we think, why French labor and management alike prefer seniority to productivity as the criterion for worker evaluation.[5]

3.1.1.3 Controlling Pay: Productivity or Seniority?

Whether productivity bonus systems are accepted or rejected depends on the strength of the workers within the company organization and, more broadly, on the strength of organized labor in industry generally. One or the other and sometimes both of these factors must be taken into account in order to explain the differences that can be observed between France and Germany.[6] The German situation is probably best understood in the light of the status of workers within the firm. When work is organized so that work teams have a fairly large degree of autonomy and supervisors are an integral part of the team, workers feel as if they control the bonus system rather than the other way around. Because the worker's professional status is high and the authority of the supervisor is based primarily on his professional competence, the productivity bonus system tends to foster cooperation rather than serve the ends of management. During periods of prosperity both workers and management find the system advantageous. At such times management is more interested in increasing output by improving methods and techniques than in reducing costs. For their part the workers have enough control over the organization of work to avoid upward readjustment of productivity standards and so are able to take home additional pay as output increases.

Boom periods do not last forever, though, and when they end, management attempts to regain part of the power that it let slip through its fingers, more or less willingly, when times were better. This is what happened in Germany during the 1960s when contractual productivity bonus systems became widespread; henceforth increases in output would not bring further increases in pay without management's consent. Still, in spite of this counterattack, the Akkordlohn system and the productivity bonus remain important.[7] German labor unions are still wary of the system, though they have not yet challenged it openly. Rather than call for the elimination of the system, they have been trying to increase their control over it. Over opposition from employers, a new law on company charters was passed with union support in 1972, giving the company works council the right to codetermine (and thus effectively to veto) productivity norms and standards, including the amount of the bonus.[8] The usefulness of this weapon depends on the aggressiveness of the council in any particular firm. At the national level the trade unions have another tool they can use: cooperation with management officials within a uniquely German institution, the REFA, or association for labor studies (Verband für Arbeitsstudien). This was founded in 1924 during a period of economic growth and rationalization of industry on the initiative of certain technicians, the so-called industrial economists. The institution consists of a board of directors and various committees made up of representatives of the unions, employers, and technical experts in the labor sciences (Arbeitswissenschaft), a group of disciplines long established in the universities and technical schools. With 45,000 members (counting both unions and firms), the REFA is a powerful organization specializing in research and education in the area of remunerative techniques. Experts working for both employers and unions, people from every level of industry down to the shop floor, supervisory personnel, union representatives, and members of company works councils—all learn the same techniques in the same classes. The DGB also runs courses on remunerative techniques and labor science in which the REFA methods are taught.

The REFA has an important effect on the way productivity bonus systems actually operate. This is because these systems are often highly complex technically, but the expertise needed to understand how they work is not limited to management because of the REFA. Not only do union experts study the theory of bonus systems alongside management experts, learning how they work and how they must change to accommodate changes in technology, but at the company level as well the union has its own Refaleute, REFA-people, who are just as familiar with the system as management specialists, having attended the same classes.

An institution like the REFA is based on a shared set of values: not only Leistung and Bildung but also the recognized value of science in general and labor science in particular, the latter being regarded as a practical science, applied and in large part developed not by academics or specialists but by practitioners themselves. The possibility of such a science has a great deal to do with the way education is regarded in Germany.

This raises the following question: Are these values not highly instrumental in character; that is, do they not endure to the extent that they serve the interests of both parties? It is true that productivity bonus systems are accepted because both workers and management believe first that they are advantageous and second that they can exert sufficient control over the way the systems operate. In other circumstances the bulk of the profits reaped from improvements in efficiency would go to the firm, which is why Marxist theory regards productivity as the source of relative surplus value. Because of the strength of the Marxist tradition in the German workers' movement, as well as the persistence among workers of Marxist ways of thinking (as shown by the well-known work of Popitz), it might be expected that German labor would be highly wary of accepting the values associated with the notion of Leistung.[9] But, remarkably, a highly dichotomous image of the society (divided between those on top and those underneath, to use Popitz's terms) coexists among workers with a strong devotion to the value of efficiency in manual labor. This goes hand in hand with the attribution of a high value to professionalism. These values come from the workers themselves and are impressed upon others (Popitz, p. 240). The worker is strongly aware of his own efficiency. Beyond that he is strongly aware of the collective identity of workers as a group (Arbeiterschaft), including the Meister, who are regarded as workers in the full sense. Because relations within the working class are what they are, based on a particular form of class consciousness and professional identity, workers are able to accept a system of productivity bonuses of which they feel they are in control.

In France the penchant for relying on seniority reflects a search for institutional guarantees of fairness and leads to a highly formalized system of pay allocation, more legalistic than economic in character. This legalistic formalism in turn tends to foster fairly wide differences in pay. By contrast, productivity bonus systems tend to smooth out differences because undue pay inequalities would cause conflict within the team and risk destroying the workers' confidence in the supervisor. This fact no doubt goes some way toward explaining why the range of worker pay is smaller in Germany than it is in France.

Another factor with a bearing on this difference was discussed earlier: the fact that variations from contractual pay minimums tend to favor b-c workers in Germany, whereas in France they are across the board for all categories from worker up to management (this is less true of the metals industry, where productivity bonuses are more important than in the chemical industry). This produces a rather surprising difference between the two countries. In both actual pay may vary widely from contractually fixed standards, but in France the variation is localized in a particular firm, which either does or does not pay well above industry norms. In Germany, on the other hand, pay variations are due essentially to productivity bonuses and are a management tool used primarily to promote worker productivity.

Thus in Germany b-c and w-c employees are treated differently. B-c labor is seen as directly related to the efficiency of production, so that the pay of b-c workers is highly elastic, rising considerably with increasing productivity. Because job assignment and technical and social supervision of the work team take on such importance in an autonomous, bonus-based work system, the authority of the supervisor is enhanced: given a relatively free hand by the firm, the supervisor controls his own workers. Management takes back some of its power during periods of recession or slowdown. The bonus system then entails a decrease in supplementary wages above contractual minimums; management is much given to pointing out that bonus pay is by its nature not guaranteed. Thus the contractual pay structure has a special significance in Germany: it is an expression of the social status of the production worker, the relation of workers to supervisors, and the economic position of the working class (which is dependent on variations in the economy). Although the bonus system may be advantageous to workers during periods of rapid growth in output, it is a powerful tool in the hands of management for coping with recession and crisis in the economy. Thus we find that the market situation has a significant impact on the pay structure of German firms (as well as on employment), which explains in part why German—as well as American—firms are so much more adaptable in the face of changes in the economy than are French firms.[10] In this connection, Krusche and Pfeiffer cite a study by the Vickert Institut showing that 86 percent of a sample of 1378 company works councils agreed to reductions in pay bonuses above contractual minimums during the 1970 recession (69 percent of these councils considered the reductions to be justified).

The social significance of the pay structure in France is quite different. First, the basic structure is laid down by a contract of indefinite duration. The actual pay figures established by contract soon become fictitious. All workers are treated in the same way by management, regardless of their training or professional capability. Companies have a more or less free hand in managing their personnel, with the proviso that they must abide by the strict hierarchical classification of jobs.

3.1.2 Role of the Firm in the National System of Wage Determination

In their struggles over the level of wages, employers and unions can concentrate on any one of three levels: the firm, the industry (either regionally or nationally), or the state (over legislation affecting all occupations). Negotiations at the industrial level are most sensitive to market fluctuations. Company-level negotiations depend much more on the balance of power between labor and management within a particular firm. Finally, negotiations at the state level are influenced mainly by the general trend of prices and the economic climate.[11]

Both the French and German systems appear to be based on industry-level contracts, where the term *industry* is quite broadly defined, particularly in such branches as metals. This might be taken as suggesting that great stress is placed on market conditions in both countries. But such a suggestion calls for two comments. First, actual wages in France vary considerably from those set by contract. Second, collective bargaining agreements are for an indeterminate period in France but for a fixed period in Germany.[12]

This second point is of great importance, for it affects the entire significance of the contract. In systems with fixed-length contracts, the decision to raise wages establishes a firm's labor costs for a period of time during which the economic situation is presumed to be known or predictable. At the end of the contract period union and management will want to reopen discussions, assuming that one or the other has not already denounced the contract as unacceptable. In Germany established rules govern the negotiating process, particularly in regard to strikes during the period of negotiations. Strikes may begin only after a certain period of time has elapsed, all conciliation procedures have been exhausted, and a referendum has been held among the workers. Negotiations are solely in the hands of the central headquarters of the union for the industry involved, although consultation with locals is allowed in order to permit information to flow between negotiators and rank-and-file members. Nevertheless the whole process is characterized by centralized decision making. In particular, although company works council representatives, who are elected by all employees, exert considerable influence over the union's wages committee, local union representatives (Vertrauensleute), who are elected by unionized employees only, are generally kept out of the proceedings.[13] Considerations of power politics are not overlooked (for example, when choosing where pilot negotiations should be held or what companies should be struck), but the timing of negotiations is generally set by the expiration of the contract, so that the economic conditions prevailing at that moment are those that bear most strongly on the outcome. Negotiations are most strongly influenced by market conditions in the particular industry involved rather than by the general economic situation or the position of an individual firm. On this point there is more or less general agreement.

No doubt some attention is paid to the general economic climate, but what is known as concerted action seems more a residue of a bygone era than an essential feature now. The only period during which the unions agreed to take part in talks concerning the economic situation in general (and the wages policy that, it was hoped, might result from a generally accepted assessment of that situation) came immediately after Karl Schiller became minister of the economy, following the fall of Ludwig Erhardt. A proponent of Keynesian demand stimulus in the wake of the 1966–1967 depression, Schiller asked unions and employers to take part in an informal commission made up of a small number of representatives of government, business, and labor. In 1968 he recommended to business that a wage increase larger than that envisioned by industry be granted. Although concerted action officially remained in place until 1976 (when the unions withdrew to protest legal actions taken by the employers against Mitbest-immung), its importance remained secondary compared with industry-level negotiations. It would be an exaggeration to claim that the unions take no account of the general economic climate in staking out their positions. With the demise of concerted action and particularly since Helmut Schmidt became chancellor, there have been regular conversations between the chancellor and top union and business leaders.[14] But these have no direct bearing on industry-level negotiations.

Industry-level negotiations seem to be much more important than wage actions at the company level.[15] Works councils do sign agreements concerning wage bonuses, but these are more a matter of applying the provisions of a new contract than of implementing far-reaching modifications, which are precluded by the fact that union locals are legally obliged not to engage in strike actions for the duration of the industry-wide contract. These local contracts are generally routine matters, except in times of crisis. It is symptomatic of the general situation that no union-led attempt to negotiate the relationship of contract-fixed to company-fixed wages has ever been carried very far. Otto Brenner, one of the leaders of the union IG Metall, at one point made company-level wage policy (Betriebsnahetarif-politik: literally, wage policy close to the firm) one of his objectives. One implication of such a policy would have been to grant a greater role in company-level wage negotiations to union representatives (Vertrauens-leute). This attempt failed, in part because of hostility on the part of employers and also in part because many DGB officials were not particularly enthusiastic about it either.

These examples show that industry-level negotiations are regarded in Germany as the one necessary and sufficient institution for the implementation of a union wages policy. No single firm provides sufficient scope for either wage discussions or any strike action that might result from those discussions. Indeed it would seem that the unions themselves are concerned about protecting individual firms from the possibly damaging consequences of limiting wage actions to such a small arena. The idea of making the firm a neutral site with respect to union activities, a tenet of management policy in France and Germany, to some extent may be regarded in West Germany as a tenet of union policy as well. French trade unionists would find such a suggestion outrageous. But the German attitude is more properly understood as one feature of a complex system, and it is by no means clear that by adopting the line that they do, German unions impair their overall effectiveness.

The situation in France contrasts with that in Germany almost point by point. They share only the fact that industry-level collective bargaining is the main legally sanctioned form of wage negotiation. But French collective bargaining agreements are unlimited in duration, so that the timing of renegotiation becomes an important bone of contention. Employers are inclined to put off negotiating a new contract as long as possible, especially if there is hope that a slack labor market and slowing rate of inflation will moderate wage demands. As a result wage movements vary sharply form one firm to the next, but companies can and do pay rates above those specified in the industry contract. Companies with ample cash reserves and strong unions tend to pay wages that rise with increases in productivity, whereas wages in other companies tend to stagnate. In the absence of any guarantee about contract renewal, unions will make the most of their effort in the most dynamic firms. Industry associations also generally prefer this system to industry-wide agreements on wage increases, which can cause friction between more and less prosperous firms or between those firms in a better position to resist wage demands and those not so well placed. Thus the use of unlimited duration contracts in France is related to the fact that French industry itself is so heterogeneous.

Industry associations will begin to move toward contract renewal talks only when the companies in the industry that are doing least well can no longer resist wage demands and begin to grant raises. Negotiations will then get underway, not so much to inaugurate a new wage settlement as to ratify one already in place. Management will then try to invoke the so-called lowest decile rule; that is, they will try to win agreement for a pay schedule based on the minimums actually being paid by the firms in the lowest decile of performance in the industry. This rule has been explicitly formulated by the Union des industries metallurgiques et minières (UIMM), the most powerful and best organized of the trade associations, especially when it comes to labor relations. The UIMM represents what is probably the most heterogeneous branch of industry in France. But still the phenomenon in question seems to be fairly general, except in the most uniform sectors, such as petroleum refineries.

These remarks help to explain what might otherwise seem paradoxical in the attitudes of French businessmen and unions. Employers and trade associations have consistently defended the freedom of each firm to fix wages and have always refused to sign contracts that would rigidly set wages that all companies must pay: contracts must establish wage minimums, no more, and each company decides how to implement changes in the minimums, contained in any new contract, whether stated in terms of percentage or absolute amounts. It might seem that under given conditions in the labor market, what is favorable to the employer is likely to be unfavorable to workers and that therefore business and labor would prefer to concentrate their efforts in different places. But in fact the contrary is true. The explanation of this paradox lies in the fact that firms are in fact quite independent of their trade associations because of the wide disparity between firms within any given branch of industry. Since the business organizations are unable to force their members to adopt a uniform policy, each firm seeks to maximize its own advantage by pursuing its own independent wages policy. Under these conditions it is in the unions' interest to concentrate their efforts at the opposition's weakest point so as to create such disparities between firms that a general readjustment becomes necessary. This objective state of affairs is reinforced by ideological factors. The values in question might be regarded as instrumental, but they cannot be explained solely by the functions they fulfill. In a situation where union structure is weak and the unions are largely dependent on the support of activists and direct action, workplace organizing activities within the firm are likely to be regarded as a better way of mobilizing workers than broader general objectives. Of the two major French unions, the CGT (Confédération générale du travail) and the CFDT (Confédération française démocratique du travail), the former is well established on the shop floor and sets great store by national strike days and other propaganda activities. More concerned with bolstering its position on the shop floor, the CFDT is interested in coordinating local activities to ensure that the strategy is appropriate to the demand. But for both unions the primary objective is to maintain or strengthen the organizing position in the workplace. In these circumstances there are two main drawbacks to industrywide contracts: industries are too heterogeneous to be governed effectively by a single contract, and the gap between contract wages and actual wages is so wide that workers take little interest in the outcome of industry negotiations. The upshot is that whereas German firms are protected against the shocks of the wage struggle, French firms are at the center of the battle.

In the French system, however, there is a substitute for wage negotiations: government-set minimum wage. In reality, though, this is more a complement to rather than a substitute for union action at the company level. Such action is governed by the situation in the labor market. The setting of the minimum wage (SMIC) takes into account the prevailing economic conditions. The SMIC serves two purposes: it enables the government to control the movement of wages and at the same time strengthens the hand of workers in those firms furthest from following the general trend. Between 1950 and 1970 the only economic indicator taken into account in setting the minimum wage was the price index. The aim of the minimum was therefore limited to maintaining the purchasing power of the most poorly paid workers.[16] But since 1970 the minimum wage has been readjusted annually in relation to actual changes in the average wage level. The SMIC now more or less keeps up with the general wage index. Accordingly it has become more common to use the SMIC as a substitute for collective bargaining. But the main purpose of the change in the manner of computing the SMIC has been to avoid the violent conflict that periodically erupted in the past whenever the disparity between the lowest wages and the average wage grew too large (in 1954–1955, 1958, 1962, and 1968). The SMIC mechanism is now virtually automatic, though the government is free to exceed the wage level determined by the formula for adjusting wages to prices. The SMIC-setting procedure has the further effect of inducing labor and management to enter into collective bargaining. If a rise in the SMIC is anticipated that would result in a minimum wage higher than the wage being paid by the least well-off firms, industry trade associations will move either to reopen negotiations or to increase their pay scales unilaterally in order to cushion the effects of the increase in the SMIC on company-set wages and consequently on the wage hierarchy throughout the industry. Clearly the nature of these forced negotiations is quite different from that of voluntary industry-wide negotiations of the sort that occur in Germany.

We can now see the significance of the differences between the French and German systems. The German system, highly centralized in structure and focused on economic conditions prevailing in a given industry at a given time, has two prominent features: industrial branches are largely homogeneous, and unions and trade associations exert strong authority over their members. By contrast, the French system, decentralized and focused on each firm's individual labor market, corresponds to the heterogeneous character of French industry and the weakness of unions and trade associations. In Germany local conflicts are subdued in order to achieve more comprehensive goals. In France results obtained firm by firm lead to agitation that is either given official sanction by means of an industry-wide contract or transmitted to the entire economy by means of the SMIC. In Germany the labor contract is implemented in the firm, but the firm is protected from disruptive labor action. In France the firm is the center of the struggle not only over wages but over which union will predominate.

3.1.3 Worker Representation and Confrontation in the Firm

Our investigation of the method of determining worker pay led us to draw a contrast between the protected German firm and its French counterpart, a veritable battlefield in the wars between labor and management. Still, work gets done in both places, and forms of cooperation between labor and management do exist, even in France. Economically French and German firms perform comparably in many instances. And labor conflicts do occur in both countries. Strike statistics are not meaningless, but care is required in their interpretation. As Heinz Markmann points out, "Contrary to common opinion ... spontaneous work stoppages, frequently characterized as 'wildcat strikes,' occur often in factories. But usually these are only brief warning strikes and are not recorded in the statistics."[17] German statistics do not reflect strikes of less than one day's duration unless they result in the loss of more than 100 days' work.[18] Also grievances and conflicts do not always result in strikes. Psychological factors may play a part: strikes are relatively rare in Germany, and for that reason, as well as for other, more deep-seated ones, they are regarded as very serious indeed, a stain on the corporate escutcheon. But there is a simpler explanation of the psychological reluctance to strike: various legal sanctions can be used against strikers in Germany. It is worth stressing, however, that conflict can also be settled without strikes by having recourse to grievance procedures, assuming these exist. Relatively protected German firms seem to have fairly well-developed grievance procedures, whereas strife-ridden French firms do not. This is true not only of the firm, which throughout this book has been described as the place where socialization and organization interact, but of labor-management relations generally.

3.2. Labor Conflict

Within the firm are two distinct spheres of action: the operational sphere and the design and control sphere. The first comprises all shop floor and maintenance activities, including production supervision; the second is administrative in nature and detached from productive operations as such. Technical and social management requires communication between the two spheres. Technical management covers the organization of production and is directed toward goods. Social management is directed toward people; it affects production, though not necessarily directly. Every production supervisor is engaged in social management to the extent that he is in contact with workers. But issues related to pay and training may relate to production in various ways. The important decisions may be in the hands of the production hierarchy, in which case social and technical management functions overlap, emanating from the same individuals, or they may be in the hands of the administrative hierarchy, whether the design office or the personnel department. Here we are distinguishing the two hierarchies in the manner of Popitz, who found in studying the German steel industry that this distinction was very clear to the workers. Paradoxically, though, it may be asked whether the sharp distinction between the two hierarchies is not important in determining where conflicts will occur. Indeed a dichotomy of this sort may imply that the production hierarchy is largely autonomous with respect to the administrative hierarchy or that the foreman and production supervisor are relatively independent of the front office and therefore capable of performing both social and technical management functions. Clearly independence of this sort is closely related to recognition by management of the professional identity of workers and foremen. In these circumstances problems that arise on the shop floor tend to be resolved on the shop floor. Social management becomes a by-product of technical management. The capacity to resolve disputes in this way can be used by production supervisors to defend their autonomy in relation to the front office, thereby assuring the workers that their immediate supervisors do in fact have the power to make important decisions on their own.

In the typical French firm, any change in a worker's job may lead to demands for a corresponding change in his coefficient and hence in his pay. Management, through the personnel office, therefore keeps a close watch on any circumstances likely to result in worker mobility within the firm, such as absenteeism or the use of rotation by the production staff. Overtime and time set aside for union activity by worker representatives are also closely monitored by time clocks, chits for excused absences and for union work, and other devices. The personnel office does more than just monitor the movements of workers; it tries to control them in such a way to avoid demands for additional wages. Some companies use a computer to keep track of work assignments: "The machine is wonderful. It keeps track of everything—overtime, absences (for illness, paid holidays, unauthorized absences, union time).... All decisions regarding transfers and qualifications that may have an effect on wages, no matter how small, must be approved by the administrative office and the general manager."

In one heavy machinery plant we studied, the personnel office monitored requests for temporary transfer of personnel from one shop to another. This kind of monitoring alters the balance of power between production supervisors and administrative staff. For example, chits recording the hours a worker devotes to authorized union activities must be signed by the personnel office, not the foreman.

By contrast, in Germany, production supervisory personnel have greater autonomy than their French counterparts, even if personnel offices still play a monitoring and coordinating role. The personnel manager and corporate executives exert less direct control over production. As a result the technical supervisors have a freer hand in the areas involving the greatest conflict. In one German petrochemical plant we were told that the production engineer spent 60 percent of his time "settling disputes" and dealing with problems of "social management." Similarly in regard to hiring, "Everything depends on the interview with the foreman and production supervisor. The personnel office plays no part in selecting candidates." By contrast, in the French petrochemical plant, job applications are sent to the personnel office, which makes the initial selection and determines necessary and sufficient levels of qualification.

In the German petrochemical plant, turning now to the question of pay, we were told that "the personnel manager rarely intervenes in matters of classification." This difference probably has to do with the fact that the basic German classification system, which consists of five or six wage groups, is more flexible (or more crude) than the French. The assignment of individuals to each group is done by the foreman, and this is based on an evaluation of the individual rather than the job (in a system where polyvalence plays a large part).

The foreman's power can doubtless result in arbitrary decisions, an often-expressed concern of French personnel managers, who worry about the danger of injustice due to the subjectivity of the foreman's evaluation. Such a danger exists in Germany, but it is dealt with differently. The foreman consults with the shift leader before making his evaluation, and the worker may appeal to the production supervisor. Thus the production hierarchy monitors its own behavior, to say nothing of the sharp watch maintained by worker representatives.

Thus a characteristic feature of French industry is the considerable influence exercised by the personnel office, which in theory should play no more than a supporting role under the close supervision of the firm's general management. The function of the personnel office is to gather information and advise management. It is a cog in the system but an essential cog. Although lacking the power to act on its own, the personnel office is likely to know a great deal about potential sources of conflict and indeed to have its fingers on all the levers of social management. The following remark, made by one personnel manager, will give an idea of the extent of the personnel department's influence: personnel problems, he said, "take up more than half the time of company management." One objective of this arrangement is to keep the technical supervisors from becoming targets in the conflict between labor and management: "You've got to keep the supervisors from being shot." Also the personnel manager is generally the only one in the firm who knows labor law and regulations, and so he is the only person who can fight the unions on an equal footing and even beat them in a domain in which argument is often highly legalistic.

Protecting the technical staff in situations of conflict is thus one of the major objectives of the personnel manager in a French firm. And yet an often-mentioned theme is the need to build up the authority of the technical staff; indeed the unions are frequently accused of circumventing the immediate hierarchy so as to address their grievances to the highest levels of mangement.[19] The almost inevitable result of this state of affairs is that the more noise a complaint stirs up, the more likely it is to be heard at the top and disposed of in a satisfactory manner.

One reason that German statistics record relatively little industrial conflict is probably that what conflict there is remains localized in a particular plant or even a particular shop. By contrast, in France, although some minor conflicts do not make their way into the statistics, most conflicts quickly engulf an entire company and are turned into public causes. One reason for this state of affairs is that French unions think nothing of taking grievances to a government labor inspector, who is responsible for enforcing public labor law and collective bargaining agreements. Whatever the legal distinction between judge and administrator (whose role is merely to monitor), it is clear that the reason for going to the labor inspector is to win his support or to embarrass the employer.

The localization of conflict, then, is related to the organization of work and the nature of the firm's hierarchy. But the general tendencies discussed are reinforced by the institutional arrangements for worker representation.

3.3 Unions and Committees: The Construction of Social Relations

The localization in Germany of labor conflict to the production sphere has to do with the fact that the productive and administratives hierarchies there are distinct. The tendency in France for labor conflicts to escalate rapidly to the highest levels of management has to do with the fact that, from foreman up, the hierarchy there is cut off from the workers; to use a phrase that came up earlier when we discussed promotion and training, the hierarchy has gone over to management. Another consequence is that the authority of the hierarchy on the shop floor is limited since the two sources of authority are professionalism and recognition of the hierarchy's functional role. This probably explains why personnel offices are constantly preoccupied with protecting the supervisors, all the more so in that the supervisors in question are generally of low rank, men whom the personnel office wishes to invest with authority, rather than highly professional production supervisor-engineers, who are less vulnerable because of their professional role.

3.3.1 Countervailing Power and Negotiating Capacity

Whatever legal forms the countervailing power of workers may take, it is structured by its interaction with management. Indeed structuring worker organizations is a crucial management function, in which the personnel office often plays a key role. In France this swells the importance of the personnel manager, who is responsible for extending the authority of management down to the level of foreman and shift leader. Despite his outsized importance, the personnel manager may not have a very free hand. He must be responsive to management decisions. In German plants, by contrast, the personnel manager is less likely to infringe on the authority of the production hierarchy, while at the same time he is probably more independent within his own sphere of action. A sign of the German personnel manager's prestige is that he is usually regarded as having executive status. In firms practicing codetermination on a wide scale, such as those in the coal and steel industries, the labor manager is one of the three company directors.

Worker organizations in the two countries contrast in so many ways that it is tempting to try to explain differences in industrial relations in terms of the legal and institutional differences observed. In Germany unions are, in theory and to some extent also in reality, excluded from the firm. Instead of the union there are representative institutions whose members are elected by all the workers, not just unionized workers. These are known as company councils (Betriebsrat).[20] These councils are organized differently from French works councils (comités d'entreprise), which were inaugurated in 1945 and are joint worker-management bodies presided over by the company president or a representative. By contrast German company councils are composed solely of workers and elect their own president. In conception and organization they are autonomous bodies representing all the workers employed by the firm.

Although unions are legally excluded from German firms, in fact unions extend their influence into the firm in two ways. First, they play an important role in elections to the company council, although they are not allowed to present a union list as such.[21] However, any worker or group of workers can propose a list of candidates in the union's name, and unionized workers avail themselves of this opportunity. According to J. M. Luttringer, 77.6 percent of all workers elected to company councils in 1972 belonged to the DGB; a 1964 study showed that 98 percent of all council presidents and 83 percent of all vice-presidents were DGB members.[22] In Fritz Strothmann's view, "The members of the company councils are the key union officials in the firm. Without their support it would be impossible to organize a dynamic and competent group of union representatives (Vertrauensleute)."[23] The second way unions influence the firm is related to the first. Within the firm there is a second elected body composed of the Vertrauensleute. Members are elected by vote of the unionized workers only. This body has no basis in law, but since 1960 contracts at both the branch and firm level have increasingly extended to the Vertrauensleute the same protections against dismissal that are accorded to members of the company council. Reality and the law are thus poles apart. It should be noted, however, that the company councils are legally independent of the union, and they can and frequently do take an independent line on the issues. The council is also independent of management, which in contrast to the French case is not represented. Its power is based on the fact that its members are elected by all workers. Finally the council commands considerable resources, especially in large firms. In particular it is staffed by a fairly large number of representatives, who are completely relieved of professional duties so as to devote full time to their duties as representatives. All of these factors contribute to making the company council a powerful and independent body.

In French firms we find not two but three types of worker organization. There are two kinds of employee representative: employee delegates and members of the company committee. In addition since 1970 the unions have had the right to establish union locals within the firm. Employee representatives are selected from a list of candidates proposed by the union; nonunion candidates are excluded from the first round of voting. Thus legally the unions are the organizers and administrators of the countervailing power within the firm. Also certain seats on company committees are reserved for union representatives.

The greatest difference between the two countries is no doubt the fact that in Germany neither the company council nor the union representatives have the right to call a strike. A strike can be called only by the union and then only after specific procedures have been exhausted. A strike affects a particular company, but it can be decided on only outside the company; in other words strikes are collective decisions, in keeping with the fact that the unions have a monopoly on collective bargaining. Both company councils and union delegates are required to enforce labor peace. By contrast French unions are almost entirely free to call for work stoppages, there being no legal prohibition against them and no restrictions written into labor contracts. In theory, therefore, French unions are in a much better position than German unions.

But this statement, based on the right to strike, takes no account of the real capacity of French unions to influence management decisions, given the fact that French management is under no obligation to enter into negotiations (though this has changed somewhat since 1981) or to reach agreement on a contract. The German situation is basically the opposite. Neither the company council nor the union local has the right to call a strike, but management in some circumstances is obliged to negotiate and to agree on a contract. This is referred to as codetermination (Mitbestimmung) as defined by the law of 1952 and amended by the 1972 law on company charters.[24] Regardless of differences in the nature of the relationship between workers and their representatives, the outcome in both countries may be the same. In France the unions' capacity to influence management decisions depends on the willingness of the workers to strike. The unions must consequently be on the lookout for worker grievances around which a strike can be organized. In Germany company councils and union representatives are not allowed to foment strikes but must seek to avert them. Still they must be alert to grievances so as to settle them before they degenerate into open conflict. If worker discontent reaches the point where a wildcat strike is unavoidable, the worker representatives are then free to lead the strike while officially regretting having been put in such a position by management. Legally their only obligation is not to take part in provoking conflict. During the labor unrest of 1969, the role of company councils and union representatives varied widely: "Although the union representatives had in many cases instigated the strikes, they played a passive role as the strikes unfolded. In the steel industry the councils played an important role, in some cases a passive or mediating role, as at Mannesmann, in others a role in organizing the strike, as at the Klockner steel plants in Bremen or at Rheinstahl in Meiderisch."[25]

If a distinction is made between the capacity to call a strike and the capacity to negotiate (and reach an agreement), it seems likely that the apparent superiority of the French system is far less than it may appear (even abstracting from specific causes of weakness in the French union movement, such as rivalry between different unions and relatively small membership). Because of codetermination, German employers are obliged not only to negotiate but also to reach an agreement. It is true that in many cases German company councils are no better off than French company committees, enjoying at best nominal rights to information and consultation (Mitwirkung). But in other cases full codetermination applies. The obligation to reach agreement is not absolute, nor could it be without risk of self-contradiction: if no agreement can be reached, the parties are required to submit their case to a conciliation commission established under the terms of the 1972 law, whose decision amounts to binding arbitration. The commission is made up of equal numbers of representatives of management and of the company council and is presided over by a third party on whom the other members must agree. Recourse to the commission is not without risks for the employer, so there is a fairly strong incentive to reach an agreement beforehand.

Codetermination can or is supposed to be invoked in a number of important kinds of conflict: these include disputes about shop floor regulations (discipline, hours, manner of pay, timing of vacations) and controversy over the effects of new technology, especially those that may require modifications in the way pay is determined. The company council may ask for the right to codetermine changes in job descriptions, including work load and environmental conditions. Hiring and transfer decisions are also subject to codetermination. This last point is particularly important because it can lead to the establishment of a virtual closed shop in companies where the council is dominated by union members. In regard to training, codetermination is applicable to certain conditions of training but not to the content of training itself: the council has the right to approve the trainers designated by the firm and to choose certain workers to receive training. Codetermination does not cover individual cases of dismissal, but, as J. M. Luttringer has observed, the German law on firing is one of the most protective in Europe.[26] Mass layoffs are associated with problems of industrial conversion; they are supposed to be dealt with in the context of negotiations concerning conversion plans (the so-called Sozialplan), which are subject to codetermination.

3.3.2 Effectiveness of Representation

Rights are always permissive. Whether the right involved is the right to strike or the right to codetermination, it can do no more than give workers' representatives a tool with which to further their demands and gain desired ends. The objective is always to resolve conflict, to reach agreement. French unions are skeptical of the German system because they believe that management will make no real concessions unless faced with a strike or the threat of a strike. If strikes are illegal, as they are in Germany for the duration of a contract, then, it is argued, the effectiveness of worker representative institutions is reduced to nil. But this argument is too narrowly legalistic. As we have seen, sporadic strikes do occur in German plants, more or less spontaneously. It is true, though, that company councils are for the most part concerned with detecting grievances and resolving them before overt conflict erupts in the form of a strike. Trying to head off grievances before they turn into strikes need not have worse results than trying to get out in front of the workers on every issue so as to organize a strike action designed to win concessions from management. In either case management will commonly respond by adopting wait-and-see tactics or by turning a deaf ear to the problem. Grievances often dispel themselves, and revolts turn out to be temporary. Besides, not every issue is serious enough for any union, even the most combative and aggressive, to try to exploit. Unions must choose where to make a stand, and they do so on the basis of the information at their disposal and on samplings of worker opinion. Some moderation is necessary if the strike weapon is not to be hopelessly blunted, so every union is forced to some extent to act responsibly. Part of their responsibility is to maintain good communications with the rank and file. This means having union representatives in every shop and department, indeed in every group where conflict is likely to arise. This is difficult to achieve, so that often a union will try to exploit conflict in certain areas while ignoring many others. Labor leaders may be just as surprised as management when certain conflicts erupt. Problems of a similar kind exist in Germany. But there both management and the company councils are afraid of a strike, and German managers are consequently willing to take steps that French managers would oppose. In this connection, it is interesting to look at where within the firm union representatives are likely to be found.

This depends, first, on the number of union representatives. Table 3.3 lists the number of representatives on French company committees and German company councils. The German bodies are twice as large on the average as the French. The French company committee has three types of members. Besides those elected specifically to sit on the committee, there are the employee representatives, elected by all employees, and the union representatives (who either sit on the committee themselves or assist the employee representatives), who are designated by the unions. Each union

Table 3.3
Elected representatives to the company committee or council

Germany		France	Representatives	
Number of employees	Repre- sentatives	Number of employees	Title holder	Aid
5–20	1	50–75	3	3
21–50	3	76–100	4	4
49–150	5	101–500	5	5
151–300	7	501–1000	6	6
301–600	9	1001–2000	7	7
601–1000	11	2001–4000	8	8
1001–2000	15	4001–7000	9	9
2001–3000	19	7001–10,000	10	10
3001–4000	23	More than 10,000	11	11
4001–5000	27			
5001–7000	29			
7001–9000[a]	31			

a. Beyond, 2 extra representatives per 3000 employees.

represented in the plant can appoint two union representatives (one for the committee and one to assist the employee representatives). Finally the union local in any firm employing more than fifty workers is entitled to appoint one union delegate, who is given job release time to carry out his functions. If the firm employs more than 1000 workers, the local can name up to four delegates.

In France representatives and delegates are granted job release time for a variety of reasons, and in some cases release time awarded for various purposes can be accumulated by a worker to the point where he is able to carry out his representative duties on a regular basis. For example, a man who is elected to the committee and named a worker representative and union delegate can combine the release time connected with each of these duties: fifteen hours per month for worker representatives, twenty hours per month for committee members, ten hours per month for union delegates (in firms employing fewer than 150 workers, fifteen hours per month in larger firms), and twenty hours per month for union representatives (in firms employing more than 500 workers). Thus a man can accumulate from forty-five to sixty hours per month of job release time. Different workers are not permitted to exchange release time authorizations, however, with one exception: union delegates belonging to the same local can transfer their individual release time (fifteen hours per month in firms employing more than 300 workers) to a single man, who can thus acquire as much as sixty hours per month. It is therefore theoretically impossible, barring special arrangement, for one man to be completely relieved of work duties and made a full-time representative. In a firm employing 2000 workers, there are three employee representatives (fifteen hours each), seven committee representatives (twenty hours each), one union representative (twenty hours), and two union delegates (per union, fifteen hours). A committee member who is also a union delegate can have thirty hours per month free. A man who combines all the posts will have seventy hours available. One other worker can then have as many as fifty free hours, five others thirty-five hours, and the remaining delegate fifteen hours.[27]

In Germany the method of calculating the number of representatives and the free time allowed to each is less complex. In a firm employing 200 workers, the company council has fifteen members, exactly the same as the number of employee representatives in a French firm of comparable size. If the company employs between 300 and 600 workers, one member of the council is completely freed of normal duties. In companies employing more than 2000 workers, this number rises to three. In large firms (9001 to 10,000 workers) the council has eleven permanent members, which makes it a kind of parallel management with considerable resources at its disposal.

Apart from the council members elected by all employees, the unions have their own representatives (Vertrauensleute). These constitute something like the French union local but without legal standing. It is becoming increasingly common, however, for the Vertrauensleute to be granted, under the terms of collective bargaining agreements, the same protection against dismissal as council members. In the chemical industry the union charter calls for one such union representative for every five to twenty workers, depending on the case. The density of representation is therefore quite high.[28] But the representatives' sphere of action is among the rank and file, and theoretically representatives receive no job release time.

Clearly the fabric of representation is more tightly woven in Germany than in France. But this is not the greatest difference between the two systems, which in our view has to do with where in the firm the representatives are found. In France the location of representatives is determined by the way in which union members are distributed among the various shops. This distribution is highly uneven. Often there are more union members in shops where skilled workers are concentrated. The distribution also depends on the willingness of union members to accept union responsibilities. Management obviously has no interest in encouraging an even distribution of representation throughout all departments. As one personnel manager said, "Where they want their delegates is their business." By contrast, in the German chemical firm, the policy of the union is not only to have a large number of representatives but also to see that representation is systematically distributed throughout the firm. Circumstances may be more or less favorable to achieving such a goal, but the fact that a high percentage of workers are unionized frequently puts it within reach.

The most important difference between the two countries is this: in Germany the employer too has an interest in achieving a balanced distribution of representatives. That this is so is clearly the case in some chemical firms, where management itself organizes the election of representatives. Other observations suggest that is true more generally. For instance, the election of delegates is organized shop by shop in production and team by team in maintenance. Thus each representative can look upon himself as the man designated by his fellow team members to represent their interests to the shift leader, foreman, and production supervisor. This attitude favors the development of a worker organization that parallels the company hierarchy and contrasts sharply with the widespread attitude in France that the way workers organize is "their own business."

3.3.3 Beyond the Law

That such an organization exists in Germany is not unrelated to the social management role of the production hierarchy. Where productivity bonuses are used, foremen become important as managers of personnel because job assignment can determine take-home pay. Establishing communication among foreman, shift leader and union representative becomes a crucial way of smoothing out difficulties and avoiding conflict. Generally the union representatives go no higher with their grievances than the foreman. If a conflict cannot be settled at that level, the union representative will generally bring in the company council. Council members deal more with the production supervisor than with the foreman. The council is normally brought in when new technology is installed that results in changes in job description and/or time allotted for certain tasks. Although many council members are also union representatives and free communication between the council and the union exists, the union delegates deal more directly with the production hierarchy, while council members have a direct line of communication to the personnel office. This is required by the rules of codetermination, but more than that it is in the interest of all concerned to resolve problems before they degenerate into overt conflict. Now that we have seen how the company council works, we can understand why F. Fürstenberg has said that it "insinuates itself into a company's command and communication structure." [29]

In France central control and coordination of decision making are necessary for reasons that we have already discussed: the coefficient system, the lack of precise standards of qualification, and the weakness of foremen in relation to worker representatives. The use of objective standards such as seniority implies that job vacancies plant-wide must be matched to available personnel, a task that only the personnel office is in a position to carry out. Thus the personnel office and its ancillary departments (payroll and training) assume particular importance. Union delegates are therefore likely to take their grievances to the personnel manager, to whom they will apply for changes in the coefficient ratings of jobs or for recognition of training and qualifications that the firm is not eager to acknowledge (particularly if acquired by the worker independently of a decision by the firm to promote him). To defend himself against such demands, the personnel manager will press for broad powers to establish a central system of regulations governing the entire plant. He thus acquires an ever-increasing monopoly of social management functions.

The upshot is that problems that come up on the shop floor must be magnified by the unions if they are quickly to reach a high enough level of management to permit resolution. Whereas German unions play the role of tension dampeners, French unions are tension magnifiers.

3.4. Collective Action and Conflict Regulation in the Firm

With respect to grievance procedures and conflict resolution, French firms can be regarded as being centralized and homogeneous in character. Although the pay systems for b-c and w-c workers are formally distinct, both are governed by the assignment of individuals to coefficient-rated jobs. The coefficients attached to each job, which determine the worker's pay, depend on centrally made decisions regarding the organization of production, administration, and control. Management has a fairly free hand to raise pay above industry-wide minimums, but it must respect the pay structure laid down by the industry contract. This induces the firm to adapt its organization to the contract, which is one of the ways that unions exert control over the pay system. Another way in which unions exert control is by monitoring individual transfers from one position to another by virtue of seniority. J.-D. Reynaud has described this system as one of "joint regulation," in which management controls the organization of work and the unions control the application of rules governing promotions by seniority. But the way the system works is determined by the fact that the various categories of workers have little professional autonomy. The positions of b-c and w-c, skilled and unskilled workers are all determined in the same way: by the industry-wide pay structure coupled with a decision, made centrally by management, about how work should be organized. Try as the unions may to gain recognition for education and other training, the imperatives of the rigid coefficient-based structure inevitably take precedence. As for the use of internal training as a means of promotion, management is entirely in control. In these circumstances the authority of immediate production supervisors is obviously limited. Lower-level supervisors can take no steps that might upset the job classification system. Conflicts that come up on the shop floor must be resolved at a higher level in order to ensure plant-wide coordination. If joint regulation does operate, it is based on the fact that the logic of administration takes precedence over the logic of production. This in turn is due to the lack of professional status of the actors in the system. The upshot is a system in which conflict tends to become centralized. The firm becomes a battlefield in which management (and especially the personnel office) squares off against unions— unions that are forced to seize every opportunity to press demands in order to bolster their position in relation to workers and management alike. Social and technical management are sharply differentiated in this kind of system, with the former invariably taking precedence over the latter.

By contrast the German firm is more heterogeneous, and social and technical management tend to overlap. As an example of heterogeneity, we may cite the differentiation of pay systems for b-c and w-c workers. Productivity bonuses are widely used in paying b-c workers. The conventional pay scale is not the major factor in determining a b-c worker's wage. The size of his bonus is what counts, and here the foreman exerts great administrative authority. In assigning workers to different pay groups, foremen and production supervisors have further latitude to exercise their authority, since promotions are made relative to a work system based not on job assignment but rather on a worker's capabilities, as revealed by rotation from job to job. But as we saw in chapter 1, professional credentials play a large role in determining job assignments.

The pay of w-c workers is more directly related to the results of collective bargaining. Again, though, professional credentials such as clerical diplomas or certification of more advanced training play a crucial role in determining a worker's job classification.

Another example of heterogeneity in German firms may be found in the existence of a fairly strict compartmentalization among skilled, unskilled, and semiskilled workers, a worker's position being determined by the type of professional credentials he holds, if any. Here seniority plays only a minor role in determining progression from one rung to another on the wage ladder. German skilled, unskilled, and semiskilled workers therefore have a stronger group identity than their French counterparts. As a result in Germany conflicts that arise on the production floor do not spread as readily throughout a plant, and skilled workers have an even stronger hold on worker representative organs than they do in France.

Furthermore social and technical management functions are to some extent associated in Germany, where the logic of production takes precedence over the logic of administration and control. This encourages problem resolution at the shop floor level. Both the company council and personnel manager seek to identify problems and facilitate their resolution. No doubt the fact that the company council is obliged to enforce labor peace has something to do with this. But this obligation must be seen in the light of the fact German labor contracts run for a fixed duration, at the expiration of which the union has the right to strike.

Still, company and union are in theory distinct entities. The union's attention is focused on negotiating an industry-wide contract, while the company is focused on peaceful bargaining with the company council. But there does seem to be a consensus in regard to the importance of keeping labor conflict to a minimum within the firm, however much reality may vary from this ideal. Thus in the German case it does seem reasonable to speak of joint regulation. But the meaning of this term cannot be understood without reference to the capability of technical managers to assume part of the burden of social management. And this capability cannot be understood without reference to the fact that the organization of German firms is solidly based on a highly professionalized work force composed of b-c and w-c workers together with the all-important supervisors.

4   Social Patterns and the Dynamics of Wage Determination

In the first part of this book we described a number of differences between France and Germany: differences in regard to inequality among workers, qualification of workers, methods of workplace organization, and institutions for dealing with labor-management relations. The results of these first three chapters have a number of common features. First, they all bear the stamp of the comparative methods used to obtain them. They are descriptive and in many cases quantitative: basic occupational training is less important in France than in Germany; the influence of seniority on wages varies considerably; cooperation in the workplace is unequally developed in the two countries; the influence of representative institutions is also highly variable, and different principles are used in setting wages. Thus far we have conducted our research in isolated areas, systematically employing a point-by-point method of comparison. This makes it difficult to determine whether the differences we find in each area are related to one another. Are there common causes for the various kinds of differences?

The problem obviously has to do with the fact that the categories of comparison (occupational training, workplace cooperation, representative institutions, and so forth) are not themselves comparable. The difficulty of making measurements is clearly the main stumbling block to systematizing our comparative results.

Matters stand quite differently, however, if we take the view that the most logical way to follow up empirical results indicating marked quantitative and qualitative differences between the two countries is to move toward a theoretical (and methodological) consideration of the reasons for those differences. The point of this theoretical work should be to explain how differences in one category are related to differences in the other categories. This is tantamount to a shift in the level of comparative analysis. Rather than list national differences category by category, we hope now to explain the pattern of differences discovered thus far in terms of broader, permanent social trends. The purpose of this chapter is to begin work toward that goal.

With this shift to a new plane of analysis, we nevertheless intend to continue to accord a central place to empirical research, but a new dimension of information will be required, and the facts must be reinterpreted to fit within a broader analytical framework. Accordingly, first we shall interpret worker mobility in terms of the professional domain within which it occurs and in terms of the firm's influence on its orientation. Next we shall be looking at the interaction between socialization and organization. In other words, we will be looking at the firm as the place where the social relations of labor are constructed, while at the same time situating the firm itself within the broader context of a professional domain. It is in this broader context that the firm must prove itself by its performance as an organization (whose behavior as such is relatively independent of the type of technology employed). Finally, the notion of professional domain can be extended even further, to what we will call the domain of collective action, within which labor management is shaped in ways that are complex and yet more or less stable. This will lead us to investigate the pattern of industrial conflict in the two countries: How are the issues defined, and what directions does conflict take?

4.1 Worker Mobility, Social Relations, and the Definition of the Professional Domain

In chapter 1 we looked at a number of concrete forms of worker mobility: mobility between firms, mobility between levels of qualification, access to occupational training and general educational opportunities, and social mobility. We also looked at some of the more persistent relationships among these various forms of mobility.

In the first stage of comparative analysis, the study of mobility played an important part in pointing up significant differences between the two countries. We found, for instance, that the two educational systems oriented mobility in different ways by establishing different kinds of barriers, both horizontal and vertical, to impede the movement of individuals. We also found differences in the intensity and interrelationship of movements from one major job category to another, between firms, and between sectors of the economy. Finally we found that such factors as a worker's social background, education, seniority, and experience, usually regarded as sufficient to explain inequalities in access to jobs and status, had very different effects depending on which of the two countries we were examining.

Looking at the magnitude and direction of worker movements no doubt takes us a step beyond more traditional comparative studies, which focus on quantifying the factors. It is interesting, for example, to know that the difference in seniority between w-c and b-c workers is greater in France than it is in Germany because of differences in the manner in which firms choose to promote people from manual to nonmanual jobs. Another salient finding is that the difference in the importance attributed to basic professional credentials is related more to the attitudes of the trainees than to the effectiveness, or lack of it, of training programs. That such observations have explanatory value, if only in a statistical and descriptive sense, cannot be doubted, since many differences between the two countries that would otherwise be incomprehensible can be understood with their aid.

Still, it must be admitted that even this more broadly based statistical approach to the problem of international comparison runs up against certain problems, problems that go to the heart of our method. Because of the importance that we accord to worker flows, we have been led to give particular prominence to the interactions among the various factors that shape a worker's identity. We found, for example, that the attitude toward professional credentials—whether they are regarded as important or unimportant—is closely related to the way in which the educational system selects people for intermediate and advanced educational programs. Similarly differences in the use of seniority as a criterion for promotion or age as a criterion for access to certain kinds of jobs reflect crucial differences between the two countries in regard to the place of formalized apprenticeship programs and the way such programs are viewed by industrial firms. Thus our comparative approach leads inevitably to this conclusion, which leaves our approach in something of an impasse: the result of comparative study is to demonstrate beyond a doubt that comparison is impossible.

We have found that analysis of differences in worker mobility is inseparable from analysis of differences in the nature of the categories between which mobility takes place. To take a particularly significant example, consider mobility between the b-c and w-c worker categories. In both countries the nature and intensity of this mobility is symptom and cause of the social and professional position of each group, not only within the firm but in the wider society as well. For example, the fact that in Germany it is difficult to pass from unskilled to skilled status has to do with the way worker status is created and perpetuated in German schools and factories.

Occupational training, which plays a general role in structuring the working class, is also important for understanding in what sense the criteria governing mobility into w-c jobs are consistent with the criteria that enter into the definition of skilled workers as a group and that determine which workers within that group will be able to move up.

The kinds of mobility comparisons described can lead at best to the identification of mechanisms of worker mobility peculiar to one country or another. This is by no means without interest, but it is inherently incapable of opening the way to a more general or comprehensive analysis.

Progress toward such a goal is possible only if one is willing to draw the logical conclusions from the empirical results obtained thus far, in which worker movements occupy the center of attention. The point is this: the primary focus of research should be neither on empirical classification of types of mobility nor on the effects of mobility on the capabilities of workers but rather on the laws governing mobility and the criteria on which mobility is based.

It is impossible, however, to shift attention from the forms of mobility to the criteria on which it is based if the only data available concern the career trajectories of workers. We must also make use of other kinds of data, of the sort presented in chapters 2 and 3. These supplementary data include information about what we call social relations: relations of cooperation, competition, and domination not only within the workplace but also in schools, training programs, and other places where individuals prepare for jobs. Once we begin to talk about social relations, we can no longer avoid discussion of organizational phenomena of the sort studied above, particularly in chapter 2.

Incorporating social relations into our analysis is the only way to break out of the vicious circle. Doing so will enable us to flesh out the notion of socialization, which we will analyze as both a form of apprenticeship, in which workers learn to relate to their human and technological environment, and a process whereby the complex social relations constitutive of industrial society are created. Accordingly a more systematic consideration of the relationship between worker mobility and social relations in industry is in order before we introduce the more general analytic categories suggested by the empirical results set forth in chapters 1 through 3. There will be three such categories: socialization mobility criteria and the notion of a professional domain. Along the way we will reinterpret the empirical results obtained thus far in a more comprehensive and perspicuous manner than has been possible heretofore.

To begin we shall consider important differences between the two countries with regard to occupational training, focusing on both the way in which training is organized and its importance in the lives of workers. The problem is to understand why the attitude toward basic occupational training is positive in Germany and negative in France.

This problem could be rephrased in terms of worker mobility since it is a question of understanding the criteria by which students select or are selected for one track or another of the educational system and, beyond the age of compulsory schooling, what criteria govern the entry into the job market. But to stop at this point is not to go far enough, for the results we have presented especially in chapter 1, show that two factors affect the orientation of pupils within the educational and training system: the relationship of the schools to occupational training programs and that of class relations in general to social relations within the educational system.

Turning first to France, the fact that the general educational system, and more precisely the system of secondary schooling, is of such paramount importance is a reflection of class relations in the society at large. There is a tendency to avoid the harsher forms of class discrimination and to rely instead on a system of open competition, a process of elimination that results in a highly selective academic and social system. Class relations insinuate themselves into the educational system in a variety of ways: nature of teaching, orientation procedures, characteristics of teachers, behavior of students and their families, and others.

The paramount importance of secondary education in France is also closely related to factors that affect social mobility within the educational system, including choice of tracks, ways of reacting to failure, and attitude toward occupational training. To be sure, these factors are in part consequences of the structure of the educational system itself, but they also contribute to maintaining the class relations whereby the system is perpetuated.

In terms of formal structure the situation in Germany is similar. Pupils are tracked at an early age, just as in France. But in Germany the tracking system is extended by an autonomous and powerful system of occupational training, which reflects and reinforces the social relations that exist not only between classes but also within classes. In particular there is a reluctance to engage in direct (nonsegregative) competition on the part not only of the upper classes but also of some elements of the lower classes, particularly industrial workers. Hence there is a broad consensus against the development of a type of educational system within which such competition could take place.

The workings of the tracking system must also be interpreted in terms of the nature of the educational system. For instance, the fact that the German apprenticeship system fulfills such a highly integrative function (reflected in the behavior of apprentices, and particularly in the low dropout and failure rates) is, we think, in large part due to the homogeneity of the school system and to the lack of competition in the Hauptschule (track 1), which normally leads to apprenticeship. The French system can be analyzed in a similar way. There, in contrast to Germany, many different routes lead to basic occupational training programs; along the way pupils are subjected to severe competition, and many have already failed to jump numerous hurdles, which no doubt makes them more likely to fail again or drop out.

From these examples, one might be tempted to conclude that our argument is based on the hypothesis that there is a causal link between student performance in early stages of education and performance later. But in fact we make no such claim. The actual situation is more complex than such an analysis would suggest because of the interaction between various phases of education and various types of instruction.

An example will help to clarify what we mean. In France students do not normally go on from the first level of occupational training (CAP) to higher levels (leading to a technician's license, a technical baccalaureate, or some other certification). This fact would be incomprehensible without an understanding of how the system of secondary education is structured. Indeed it is the results of competition, selection, and elimination in the secondary schools that determine which students enter occupational training at the basic level and which enter at higher levels. It follows that the absence of vertical mobility within the occupational training system itself is due to the relationship between this system and the system of secondary education (where vertical mobility is possible). This relationship itself reflects class relations in general as they bear on the educational system as a whole. A similar remark could be made about Germany, where there is considerable vertical mobility from basic-level apprenticeship up to intermediate and advanced training. This is consistent with the fact that there is real social competition for the corresponding positions in German society.

These observations, based on our study of two concrete cases, suggest a number of generalizations useful for developing a more theoretical analysis of educational systems and of the supply of and demand for educational goods.

The notions of social structure and social system are widely used by sociologists. Our discussion suggests, though, that as these notions are generally used, they are too narrow because they take no account of the social interactions of which the structure or system is the expression or reflection. Thus in analyzing the French and German educational systems, we have tried not only to show their importance and stability but also to indicate in what sense they are the organizational crystallization of class relations and processes of social mobility.

Second, our work has led us to take a closer look at such economists' notions as the supply of diplomas or the demand for education, on which many labor market analyses are based. We have no wish to deny that knowing the educational composition of the work force is useful for analyzing inequality among workers, access to jobs, and tensions within the working class. But the differences between France and Germany are such that the present distribution of diplomas and credentials cannot be taken as a given. Rather the reasons why it is what it is must be analyzed. Simple supply-demand notions are not useful here.

Such notions derive from a market-centered analysis and are based on an implicit assumption that the decisions made by the actors in a social system are in large part socially neutral, as we shall argue in the appendix. When educational mobility is analyzed in this way, the reasons for the actors' decisions are thus disregarded and only the actual results are taken into account. But our comparison of France and Germany shows that the supply of credentials reflects the effects of class relations on social mobility. Thus observed correlations among mobility, type of credential, and relative scarcity or abundance of education and training merely express social relations. These correlations characterize the form of mobility that has developed in the particular society being looked at. Before distinguishing between stocks (supply of credentials) and flows (worker mobility), it is essential to ask how (through what intermediaries) the two interact. But this question takes us away from a market-centered approach.

In exploring the question of how these stocks and flows interact, it is wrong to limit the investigation to the relationship between mobility and social relations within the educational system alone. As the results of chapter 1 make clear, it is essential also to look at how qualifications and hierarchies are shaped by the firm. What we have to try to understand, then, is the relationship, within the context of the labor market, among three phenomena: social mobility associated with education, social mobility associated with job experience, and the kinds of social relations that exist within industrial firms.

The results obtained thus far, particularly in chapters 2 and 3, suggest that German and French firms are organized quite differently and that the worker hierarchy in the two countries is not the same. In Germany we found evidence of both cooperation and competition among workers. We also found that supervisory personnel, particularly those directly in charge of b-c workers, are interested mainly in monitoring worker performance and organizing workplace relationships.

There are two dimensions to social relations within the firm. One dimension pertains to the relationship of performance-oriented hierarchies to power-oriented hierarchies. The other pertains to the relationship between the technical division of labor and the social division of labor.

In both respects worker attributes play an important role in determining what groups will become important actors in the system and what criteria will distinguish these groups and determine their collective identities. In other words, social relations within the firm, whether pertaining to command and control functions or to technical job performance, are mediated by social relations of another kind, based on worker attributes that are more or less independent of the way a particular firm is organized and managed.

The fact that German firms attach great importance to occupational training is not, in our view, due to a desire on the part of workers to equip themselves with the technical skills necessary to do their jobs. Rather it has to do with the way workers relate to one another in carrying out their assigned tasks. Thus the purpose of occupational training is not to match worker skills to extant jobs; it is to prepare workers to effect the required mediation between the exigencies of technology and the methods of organization employed by the firm.

Stated another way, the importance attached to occupational training may be viewed as due to the market demand for trained workers, which in turn is an effect of the way German firms are organized, specifically, with technical and social management tightly intertwined. Because work teams in such a system are given a fairly free hand, the emphasis in selection is on a worker's intrinsic capabilities rather than on criteria such as seniority, which have to do not with capability but with the individual's relationship to the organization. There is an obvious paradox in this situation: it is because firms are organized in such a way as to allow considerable autonomy to each work team that a system of qualification based on social and professional norms largely independent of any particular firm has been able to develop.

We can go on to examine divisions within the German working class. Consider, for example, the relations between skilled and unskilled workers. Because of the way each work team functions internally, a worker has only limited chances of moving up from relatively simple to more complex jobs. Jobs are not distributed along a continuum running from low to high technical requirements. Rather discontinuities develop among jobs, discontinuities that are not purely social but the result of social relations that develop within the work team and are reinforced by the nature of the apprenticeship system. Because of these discontinuities, a man's chances for promotion based merely on seniority or experience are limited. Thus unskilled workers do not acquire skills merely by staying on the job for a certain length of time, and the labor market continues to place a low value on a man's experience if he is classed as unskilled.

It would be wrong, however, to ascribe this lack of upward mobility from unskilled to skilled status simply to an arbitrary decision by industry to attach a greater value to training than to experience or, alternatively, to the fact that enough apprentices are certified each year to fill industry's need for skilled workers. This may be an accurate—perhaps one should say a statistically correct—account. But things happen to be this way because of more general social factors. This was brought home to us with particular force in our studies of individual firms. There we found that the development of practices that might have encouraged raising the value attached to experience and seniority was hindered by the way the organization worked (with respect to shop floor–personnel office and worker-foreman relations) and by the attitude of the unions (which were intent on maintaining the status of skilled workers). Although firms prefer training to experience and demand qualified workers on the job market, it is wrong to ascribe this preference to a decision on the part of the firm, since the decision merely reflects the nature of the professional domain within which it is made.

Social relations in the workplace determine professional norms, which in turn shape the sphere within which mobility takes place. The social mobility of workers undoubtedly reflects both worker strategies and industrial demands, but these strategies and demands make sense only within a given professional domain. Otherwise it would be impossible to explain, for example, why so many apprentices eventually take jobs in firms other than the one in which they trained, or, to state it another way, why firms are willing to set up costly training programs and then allow those they train to go to work elsewhere. What might at first be characterized as market behavior is, we think, in a more fundamental sense a form of behavior characteristic of a particular professional domain, which we think of as the crystallization of organizational practices, professional norms, and forms of mobility.

In Germany we also found a second discontinuity, this time between skilled workers and w-c workers assigned to supervisory or technical jobs. In German firms supervisory authority is based in part on the same professional criteria that enter into the stratification of the manual labor force, as is exemplified by the relationship between workers and foremen. This relationship is shaped during apprenticeship, when the worker not only acquires general technical capabilities but is also subjected to a fairly strict regimen of social control. Authority relations can therefore be established without hindering the development of a strong sense of professional identity among skilled workers. This identity is legitimated, moreover, by the fact that foremen have acquired even more advanced technical knowledge than those working under them.

In other words intermediate or advanced training becomes a prerequisite for access to supervisory posts. Hence the essential gap in status between manual and nonmanual workers does not coincide exactly with the nature of the work done or the degree of supervision to which it is subject. Rather it reflects a broader system of social and occupational stratification, in which the criteria that govern vertical mobility are the same as those that guarantee the autonomy and professional status of skilled manual workers.

Here again we see how class relations and worker mobility interact to create what we earlier called a professional domain (or skill domain). The professional status of w-c workers is founded first on the way German firms are organized and second on broadly general criteria whose nature and objective determinants, such as credentials and background, ensure their applicability beyond the confines of any particular firm.

The forms of work force stratification we found in France were quite different from those in Germany. Nevertheless they can be explained in terms of a fairly similar kind of analysis. Once again we shall start with certain organizational characteristics of industrial firms, characteristics with an important bearing on how firms are managed and what kinds of social relations develop within them.

At several points thus far we have stressed the heterogeneous character of jobs in French firms and the important influence that this heterogeneity exerts on worker stratification and mobility. Clearly, however, this does not mean that a worker's place in the hierarchy is rigidly determined by the objective nature of his job, nor does it mean that relations between workers are determined solely by the technology-related interdependence of their functions. Rather the French form of work organization corresponds to a certain conception of what qualifications are all about, and because of this there is a greater need than in Germany for the workers as a group to exert some control over the way the industrial hierarchy is constituted (for, once constituted, it remains fairly stable despite changes in specific job descriptions). Objectively the form this worker control has taken is the following:

at the firm level and even the shop level, seniority has become the main criterion for determining a worker's place in the hierarchy. Like occupational training in Germany, seniority has proved the most effective way of mediating between the existence of a hierarchy in the workplace and the fact that all the employees of a firm share a common history of working in a joint endeavor. Still, although French firms give greater weight to the nature of the job than to the qualification of the worker, this does not rule out the possibility of other processes for establishing hierarchical status, processes rather more independent of the immediate production process than are job descriptions and measures of worker efficiency. Whenever such processes exist, they reflect stable patterns of social relations (between various segments of the work force) within a given organization.

The fact that the status hierarchy corresponds closely to the job structure tends to diminish the importance of criteria of stratification related to training acquired by workers before they enter the work force and to increase the importance of criteria that tend to promote certain career patterns. Any level of skill attained by a worker at a given moment may be regarded, in theory at any rate, as a transitory state rather than a status defined by membership in a highly stable group defined by strict social and professional standards. This system of stratification tends to break down the barriers between different echelons of the hierarchy; the continuities that develop within the job system outweigh whatever social and professional discontinuities may tend to establish themselves within the work force.

Still we must be clear about what we mean when we say that barriers are broken down. We found that certain characteristics of French industrial organizations, such as the importance attached to the job (and the job coefficient) and the distinction between technical and social management, tend to create a more centralized, bureaucratic (and in a sense more individualized) style of worker management than in Germany. This opens the possibility of upward mobility within the organization, even if actual upward mobility is dependent on the existence of job vacancies and thus on deaths, resignations, or the creation of new jobs.[1] Thus barriers that are broken down in theory, because of the way in which qualificational prerequisites are conceived, may not be broken down in practice. But the conception of qualification or professional status in question goes hand in hand with a centralized, bureaucratic style of management. These observations lead us to make the following hypothesis (a fundamental tenet of our approach): organizational practices are inseparable from the ways in which workers develop their professional status. Hence the effects of organizational practices extend beyond the limits of the organizations within which they develop to help shape the labor market and the way it operates.

If barriers are broken down in this way, it is possible for firms to promote self-taught workers who learn what they need to know on the job rather than to reinforce, as German firms do, the fairly stable dividing lines that in Germany separate one group of workers from another. In the French system the kinds of individual and collective mobility that will develop most fully therefore depend on contacts determined by the organization of industry (workers can move up within a shop or a firm or within a particular branch of industry). As for making the jump from b-c to w-c status or even up to management level, the main control over this kind of mobility is exerted by the relationship of the worker to the firm and its system of authority (the tendency is to promote the most senior workers and to emphasize leadership capabilities). In short the stratification of the industrial work force in France is a result of the interaction between a fairly administrative (and therefore potentially egalitarian) conception of worker qualifications and professional status on the one hand and the differentiating effects of the division of labor on the other hand.

It is probably wrong to claim that the importance attached by French firms to experience in general and to seniority in particular is a way of compensating for a presumed failure on the part of the educational and training system to turn out workers with technical know-how adapted to the needs of industry. We have seen that in fact occupational training does not play such a role in Germany. There the training system is regarded as legitimate because it provides workers with professional skills that are largely independent of the specific needs of industrial firms, and therefore with an autonomous professional status.

In France the logic that governs the social determination of qualification is in contradiction to the logic underlying the hierarchy of diplomas and credentials associated with education acquired prior to entry into the work force. The fact that only a small number of workers have received occupational training is inseparable from the fact that the relationship between level of credentials and actual qualification is highly indeterminate. Both are due not only to the way the educational system operates but also to the practices adopted by industry and the forms of professionalism that tend to develop within industrial firms. The organizational practices of French firms constitute a professional domain in which two types of mobility are possible: mobility within the educational system and mobility within industry based solely on professional experience. Both forms are the result of strategies adopted by individuals in a labor market that makes such strategies possible and even profitable. In our view, however, the important point is that these strategies are legitimated by industry and thereby become a structural feature of work force stratification within the firm. Here we are emphasizing the relationship between mobility and social relations. We thus find a close relationship between the strategic behavior of the actors in the system (workers and firms) and the structures in which their behavior crystallizes. It is within these structures, moreover, that the actors' behavior becomes efficient (in the social or economic sense) and can be seen as legitimate.

These remarks, which are directed toward the specific role of occupational training in shaping the stratification of the work force, are not intended to suggest that a worker's educational level has no effect on his level of skill or the position to which he may rise within industry. Education does play a role. But this role is one of establishing a worker's potential to advance within the system of employment, and in this regard the importance of occupational training does not outweigh that of general educational achievement—in fact, the reverse is true. This is clearly the case even at the highest levels of the hierarchy. Consider graduates of the grandes écoles, for example. The professional worth of a degree from one of the grandes écoles, the precedence of one kind of degree over another, and the value of an elite degree as compared with the value of other degrees all depend strongly on criteria laid down by individual firms. In other words the value of a degree depends on how it affects an individual's chance of moving up in an organization: the importance of career experience outweighs that of previously acquired training; a man's future potential counts for more than his present skills. Similarly basic worker training, even when offered by a large firm and sanctioned by a professional diploma, is valuable mainly because it puts a man in line for internal promotion. Workers trained by a firm can hope one day to rise to in-house management positions. It is this hope that makes such internal training programs attractive to workers.

The situation in France thus contrasts with that in Germany in the following essential respect: occupational training does not play a key role in the process by which firms establish, stabilize, and legitimate the stratification of the work force. This explains why occupational training is so little developed in France. Indeed it is far better to explain this fact in this way than to adduce supposed structural or cultural rigidities inherent, as some would claim, in French society in general or in the French educational system in particular.

With these remarks we have begun to work toward a synthetic

overview of our subject. Several times we have referred to the notion of a domain or span (professional domain, organizational domain, and so forth). We first began using this term when presenting the data concerning the role of the educational system and the nature of social relations within the workplace. It has also figured in our international comparisons. Having pointed out that the terms generally used in making such comparisons do not necessarily designate the same objects in different countries, we were forced to give prominence to differences in the context of social action, socialization, and industrial conflict. In other words we have found it necessary to examine how the professional, educational, and industrial domains vary from one country to the next.

In the last few pages we have tried to give a somewhat clearer definition of the notion of a domain by introducing the concept of a form of socialization in order to emphasize the relationship between worker mobility and social relations. We have gone into some detail about the way in which German society gives prominence to what we have called the professional domain or domain of qualification, whereas French society emphasizes the organizational domain.[2] In this discussion we made it clear that the nature of the typical firm and the criteria that govern worker mobility are important aspects of the notion of domain.

In regard to the nature of the firm, we must dispel an ambiguity that may remain. French industrial firms seem to bear the major part of the burden of establishing criteria and procedures whereby work force stratification is institutionalized. But this does not mean that individual firms have control over these criteria and procedures since it is quite clear that there is a general pattern to which each firm must conform. Minimal expectations exist in regard to career progress, and educational achievement is generally recognized as an important factor. Thus factors that can be regarded as external to industry create a situation in which all firms behave in accordance with a general model.

By contrast, in Germany the professional domain is paramount. This is another way of saying that work force stratification is determined by a unique standard external to each individual firm; the level of occupational training received. But our analysis has shown that this external standard is inextricably intertwined with organizational practices in industry, such as the type of hierarchy and the nature of skill differentiations within German firms. Saying that the skill domain is paramount is a shorthand way of saying that, in classifying workers, German firms rely on criteria relatively independent of factors over which they exercise direct control (such as internal promotion and type of authority relations).

We are now in a position to clarify how the notion of a firm relates to the notion of a domain. The role of the firm is in fact central but only insofar as the firm helps to create the specific constraints (specific to each country) to which it must submit.

It is also important to explain how mobility is related to criteria associated with the socialization process. Our approach to the question of mobility contrasts with that of human capital theorists in the following respect: rather than think of mobility as productive of skills, we think of it as movement within a system of qualifications. Thus the way in which the educational system channels students into worker training programs should not be regarded as an adjustment of supply to demand but as a flow intimately associated with the social relations that define worker skills and professional status. We therefore do not think that a high degree of mobility necessarily tends to unify the labor market. For example, the fact that wages are more uniform across branches or within firms in Germany than in France cannot be regarded as due to a higher level of horizontal job mobility. Instead the uniformity of wages and positions is more fundamentally a reflection of the fact that highly developed professional norms are accepted as legitimate throughout German industry. These norms define a professional domain within which mobility has an equalizing effect on wages insofar as it reflects the norms and reinforces their legitimacy. Conversely it is easy to show that the relatively high level of mobility between b-c and w-c worker status in France goes hand in hand with marked and enduring inequalities between the two categories. To understand why this is so, it is necessary to refer to the criteria that govern worker mobility in France. These have to do with organizational discontinuities and are not based, as in Germany, on generally applicable standards of qualification.

It would be wrong, however, to think of the relationship between the professional domain or domain of qualification and the pattern of worker mobility as a one-to-one correspondence. To do so would be to argue in favor of a kind of structural determinism, which goes beyond the evidence. But in fact it is the workers themselves who establish a mobility pattern in response to professional norms and other factors associated with the skill domain.

In France where the organizational domain is paramount and characteristics and capabilities acquired on the job play an important role in determining the course of a worker's career, it is nevertheless the education received before entering the work force that largely determines the kind of job the worker will get and hence his ability to manage his own career.

Education tends to broaden the range of jobs accessible to a worker rather than to assure him a place in a more or less autonomous professional group. As a result the criteria that govern worker mobility in France are quite different from those in Germany, where professional credentials play such an important role.

Furthermore in Germany the criteria that govern mobility give prominence to the professional autonomy of workers by enhancing the capability of groups of workers to carry out various tasks with minimal supervision. The importance attached to credentials is the formal (legtimating) counterpart of a work system based on collective capabilities of this sort. It becomes clear why any attempt to broaden the range of worker mobility by using criteria other than professional credentials (such as seniority or general work experience) will be seen as a threat to the legitimacy of the whole system. Hence no such attempt is likely to succeed in establishing new standards that will be widely recognized by all workers and taken into account in individual planning of career strategies.

The labor market is frequently analyzed by classifying workers according to their capabilities, based on such identifiable characteristics as type of experience, nature and level of training, and social origin. Usually these are related to wages, which are regarded as the principal market reward for such capabilities. These characteristics are the ones on which firms rely in making hiring decisions, and the associated capabilities are most commonly related to the needs of the productive system. But our comparative analysis of France and Germany has shown that these presumed needs can vary considerably from one country to another. They are shaped by a complex series of mediations. Thus the characteristics that are valued or not valued, and the resulting hiring policies, are by definition a product of worker mobility. Hence they are a consequence of the way firms are organized and the state of class relations in the wider society.

We can now understand why formally identical characteristics can have such different meanings and such different effects on worker stratification. We can also begin to work toward an answer to the question of what is comparable and what is not. In particular it should be clear that comparisons based on such apparently objective measures as differences in average worker productivity and wages are not as legitimate as they may seem at first.

Indeed our results suggest that worker productivity can be analyzed in causal terms only by studying the effects on economic efficiency of the interrelationship between autonomy and control. Further research is needed before we can hope to elaborate more precise and operational models.[3] A similar remark applies to wage inequalities (which are different in France and Germany).[4] We take for granted the fact that wage differences are the economic reflection of class relations, organizational practices, and mobility-governing criteria and hence a characteristic feature of what we have been calling the professional domain. Here we can perhaps take the argument a step further by suggesting that the importance attached in Germany to professional autonomy within fairly uniform strata of the work force (and to controlling worker movements within the organization) tends to make constant expansion of the job spectrum (and thus constant increase in the ratio of highest to lowest wages, which measures the width of that spectrum) less inevitable than it is in France. By contrast the fact that the stability of the French system results from worker mobility within the firm tends to widen the gap between the highest and lowest wages.[5]

4.2 How the Firm Shapes Workplace Relations: Cooperation and Hierarchy

The previous analysis sheds light on the relationship between worker mobility and social relations associated with the production process. Conditions in the workplace and characteristics of various relations between groups of workers have been related to the processes whereby workers acquire their collective identities as well as to phenomena of worker mobility (or lack of mobility)

In this analysis we focused primarily on the contribution of various socialization processes to worker mobility and of occupational training to the formation of social relations between different categories of workers. It is now necessary to complete the analysis with further investigation into the effects of organization, which are not reducible to effects of socialization. We can then analyze how the two kinds of social facts interact.

In particular we shall give a more systematic account of some of the differences between French and German firms brought to light earlier, especially in chapter 2. At this point in the argument we shall introduce a new concept of the firm. Rather than go on thinking of the firm as the site where organization and socialization interact, we shall begin to look at it as an organizational actor in its own right (in other words, as a relatively autonomous center of decision making), which acts in such a way as to produce further effects of organization and socialization (associated with particular social relations) beyond those already discussed. In effect we are taking the firm as another level of analysis. It is the source not only of organizational rules and norms but also of specific forms of authority and domination, specific work relations.

Hence it is wrong to look at the firm as a neutral site where the relationship between worker mobility and collective professional identities can be observed. The firm plays an active role in shaping this relationship in several respects; among these are the way it divides and organizes work, the kinds of norms and rules it promulgates and enforces, the kinds of authority and control it chooses to establish, and the technology it chooses in relation to its administrative and organizational policies. Taken together these choices establish specific conditions with regard to worker mobility, professional group formation, and the development of cooperative and/or hierarchical work relations. It should not be forgotten, however, that the firm itself is constituted by interrelated processes of socialization and organization set in motion by other complex actors (institutions and organizations) with which the firm maintains more or less selective relations (the educational and training system, unions and professional groups, industry associations, governmental agencies, and public services).[6]

This way of approaching the problem enables us to reformulate the question of what the boundaries of the firm are. What is internal to the firm and what external? How does the firm relate to its environment? The autonomy of the firm as an actor is never more than a relative autonomy. Autonomy depends on how open or closed the firm is to influence by other organizational and institutional actors. It also depends on how far it can influence those actors in turn—for example, by producing effects of organization and socialization in its own right. We shall have more to say later about these aspects of the firm's behavior when we try to relate our work to other work in the sociology of labor and organization theory.

4.2.1 Cooperation and the Division of Labor

In order to isolate certain organizational effects and emphasize the special role of the firm in producing them, it will be worth reviewing some of our previous observations.

Let us start by recalling the importance of polyvalence in a number of the firms we looked at.[7] For our present purposes we are interested in polyvalence because it reflects the influence of both organization and socialization while showing that the former is not reducible to the latter.

In the German firm where polyvalence was practiced, it was related to a particular form of work organization, based on the idea of work stations. Insofar as the technology allows, each work station is defined as a set of tasks to be performed by the worker assigned to it. The Meister determines what these tasks will be in the light of the specific qualifications of the workers under him. Workers are then rotated from station to station, and this, coupled with training by the Meister, helps to socialize new workers.[8] As a result the "Meister's group" (the terminology itself is significant) acquires a collective capacity to function within a system that would seem to be a particularly efficient way of organizing work. In this particular case a polyvalent form of work organization was chosen no doubt because of certain organizational requirements (the need to ensure continuity in the production process in cases of absenteeism or technical failure). But the efficiency of the system is surely enhanced by the fact that workers are trained to meet its specific needs. Thus we have an effect of organization produced by the firm, which contributes directly to shaping the collective identity of the workers and the social relations on which that identity is based.

The significance of polyvalence in the French firm where it was practiced was quite different in that it was based on another sort of work system. Here the organization of work stations and the assignment of workers to particular stations were predicated on criteria more administrative than professional in nature.[9] Each work station in the French plant was assigned a coefficient established by an industry-wide contract. Since the coefficient determines a worker's wages, giving a man a raise means moving him to a new station. All the work stations figure in a classification plan for the firm based on the contract-fixed coefficients. This plan in effect lays down the internal architecture of the firm. It cannot be changed piecemeal without calling its internal consistency into question.

The consequences of this kind of system are numerous (and do not seem to have been affected by recent contract changes).[10] Assigning a worker to a work station immediately assigns him to a specific place in the organization chart (in the formal structure of the organization) rather than to a place in the work domain. The worker's classification recognizes not his personal qualifications but the technical requirements of the work station to which he is assigned, requirements that are defined in the abstract without reference to the actual capabilities of the work force. The advantage of this system (which lends itself to centralized labor management) becomes clear when we remember that promotion is based largely on seniority; it eliminates any need to rely on judgments of a worker's professional qualifications, judgements that are liable to be challenged.[11]

In this kind of system promotion is based not on a worker's capacity to master all the tasks associated with a given work domain but rather on his potential capacity to perform well in a higher-level post than the one he currently holds (where level is defined by coefficient and by the organization chart).

What can polyvalence mean in a work system of this sort? In the firm we studied it seemed directed not so much at training the work force as at responding to certain problems of management (such as coping with absenteeism, ensuring continuity of production, and integrating certain maintenance functions into production departments). The logic of the system of job classification would seem to stand in the way of the development of polyvalence based on the professional capabilities of the workers. Whereas in Germany polyvalence was not only a form of work organization but also a kind of apprenticeship, in France it merely equips workers to perform a number of different jobs, accumulating specialized bits of training, rather than expanding their professional horizons through combined practical and theoretical instruction.

The example of polyvalence shows how the organizational characteristics of a firm can influence the collective professional identities of its workers. Every organization contains an implicit model of what practical and technical knowledge is, a model based on specific social relations. Hence every organization is also an agency of socialization, which embodies a certain theory of practice and instructs workers not only by putting them to work in very specific ways but also by laying down certain norms specifying how work should be done. As socializing agencies, then, French and German firms have very different capabilities.

In both French and German firms, as indeed in any other organization, we find processes of role and status differentiation and integration at work. But the nature of these processes varies from country to country. In particular the influence of organizational factors on the formation of collective professional identities is not the same.

In Germany the classification of workers is relatively independent of the structure of the organization within which they work. This is reflected primarily in the fact that wages tend to be fairly independent of the post to which a worker is assigned. Firms value (and reward) a worker's capacity to master all the tasks associated with the production process. In this respect organization has a direct effect on the formation of (individual and collective) professional identity in that the form of work organization reflects the fact that the firm values professional competence as a personal attribute of the worker and not as a reflection of his position in the organizational structure. Work is organized in accordance with this normative notion. For example, jobs must be flexibly organized so that workers of all classifications can gradually acquire the skills needed to master all the work stations in a production facility. Considerable room for maneuver must be left to the Meister, who defines work stations and assigns workers with the idea of increasing their professional competence. To the extent that wages depend on productivity, evaluations of a worker's productivity must be decentralized; these decisions are usually left up to the Meister and Produktionsleiter (production supervisor). In such circumstances workers have an incentive to develop their productive capacity by taking supplementary training courses and by taking the initiative in the workplace (or by enrolling in an apprenticeship program if they are not already Facharbeiter). The bonus system, which is controlled by the workers themselves, is a mark of how individualized (and autonomous) the payment of productivity allowances has become.[12]

All of these practices tend to enhance the professionalism of the work group as a whole while distinguishing both qualitatively quantitatively between the contributions of the group's members. This has an impact on the relationship of the worker to his work; his capacity to acquire professional know-how or his "willingness to acquire the training he needs to do his job better" can actually affect the content of his work.[13] Although this capacity is influenced by the socialization process (occupational training, mobility), in which industry plays a role by setting standards and adopting specific organizational practices, it can be capitalized on only to the extent that the actual organization of the work process allows and indeed encourages. A man's chance of broadening his skills and developing his professional capacity depends largely on the autonomy of the Meister and Vorarbeiter, who assign individuals to work stations and thus exert effective control over how each worker spends his working hours.

Thus the German work system and, more generally, the organizational structure of German firms play an important role in shaping the professional identity of the German work force. Because work is organized in such a way as to encourage polyvalence, working life helps to socialize and educate the worker. The fact that the density of trained and skilled workers is high nationwide (because of the organization of German industry as much as to the socialization process) allows industry to accommodate itself to a work system that makes occupational training attractive to workers.

The situation is quite different in France, where the job structure and job content are closely related to the formal structure of the firm. Jobs are defined in the abstract, without reference to the capabilities of the workers. The pay scale is determined by the job coefficients and thus ultimately by the formal structure of the firm. A worker's pay therefore reflects his theoretical job description rather than his actual productive capacity.[14] With this kind of system, the job structure is "highly collective in nature, and so too are demands for changes in that structure.[15] This collectivization is based on administrative rather than professional considerations, however. It is the organization chart that determines job content rather than the qualification of the person who holds the job. Bureaucratic logic tends to outweigh professional concerns. This affects not only the organization and management of the firm but also social relations in the workplace.

Centralized personnel management at the company level becomes essential in this kind of system because there is no other way to coordinate policy, whether in regard to hiring, work assignment, productivity evaluation, promotion, or pay. As a result social management tends to become distinct from technical management, and this in turn reduces the autonomy of the direct production supervisors, particularly the foreman.[16]

Worker training is one of the responsibilities of the personnel manager in both France and Germany, but the role of training varies from one country to the other. In French firms training is not as integral a part of the workday as it is in Germany, where jobs are organized with training in mind. On the other hand, educational criteria play a greater part in determining a worker's job assignment and classification in France. Thus education and training tend to play an important part in decisions regarding promotion (by change of job), even if there is little direct relationship between the course content and the job requirements. A worker who possesses a degree or certificate specified in an industry-wide labor contract can claim that he has a right to promotion (provided an opening is available). Thus training-related issues become a central focus of labor-management relations as unions try to win formal recognition of such a right to promotion for workers possessing certain kinds of training.[17] In this respect training tends to be incorporated into the logic of the job classification system without necessarily having any real impact on the actual work system or the professional qualification of the work force.

It is true that in both France and Germany employers look at training in an instrumental way, thinking primarily of how it may contribute to worker productivity. But in France training plays more of a role in questions of personnel management than it does in the actual work process. Training often comes after a worker has been assigned to a job.[18] In Germany, on the other hand, the function of training is to broaden a worker's professional competence; it is a necessary but not sufficient condition for promotion, which it therefore precedes rather than follows.[19]

These organizational effects help to shape both the individual and collective professional identities of workers. A distinction should be made between the administrative management of the various job assignments (based on some system of worker classification) and technical labor management (based on the organization of work on the shop floor). Where these functions become separate, as in France, the worker's professional identity becomes fragmented; it is at once collectivized and individualized.

The French worker's professional identity is collective because it relates to a system of classification based on identical standards for all workers (or at least all workers in a category). Such a system no doubt promotes unity but in the same sense that Max Weber had in mind when he said that bureaucracy promotes unity: it establishes equality (equality before the law, as it were).[20] In other words any worker classified as having a 170 coefficient is the equal of any other worker with the same coefficient in some abstract sense but not necessarily in regard to working conditions, professional capacity, or even real wages (it should be remembered that the coefficient determines a worker's base pay but not his actual wage.)

At the same time the French worker's professional identity is individualized in the following sense. Each man is asigned to a job with a specific coefficient and job description. This tends to isolate him from other workers in the production process because the coefficient abstractly determines what each individual's contribution is supposed to be. This tends to set limits to the development of polyvalence since a worker cannot be moved to a position with a different coefficient unless a vacancy opens at that level of classification. Thus, somewhat paradoxically, the formal administrative collectivization of work stations goes hand in hand with individualization of the actual work process, which hampers the development of broader professional competence in individual workers.

Anything that makes the work process less flexible and tends to make each job relatively autonomous with respect to other jobs impedes the development of cooperation in the workplace and tends to make professional competence an individual rather than a group attribute. This is what happens, for example, in firms with centralized, bureaucratized systems of personnel management: while personnel policy may be coordinated at the company level, decisions tend to be made on an individual basis, without regard to the way a given worker relates to the others who work alongside him. This inevitably affects the relationship of the worker to his job and to other workers. Professional competence tends to be defined primarily in terms of qualifications (in the administrative sense of the term, that is, formal criteria in virtue of which a coefficient is assigned to an individual worker).[21] Work assignment is then made in the light of a worker's formal classification, as though a man's contribution to the productive process were a matter of his individual prowess rather than his relations with other workers. The formal organization chart exerts a powerful influence on actual job descriptions. Each position in the firm comes to be seen as independent of every other position. The whole is merely the sum of all the individual parts. This leads to compartmentalization, which further hampers the development of broad professional competence.

The narrower the definition of worker categories and job descriptions and the less a worker has the opportunity to develop his professional capabilities, the more he will try to keep his cooperation with other workers to a minimum. Promotions will tend to be confined to narrowly defined job hierarchies (whether within a given category or between different categories). Thus a worker will tend to deepen his skills in a narrowly defined area rather than broaden his competence over a wider domain. In fact it is common in France to speak of a typical career pattern for certain kinds of workers, who frequently move from job to job along a well-trodden pathway, sometimes moving up to higher echelons of the hierarchy along the way but without really broadening their base of skills.

The socialization process, then, is shaped by the relationship of the worker to his work. In this kind of system promotion generally breaks with a worker's previous professional experience rather than builds on that experience. Thus upward mobility tends to destabilize the professional group.

The analysis has focused on the organizational processes that help to shape group identities. Now we must look at how these processes are affected by the actions of employers and labor unions. In the case of France we have called attention to the complementary effects of the apparently contradictory tendencies toward individualization and collectivization of the system of worker classification. In regard to the latter tendency, it is significant that many labor conflicts have revolved around issues of classification.[22] A good example of what is at stake is the frequent demand for a unique grid of classifications running from the lowliest laborer to the highest-ranking executive. For the unions the unique grid symbolizes worker solidarity, whereas for the employer it is a "political problem, in that employers look upon management personnel as potential support for the firm's choice of goals."[23] This is an issue that unions can use to mobilize all workers (or perhaps one category of workers that happens to be of particular strategic significance at a given time) on the grounds that everyone will benefit from a change in the system of classification (a claim that employers tend to disparage as political).

But the complementary tendency toward individualization must not be forgotten. It is responsible, for instance, for the considerable gap between the base pay (established by the job coefficient) and the actual wage (which includes individual, seniority, and productivity bonuses). Compartmentalization further reinforces the tendency toward individualization.[24] To be sure, we earlier encountered some evidence of individualization in Germany as well, notably in regard to the close relationship that exists there between an individual worker's professional competence and his take-home pay. Still German workers have more scope than French workers to develop their professional competence because of the collective organization of the work system and the relative autonomy of the Meister in evaluating what each worker contributes to the overall productive effort.

Institutional analyses of the structure of the work force (such as the analysis of classificational and pay systems) therefore cannot hope to explain very much unless they are related to an analysis of social relations in the workplace. In other words the twin tendencies toward collectivization and individualization in the French classificational system must be regarded as being due not only to the system's institutional nature but also to the structure of social relations in the workplace; the two dimensions interact.

It is probably true that unions generally try to take advantage of the fact that working conditions are individualized in pressing their collective demands. In the French classificational system, unions have been successful in using the system as a focus of their organizing efforts. It may be asked, however, whether this type of action, waged as it were in enemy territory, does not inadvertently reinforce the system that it seeks to modify. Paradoxical as it may seem, the union goal of establishing a uniform system of pay (the counterpart of the management goal of coordinating the system of classification) may actually help to depersonalize the relationship of the worker to his job still further by emphasizing a bureaucratic system of classification rather than a system that would give workers an incentive to broaden their skills by rewarding their overall contribution to the collective process of production.[25]

It might seem to be the case that the classification system itself is decisive in determining the collective identity of each group of workers. But the logic of our approach suggests that although this may be the most important factor, other factors must also be taken into account. The significance of the classificational system appears fully only when it is seen in relation to the way the firm is organized and labor is divided.[26] The classificational system itself might be regarded as an effect of organization.

But at the same time the example shows how organizational effects can influence the socialization process.

Indeed this is particularly clear in France. The system of job classification is not only an effect of the organization of individual firms but also a feature of French industry in general (where classification by coefficient is enshrined in industry-wide labor contracts). It is all the more important because, in evaluating a worker's status, French firms pay less attention than do their German counterparts to such other factors as occupational training. The system of classification is thus one aspect of the French firm's relationship to society in general. We shall have more to say about this relationship later: specifically, the less value an organization attaches to socialization by educational institutions, the more it will try to institute a socialization process of its own in order to instill its norms in its employees, and vice-versa. In other words the extent to which an organization is open or closed to socialization accomplished by other institutions will affect the modes of social control, and therefore the kinds of social relations, that will develop within it.

Before proceeding further in the attempt to systematize our empirical results, we must introduce a new element into our analysis: technology and its influence on organization, which a number of earlier studies have described as decisive.

4.2.2 Technology, Organization, and Hierarchical Relations: The Foreman's Span of Control

Studies of organizations commonly emphasize such variables as the ratio of supervisors to workers or the span of control (the number of workers working under a supervisor at a level of the hierarchy). Beyond these considerations, we have tried to discover the influence of two additional factors: the technological factor, which has also been studied by Joan Woodward, among others, and what we have called the social factor. By themselves our statistical results might suggest that the importance of the social factor tends to outweigh that of the technological factor, since we found that no matter what organizational variable we considered, the results seemed to be determined not so much by the technology used in a firm as by the country in which it was located. This might lead one to think that the effects of techology are overdetermined by social factors. It is more in keeping with the logic of our overall approach, however, to regard technology as an intervening variable between the effects of organization and the effects of socialization. Technology is not an exogenous independent variable, capable by itself of explaining the differences we observed but an element in the process that shapes social relations in the workplace and the collective identities of various groups of workers. Not that the influence of technology is unimportant: firms using unit production technologies have a different supervisory structure and organization from firms using line or continuous process technologies. But technology is just one factor among others that help to shape workplace relations, organization, and processes of socialization.[27] It might be said that technology alone does not suffice to explain a firm's authority structure. Rather it is the processes of control (of tasks and workers) that a firm puts into practice that explain how the labor process is structured, both functionally and hierarchically.[28] These processes may well depend on the degree of uncertainty associated with various kinds of technology and production processes, but they also depend on the nature of social relations in the workplace. Indeed one major result of our work is to show that latitude is left to firms in deciding what system of control to institute in connection with a given choice of technology. But the range of possible choices is limited in each social context by a coherent set of factors pertaining to organization and socialization.[29]

To make this point clearer, we want to consider a classic problem of organization theory: the problem of the span of control of first-line supervisors—for present purposes, the number of workers working under each foreman.

Our empirical findings show the same general pattern as Woodward's. If we plot the span of control starting with unit production on the left, line production in the middle, and continuous process production on the right, the resulting curve looks like an inverted J. But the shape of the curve is not the same for French and German firms; it rises much less steeply for the former than for the latter. The gap between the two curves is widest in the case of line production and smallest in the case of continuous process production.

These results are not easy to interpret, and they cast some doubt on Woodward's analysis and other work suggesting that some sort of technological determinism is responsible for observed variations in organizational structure. It is as though the way technology is used in France is conditioned by factors different from those that hold sway in Germany, assuming that one agrees that technology itself is a social product whose economic value depends on how well it fits into particular industrial organizations and adapts to particular systems of socialization. To employ a technology is a social act; hence some latitude is left to the actors who do the employing. On the other hand, any technology itself conditions the actors who use it (to some extent at any rate—never entirely). Using a technology requires the acquisition of certain theoretical and practical capabilities; it requires learning. Undoubtedly because technologies are shaped by the social conditions under which they are created and used, seemingly comparable technologies are compatible with quite different forms of work organization, job structure, and workplace relations. In this regard technology is inseparable from the social relations of production (in the broad sense), but it is not reducible to these relations.

If, however, we assume that in each country, one of two possible logics of work organization is paramount—either administrative logic or the logic of professionalism—then it becomes possible to explain why the span of control is larger in German firms than it is in French firms. Indeed each logic implies a different conception of labor control.

The logic of professionalism, which emphasizes professional socialization, tends to play down nonprofessional forms of supervision. The resulting system of labor control is designed to encourage both (professional) autonomy and productivity (Leistung) in the workers. Furthermore the system tends to stress technical-instrumental skills rather than social-normative skills.[30] Production departments carry great weight in such a system since technical support services are regarded primarily as adjuncts of production. Workplace relations are cooperative rather than hierarchical, and what authority relations do exist are legitimated by the recognized professional competence of the superior.

By contrast, administrative logic is associated with a different kind of work organization and different worker attributes. In hiring, firms are less selective in regard to occupational training and worker credentials. On the other hand they take a more active part in socializing workers, shaping workers to fit their own productive requirements. Social-normative qualities are emphasized, with workers being encouraged to adapt themselves to company norms. Control functions tend to be assumed by the supervisory hierarchy and the technical support departments, which take precedence over production. Workplace relations in this kind of system are oriented more vertically than horizontally (because of the compartmentalization associated with administrative rules and/or contract-fixed worker-worker relations). Authority functions in such a system will be more distinct from technical functions, so that the chain of command will tend to be longer. Finally, there will be a greater separation of design, management, and planning functions on the one hand and execution functions on the other hand than in the other kind of system. As a result operatives will have less autonomy.

Each logic—administrative or professional—is itself the expression of the complex interaction between organization and socialization. Although the span of control in any organization is affected by the logic that dominates that organization, this merely reflects the effects of different types of social control. The concept of an organization can in fact be subsumed under the concept of a social relation; the formal structure is in this sense shaped by a social relation, while the type of social control is yet another aspect of the social relation of which the organization is the embodiment. With these remarks in mind, we shall now reinterpret the effects of technology on organization.

Since we are thinking of an industrial organization as the embodiment of a social relation, the use of a particular technology must be thought of as conditioned by that relation. In other words a technology cannot be specified in purely technical terms; its social aspects must also be taken into account. Thus technology cannot be treated as an exogenous variable or an objective, all-but-universal condition of production, indeed a quasi-natural object, as it sometimes is.

Some of our results up to this point may seem rather paradoxical in the light of certain classical theories of organization and of the relationship between technology and work. We are now in a position to dispel some of these paradoxes. But first we must take up a question to which the theory of the span of control offers no answer: how does it come about that b-c workers consistently account for a larger proportion of all employees in German firms than in French firms, no matter what type of technology is used?

Partial answers to this question may be found scattered throughout the book. Here we stress the relationship of this question to the question of technology, or the social use of technology. It is possible to argue (without falling into the trap of culturalism, which we wish to avoid) that the status of b-c workers is higher in Germany than it is in France, and similarly that the importance of production is held to be greater within the firm. But then we must ask how this came to be so and what its social significance might be. The study of history is an interesting approach but does not seem an adequate way to deal with the problem. Although it is relevant to introduce a historical dimension into the discussion of how the social actors come to be what they are, history cannot by itself explain why the characteristic structures of German society and German industry have remained stable over a fairly long period of time.[31] It seems more appropriate to look for an answer to the question by examining the social and technical division of labor. These are both produced by and productive of social relations not only in the workplace but also in society at large. Stated another way, the value attached to production and the status accorded to b-c workers must be interpreted in the light of class relations in German society as a whole as well as in relation to the influence of educational and organizational factors (where these factors are particular aspects of the fundamental social relations that obtain in the wider society).

It can be seen how our approach differs from others in which appeal is made "in the last instance" to some unique causal factor. [The allusion, which may be lost on non–French-speaking readers, is to work inspired by the Marxist philosopher Louis Althusser—Trans.] Instead of a unique cause we emphasize the complex interaction of actors, processes, and social sites or individual firms and society at large. By doing so we are able to go beyond the economic reductionism often implicit in the notion of social relations, which are too commonly seen as one-dimensional and everywhere the same ("the bourgeoisie versus the proletariat"). But this kind of approach makes it impossible to explain differences in the b-c to w-c worker ratio as being due solely to the effects of technology, conceived as a socially neutral variable. Such differences can be interpreted only in relation to the complex social relations that obtain in the society under study, particularly as these manifest themselves in organization and socialization. It is not that the forms of organization and socialization in a particular society are immutable, though they do tend to remain fairly stable over long periods of time. Still the nature of social change itself is strongly conditioned by the kinds of organization and socialization in any society.

The fact that the proportion of b-c workers in German firms is relatively high must be interpreted in relation to the importance attached to occupational training and to the stratification and professional characteristics of the work force. The division of labor must also be taken into account because it affects industry generally and the structure of industrial organizations in particular. Taken together, all of these factors explain why the b-c group is more stable as a group in Germany than in France.[32] This no doubt has consequences for the nature of class divisions in German society as well as for the nature of the working-class movement and the unions.[33] The fact that b-c workers (and low-level w-c employees) constitute a relatively unstable group in France is not unrelated to the fact that there is a relatively large number of low-level management personnel (particularly production supervisors and other petty bosses) on the shop floor as well as in administrative offices.

We find the same characteristic differences in regard to job structure no matter what kind of technology is used. Indeed the differences between the two countries are particularly marked in firms using line production technology. In these firms we find the greatest gap between French and German firms in regard to span of control, which is much larger in Germany than it is in France. In other words the greatest difference occurs where the division of labor is most extensive, the workers are least qualified, and labor discipline is built into the technology (because of the highly mechanized nature of assembly line production). Accordingly German firms using this kind of technology tend to use fewer supervisors, since the situation offers little scope for employment of their characteristic training. On the other hand French firms using batch technology are more likely to use a larger number of supervisors, as though they believed that relatively unskilled workers required that much more supervision.[34]

This brings us to another result: differences between the two countries concerning changes in the worker-supervisor ratio with respect to changes in technology. Specifically we found greater variation in Gemany than in France. It is as if German firms were more sensitive to the effects of technology than French firms. This does not mean that technology is the sole and direct determinant of the division of labor in German firms anymore than in French firms.

This leads to the following hypothesis: similar technologies are used in different ways in different societies. The use of a technology is a social act and as such an integral part of the social relations inherent in any society. When a technology is put to use, it becomes in a sense socialized in systems characterized by different kinds of social relations. Technology is therefore not an exogenous but rather an endogenous factor in any social system. It is impossible to conceive of a technical organization of labor that is not also a social organization.

Thus the firm's relationship to technology (or the way in which the firm, as a complex social actor, integrates technology into its social relations) is different in France than in Germany. To the extent that the work domain in each country is structured by specific social relations, the effects of technology (on the division of labor, worker-worker relations, and worker qualifications) will vary from one country to the other.

In Germany, where the logic of professionalism predominates, technics (Technik) has a more direct bearing on organization than in France.[35] The firm's relationship to technology is conditioned by factors such as dual apprenticeship associated with socialization and by organizational factors such as polyvalence and interdepartmental and interdepartmental cooperation, which make industry more sensitive to the technical-professional requirements of each type of technology. This in turn serves as the basis of the culture of labor relations in Germany, in which technical-instrumental qualification plays the leading role.

By contrast, in French firms, the predominance of administrative work relations tends to attenuate the expected technological effects. Social-normative qualifications take precedence over technical-instrumental ones. No matter what type of technology is used, labor discipline is more a matter for bureaucratic management than an integral part of technical control of the work process. To be sure, the technological base of production does still exert some influence but much less than in the German case.

In the end it is as though what we have been calling the social factor were somehow reinforced by the intrinsic requirements of each type of technology. This is particularly clear in regard to the relative numbers of various kinds of supervisory personnel. Thus French firms using line production tend to use more direct production supervisors than comparable German firms, which are likely to employ more technical supervisors (technicians and graduate engineers in the various technical departments). By contrast in firms using unit and continuous process production technologies (which rely more heavily on technically qualified workers and on cooperation between production and technical departments), French firms are likely to require a relatively large number of maintenance supervisors and technicians, whereas German firms prefer to rely on polyvalent skilled workers in conjunction with graduate engineers (this is particularly true of maintenance departments in process production facilities).

We began by asking what the reasons were for differences in the span of control between French and German firms. Our answer is now clear. It does not revolve around the factors generally invoked in classical organization theory, such as technical complexity and predictability. We focus instead on the nature of the interdependence (hierarchical or functional) between different kinds of workers and different professional groups, or, to put it another way, on the contrast between cooperative work relations and compartmentalized work relations. We think that this approach is more helpful for understanding the nature of authority relations in industry than such merely quantitative measures as the span of control. The qualitative differences between French and German firms using process production technology show quite clearly some of the shortcomings inherent in an approach as formalistic as the so-called theory of structural contingency, which is incapable of explaining how organizations actually relate to their social environment.

In classical organization theory, technology and the social environment have generally been conceptualized as contraints to which the organization must adjust. By contrast the kind of social analysis we have been developing here conceptualizes the relation between the organization and its environment as a social relation. Although it is true that any technology, once in place, embodies a certain kind of rationality and entails certain kinds of social relations, it is equally clear that each society makes use of technology in ways in keeping with its own characteristic social relations.

Accordingly the current state of social relations in a society may be regarded by an organization not simply as a constraint on its own development but also as a resource on which it can capitalize.[36] Assuming constant technology, social differences in the way labor is divided merely manifest differences in the ways different societies put the technology to use, reflecting what resources are socially available and what constraints are socially imposed. It is not hard to understand why attempts to transfer technology sometimes run into difficulties. A given technological resource may not be appropriate for use in the importing society. The attempt to import such unsuitable technology is made without regard to the fact that every technology depends on certain (preestablished) social relations. In some cases, therefore, a transfer of technology may be tantamount to an act of imperialism, to an exercise of technological hegemony. In other words it may be seen as an attempt to impose constraints on the possible evolution of social relations in the importing country.

This analysis may leave readers with the impression that the organization of the firm is ultimately determined by an externally imposed social process. Nothing could be further from the truth. We therefore turn to a consideration of how the firm itself plays an active role in producing the social relations that play a more important role in determining its organization than does any alleged technological determinism.

4.2.3   Socialization, Organization, and Social Control: The Active Role of the Firm

There is a connection between the forms of social control promoted by a firm and the forms of socialization that it institutes in order to integrate new workers and establish distinctions within the work force. The criteria used in hiring new workers are crucial in this regard. An organization may choose either individuals who have already been socialized elsewhere, particularly in the schools, or individuals whom it intends to subject to its own forms of socialization. If professionally competent individuals are selected, then the organization will have less need to develop internal control mechanisms.[37] This is just what German firms do. By hiring trained individuals and incorporating criteria associated with the training system into their internal management policy, they are able to reduce the need to rely on other forms of organizational control. By contrast French firms are far more likely to rely on internal control mechanisms, since they regard newly hired employees as requiring indoctrination in company norms.[38]

The professional competence and identity of German workers are formed in large part outside the firm. A worker's skills are generally recognized as standing apart from the position to which he happens to be assigned by a particular firm. Thus the worker is more independent of the firm, and his chances of moving up in the world are associated with his socially acknowledged skills rather than with his relations with a particular company. By contrast, in France a worker's professional status depends primarily on socialization within a particular firm. Hence it is more directly related to company norms and standards. A man's professional identity in France corresponds to his position and status within the organization, on which he is therefore more dependent than his German counterpart; his professional capital is not necessarily recognized on the labor market.

The way in which workers are integrated into the firm helps to shape their collective identity and beyond that to shape the kinds of social relations that develop inside and outside the firm.[39] In this we see how the firm shapes its own identity while helping to shape the identity of its employees. We also see how forms of organization and social control are related to forms of socialization and professional training. When a firm agrees to accept training provided by other agencies and organizes itself internally in such a way as to encourage technical-instrumental forms of professionalism, it thereby reduces the need to rely on other, nonprofessional modes of social control. Hiring and promotion are based on criteria of professional competence, and this in turn encourages competition among workers to improve their skills. Social control is more internalized: for example, the Leistungsprinzip, or productivity principle, takes precedence in Germany over the principle of equal pay for equal work. The authority of supervisory personnel is based on technical competence and is used not so much for disciplinary purposes as to help workers master new skills. Authority and expertise tend to reinforce one another, and the contrast between line and staff personnel is diminished. The result is a less cumbersome supervisory apparatus and an increased span of control.

In sharp contrast is the situation in France, where firms assume part of the burden of socializing their employees. Their purpose is to shape the professional qualifications of workers to suit company needs. In such a system social control mechanisms serve primarily to enforce conformity with company norms; an impersonal code of rules applies to all employees.

The measure of the system's efficiency is its capacity to take relatively untrained workers and train them to some uniform minimum standard; here integration and differentiation must respect the principle of equality. Supervisors concern themselves primarily with enforcing the rules rather than with worker training. Social control is more impersonal, more bureaucratic than in Germany. Norms are less internalized by the workers. There will tend to be more supervisors, technicians, and specialists whose job is to simplify the tasks assigned to ordinary workers, thereby helping to adapt technology to the needs of labor discipline. The professional status of the ordinary worker is based primarily on the length of time he has worked for the firm rather than on qualifications generally recognized on the labor market.

At this point we are in a position to amplify somewhat the conclusions of Joan Woodward. No organizational structure, Woodward argued, is good in itself. Rather, that structure is good that is best suited to the constraints laid down by technology (the conclusion of her 1965 study), or, better still (as the argues in her 1970 study), best suited to the type of control chosen by the firm in order to deal with uncertainties in production (mainly connected with the type of technology employed). Accordingly we may summarize the discussion by saying that the various types of industrial organization found in France and Germany reflect specific mechanisms of social control, which are in turn related to certain characteristics of the collective identities of the social actors and to the social relations between those actors.

4.3 The Professional Domain and the Domain of Collective Action

In the course of analyzing the interaction between socialization and organization, we introduced the notion of the professional domain associated with a social system. Our empirical work culminated in a description of the professional domains associated with French and German society and in discussion of differences between the two. In one sense the notion of a professional domain is a necessary analytic construct, without which it would be impossible to grasp the underlying unity of diverse organizational practices and phenomena of social mobility. But it is also more than that: it is a starting point for a more thorough and rigorous analysis of organized collective action than any we have undertaken until now.

Different professional domains are distinguished by characteristic features of two kinds: the criteria that unify the elements within the domain and those that differentiate between elements. By taking both sets of criteria into account, we hope now to elucidate the structure of social relations in the two countries and to explain where in the social structure, and around what issues, the most significant conflicts are likely to materialize.

We begin with France. There the criteria that unify the professional domain are educational achievement and seniority. The predominant role that these criteria play, through the labor market, in determining the administration of workers' wages and qualifications tends to level out differences between workers and to reinforce the social homogeneity of the working class. Another factor that contributes to this homogeneity is the scarcity of occupational training available outside the firm. As a result conflict tends to focus on the firm itself, particularly conflict over wages. This tendency is enhanced by the centralized, bureaucratic character of decision making in the firm, particularly in regard to job content and job assignment. Since there is a single center of authority, all worker complaints are directed toward that center. (A recent instance of this was the demand—eventually acceded to—for payment of wages on a monthly basis along with the introduction of a single grid of classification for both b-c and w-c employees.)

But there is another side of the coin: workers of all sorts tend to be reduced to uniformity in the face of the firm's authority, yet there is much disparity in industry as a whole. We find variations in the wage level from industry to industry, from firm to firm within a industry, and from one region of the country to another (with a particularly sharp contrast between the Paris area and other regions). These disparities make it difficult for unions and employers to adopt coordinated policies. This accounts for another feature of the French system of industrial relations: the tendency to rely on negotiation at the national rather than the local level in order to overcome difficulties of coordination. In practice, what this means is that labor contracts, often worked out in conjunction with the government, generally include clauses stipulating certain minimum criteria (in regard to working hours, layoffs, discharge, and so forth) applicable to all firms. French minimum wage legislation is only one example among many of the tendency to resolve problems at the highest levels. There are two reasons for this: one is to cope with the fact that the centers of power are so heterogeneous in character, and the other is to move negotiations on a large number of topics away from the firm, where the atmosphere is often highly charged. In sum, the foregoing amounts to a description of what we might call the domain of collective action associated with French society. The specific characteristics of this domain are not without influence on the determination of wages and social benefits in France.

Having discussed the levels at which conflict and negotiation are situated, we now turn to a consideration of the issues and the strategies of the various actors. Since there is little professional differentiation in France between b-c and w-c workers, in theory it should be possible for unions to mobilize all of a firm's employees in case of conflict with management. Employers try to deal with this by reducing the unions' capacity for mobilization—no mean feat given the uniformity of the work force. But management can resort to the device of setting wages on an individual basis. This is possible for two reasons: actual wages may vary from the minima fixed by contract and wages are in part determined by the job coefficient, the job coefficient is determined by the job assignment, and the job assignment is made at management's sole discretion. Furthermore the fact that the number of management personnel is relatively high in France can also be interpreted as part of a strategy to discriminate between workers while reinforcing some of the basic criteria that unify the professional domain: seniority (some autodidact senior workers are promoted to the ranks of management) and educational achievement (many managers have advanced degrees). To sum up, French union strategy is directed toward mobilizing all workers in a given firm, and management parries by discriminating between workers individually and by trying to shift conflict away from the firm and into the national arena, often with the tacit concurrence of the unions.

The German professional domain is opposed to the French point by point. Whereas the French work force is homogeneous, in Germany there is a traditional division between b-c and w-c workers. Where French industry is diverse, German industry is fairly uniform, so that German firms are more likely than their French counterparts to accede to the authority of industry associations and business groups.

Futhermore the German professional domain is unified by the importance attached to occupational training, based on apprenticeship and continuing training for the most part open to all workers. The sharpest divisions in the work force are between industrial workers and nonindustrial workers and within the former group, between b-c and w-c personnel. The latter division has proved ineradicable, even within the DGB, which counts both b-c and w-c unions among its members. This is one division in the ranks of the working class that employers did not need to create. Although w-c workers are subject, in part at the request of their own unions, to different rules from b-c workers, the gap between the two groups is lessened in some respects by the way pay is determined (for example, through productivity bonuses for b-c workers), so that pay differences are far less pronounced than they are in France. Another source of heterogeneity in the German work force is the existence of a fairly large group of so-called noncontract employees: workers earning more than a minimum threshold salary above which pay is negotiated bilaterally between employer and employed (such workers need not be union members).[40] The difference between these and other workers is more theoretical than actual, however: both unions and company councils have an interest in seeing that the pay of noncontract workers remains in line with the rates established by collective bargaining.

The structure of the professional domain reinforces the structure of the domain of collective action and viceversa. The unions recognize the distinction between b-c and w-c workers, and there is a dual system of collective bargaining, supplemented by negotiations at the firm level between worker councils and company management. Negotiation at this level is subordinate, however, to industry-wide negotiation, important not only because of its impact on real wages but, more fundamentally, because of the homogeneity of German industry and the resulting power of business organizations.

Thus industry-wide collective bargaining is central to the German system of industrial relations. Labor conflict generally takes the form of a strike throughout an entire industry, to which the industry often responds with a lock-out.[41] Strikes at individual firms are of only secondary importance. Local conflicts are resolved through the mechanism of codetermination, which, while not eliminating conflict entirely, does commit both sides to the resolution of disputes by negotiation between management and the company council. The major source of conflict at the national level in Germany is not wages but the political question of whether to maintain, extend, or do away with institutionalized large-scale comanagement (guaranteed labor participation on corporate boards). In France labor conflict either revolves around the firm or is directed toward such national goals as an increase in the minimum wage. Apart from wages, other national goals include changes in the length of the work week, rules concerning layoffs and firing, social security, and so forth. Somewhat schematically, it is therefore possible to contrast the industrial, work-issue-related character of the union movement in Germany with the panindustrial, class-related character of its French counterpart. The social homogeneity of the French work force helps to explain why this is so. The German scene, by contrast, is dominated by industrial trade unionism and the distinctive character of German industrial workers as a group. Although the formal structure in both countries is that of industrial unionism, the two systems in fact operate quite differently. The operational differences are fundamental and are reflected in the difference between the sources of the unions' power.

Historically the unions' power derived from the force of numbers and the potency of revolutionary ideology, though the latter quickly accommodated and later gave way to more pragmatic concerns such as collective bargaining. But the power of the unions has also been based historically on the high status accorded to industrial workers and on the development of a system of occupational training in which industry plays a part and the value and importance of technology are emphasized (in contrast to the general educational system, where the accent remains on the humanities). No such sustem of training could have developed apart from industry or in opposition to industry. Together these facts explain how it is possible for German workers to have a dual allegiance: to the employer and to the union movement. By contrast, in France, where industry is not so highly regarded and attempts by industry to intervene in education are regarded with suspicion, such a dual allegiance is harder to come by; loyalty to the firm is in a sense contradictory to loyalty to the union. This, together with the fact that French workers must choose between rival unions of very different political hue, may help to explain why the unions have had a rather difficult time organizing in the private sector of French industry.

The fact that German workers and German employers recognize union values along with company values (a statement undoubtedly more true of workers than of employers) explains why the unions find it relatively easy to separate company-related activities from wider social actions. The aim of the former is to limit the employer's discretionary authority in matters pertaining to work organization. This is the role of the union representatives and the company council, and the methods used are not unlike the grievance procedures employed in American firms. Beyond the limits of the firm, the unions are interested in industry-wide collective bargaining and, in a still larger sense, in the problem of comanagement (though efforts to extend comanagement as practiced in the coal and steel industries to all large firms have been cut short). Comanagement affords worker representatives fairly extensive powers to control investment and rationalization decisions, probably not so much because of the powers explicitly granted under the law as because of the strategic opportunities that are opened up in a country that is largely fearful and harshly critical of labor conflict. Thus the main union effort outside the firm is directed toward the extension of large-scale comanagement; to date the business counteroffensive has proved invincible.[42]

Comanagement is distinct from codetermination (Mitbestimmung, instated by the laws of 1952 and 1971) on the shop floor. Comanagement pertains to broader economic powers exercised at a higher level and involves equal representation for labor and management on monitoring boards (or demands for equality of representation) and, in the coal and steel industries, the presence of a labor representative, often a union official, on corporate boards (see the law of 1951, amended and weakened in 1976).

Codetermination as practiced on the shop floor is a way of resolving everyday management problems. As an institution it is based on the close relationship that exists in German firms between social management and technical management. It is not codetermination that reduces social conflict on the shop floor but rather the attenuation of shop floor conflict that permits codetermination. The less conflict there is, the less management needs to take steps to weaken worker opposition (of the sort discussed for France), and so the less disciplinary supervision is necessary; in the opposite situation, the difficulty of breaking out of the vicious circle hardly needs emphasizing.

French and German unions behave differently. French unions wage their battles first against individual firms and second against the government and the central employers' organization. German unions shape their demands to fit the economic conditions prevailing in particular industries, whose capacity to pay is exploited, if need be, by an industry-wide strike.

4.4 Conclusion

At the outset our two objectives were to compare two highly industrialized countries in order to show empirically and analyze theoretically differences in the structure and organization of the work force, and to move beyond specific differences to consider more generally the theoretical implications of this kind of comparative work. Our results suggest that it is important to understand how the various factors that shape the wage labor relation interact with one another in a society. In emphasizing interaction we part company with the classical analyses of educational sociology, industrial relations, and production. In all of these the traditional approach has been to look only at the economic or historical laws presumed to govern the single factor in question. For these analysts, the wage labor relation is thought of as having a number of different dimensions, each autonomous of the others. We have shown that there are interdependencies at work that ultimately structure the wage labor relation. We believe that this represents a methodological breakthrough, which has enabled us to move from the descriptive to the theoretical level. Comparative study has made it possible to show that the factors that enter into the structure of the work force are not those that theorists have traditionally assumed to be important.[43]

By systematically studying these new factors, we have been able to show that the differences between the two countries were not merely reflections of residual cultural differences or crystallizations of accidental historical differences. Rather they form a pattern that can be related to fundamental features of advanced capitalist societies and economies. Making this relation explicit is the fundamental goal of comparative social analysis.

We hold that the structure of the wage labor relation points to certain general laws. Because we believe that this relation is in large part autonomous, we think that its importance is not merely functional; it is of general significance, and one may reasonably propose a theory to account for its structure. We have tried to do this by introducing the complementary ideas of the domain and the actor. We think of the actor in relation to the flexibility inherent in the wage labor relation. Hence we do not attempt to establish a one-to-one correspondence between actors in our theory and specific groups in the workforce, whether b-c or w-c workers or management personnel (though we began with such specific groups in the empirical phase of our study before moving to greater generality). The idea of the actor, as we conceive it, is intimately related to the autonomy of the wage labor relation—that is, to the fact that the structure of the work force is determined by a law unto itself.

Our theory of the firm is premised on the same principles. We think of the firm as an autonomous organization and an institution shaped by the same forces that help to mold the wage labor relation. The rationality that guides the firm's actions is formed under the influence of these factors. Thus our approach to the firm goes beyond the approaches taken by other theorists of organized action. We have been able to do this by systematically taking notice of how the workers are socialized and how this shapes the social relations in which they subsequently become involved.

Thus the theory we are proposing differs from both traditional economic theories and traditional organization theories. Our purpose in suggesting our theoretical innovations is twofold. We want to analyze the firm not as a universal institution but as a social construct. We also want to analyze the way in which the structure of the firm, whether French, German, Japanese, or British, is influenced by the interaction of the various factors we have elucidated.

Such an approach to the firm can be fruitful and, furthermore, increasingly necessary for empirical and theoretical purposes. Promising though this new approach has been, we do not regard it as an end in itself. The firm relates to many things: the market, science, and technology, to name a few. To analyze the firm, as we have done, in relation to society, is merely to inaugurate a methodological debate; it is not to determine once and for all the limits of comparative research. Such a debate will make sense only if it succeeds in identifying the concepts necessary to restore the proper balance between the work of economists and the work of others who, using the tools of sociology and institutional analysis, have become aware of the importance of factors that cannot be reduced to market forces.

Appendix: Societal Analysis as a Critical and Theoretical Tool

To conclude this work we would like to relate our approach, which we call societal analysis, to various theories currently prominent in the several fields on which our work touches: labor economics, organizational sociology and sociology of work. We hope in this way to avoid having our comparative study classed as nothing more than a method for identifying national differences, for it is our belief that comparative research is a useful tool for understanding how the stratification of the work force has been affected by a number of important and enduring social phenomena.

Although this appendix may be formally disconnected from the chapters that precede it, it provides answers to a number of questions that may have occurred to readers. In particular it deals with the important question of why we have refused to make use of such powerful and well-honed tools as the economic theory of education and mobility, strategic analysis [as developed by sociologists Michel Crozier and Erhard Friedberg—Trans.], and the Marxist theory of the relations of production. We also hope to make clear what our own method has to offer in a positive sense. This positive contribution will emerge, we hope, as we submit rival theories to critical examination. Our criticisms are neither novel nor original. Yet we believe that our results lend cogency to some earlier critiques and show how they may be usefully extended.

A.1 The Theory of Human Capital and the Structure of the Labor Market

The neoclassical theory of the labor market focuses on the activities of two actors: the worker and the firm. What makes sense of these activities is the existence of something called human capital. Indeed the function of the labor market is merely to direct the flow of human capital. On this view of the matter, the two key questions are: How is human capital produced? How is a value placed on it by industrial firms?

A.1.1 Worker Mobility and the Formation of Human Capital

Human capital consists of a worker's capacity to perform services that have value. It is amassed by investment, in the sense that satisfaction that might otherwise have been derived from income (through the purchase of useful goods and services) is forgone for a certain length of time for the purpose of accumulation. A value is attached to a worker's investment in human capital because it is possible to establish an equivalence between that investment and a certain quantity of goods and services (among which must be included the individual's leisure time). Human capital is thus the essential mediator between the individual and the market. There is a temporal dimension to a worker's investments (in labor time, education, physical moves from one region to another, initiative on the job, and so forth); the value of any investment is related to the value of satisfactions forgone over a specific length of time in order to acquire the given stock of human capital. Mobility may be thought of as a sum of investments in human capital. The result of the mobility process is to increase the amount or to change the nature of the human capital that a worker has to offer for exchange on the labor market. A characteristic feature of the neoclassical analysis of mobility is that although the process of amassing human capital extends over time, the value of a stock of accumulated capital at any moment is determined, like the value of any other commodity, by the amount of goods and services the accumulated stock commands at that moment.[1] By definition, then, mobility is the process by which a worker's time is crystallized in the form of capital.

With these definitions in mind, we can now see how the actor (the worker) involved in the mobility process is central to the analysis of that process and yet ignored as a social reality. He is central in that decisions made by the individual worker are responsible for the existence of human capital and for changes in the stock of available human capital in response to the changing demand for goods and services. But an actor so defined has no social existence; in other words, the influence of the social setting in which he makes his decisions is not taken into account in the analysis. Mobility is analyzed merely as a capital flow, and the time dimension that figures in the analysis is a purely abstract one, suited to the evaluation of capital stocks. Such an abstract time must be sharply distinguished from what sociologists refer to as social time.[2] The failure to take social time into account is no accident. Indeed it is crucial to the concept of human capital. This concept makes sense only in a framework in which it is possible to establish an equivalence between one stock of capital and another, regardless of how and when those stocks were amassed.

Thus economic analysis has no choice but to abstract from time as it is experienced by the worker, since this is the only way to establish the necessary equivalence between human capital and other commodities, which for the purposes of economic analysis are regarded as existing in an idealized, atemporal domain.[3] Embodied solely as human capital, the economic actor ceases to exist as an actor. The rationality of the actor—here, the worker—on which the market model is based is reduced to a question of rational management of capital.[4] Economic rationality in this sense is one-dimensional. Abstracting from social time, economic analysis reduces the worker to a mere stock of capital, to a one-dimensional existence.

Economic analysis further neglects the existence of any significant structure of the actor's choices. Such diverse activities as apprenticeship in a trade, classroom study, accumulation of on-the-job experience, and moving from one region or one job to another are all analyzed as so many phenomenal forms of a single underlying reality: the accumulation of human capital. The result of the process is a stock of capital, and it makes no difference what trajectory a worker has followed to arrive at the end state. No account is taken of any pattern that may exist in the choices involved in amassing human capital. In other words the social time in which such choices are made is ignored.[5]

How good an account of reality does this theory provide? We will not presume to sum up in a few words the enormous volume of empirical work (done in France and elsewhere) on the labor market, human capital formation, and the evaluation of human capital as reflected in wages. We think we do no violence to the burden of that work, however, in making the following assertion: worker mobility and its economic rewards are significantly influenced by many factors that cannot be reduced to the notion of human capital.

The factors most commonly shown to have an important bearing on the question include sex, race, age, occupational category, place of residence, and social origin. Systematic distortions of this kind (which may be classed broadly as effects of segregation) indicate the existence of what economists like to call market imperfections or obstacles to mobility. Using the terminology of sociological theory, we may say that the flow of human capital is structured by social time in a way that cannot be explained in purely economic terms. In other words a worker's decision to produce human capital and his management of that capital cannot be explained solely in terms of the valuation of that capital by the market.

Empirical research has thus thrown down a basic challenge to the neoclassical theory of the labor market. The problem is not how well neoclassical theory approximates reality but rather whether neoclassical theory is internally consistent.

The existence of socially structured forms of worker mobility cannot be explained using the conceptual tools available to economists. They then have no alternative but to assume that, for social, cultural, or institutional reasons, the labor market is imperfect. Economic analysis recognizes social, cultural, and institutional factors only by their effects; they have no place in economic theory as such.[6]

Economic theorists have not been idle, however, in the face of a proliferation of such effects as revealed by empirical research. While acknowledging that actual labor markets may function imperfectly, they have constructed various models that try to explain the imperfections without sacrificing the central idea that worker mobility is explained by rational investment in human capital. Many of these models involve the introduction of a new good, information, which individuals or groups may possess, acquire, or dispense.[7] Importance is attached to worker itineraries in this work but only insofar as these influence the use, availability, or value of information. The so-called structure of supply is related to the structure of information about the labor market and to the way the latter structure is produced. Ultimately it is still human capital that mediates between the worker and the labor market.

This approach has the virtue of conceptual unity. Insofar as social structures manifest themselves in effects on labor supply, they are treated as influences on the way human capital is produced.[8] The theory is no longer atemporal because these influences may vary over time, yet it remains completely general. The basic principle of neoclassical labor market theory remains intact: the purely economic concept of human capital is the key to understanding the labor market, whose structure is presumed to be endogenously determined.

A.1.1.1 The Labor Market and the Firm

Also implicit in the economic theory of the labor market is a theory of the firm. The firm plays a key role in the theory of human capital on which the theory of the labor market is based. Indeed workers' decisions in regard to mobility would not count as investments were it not for the value that firms attach to certain kinds of skills and other individual qualities.[9] The variables ordinarily used to characterize a worker's situation, such as educational level, experience, or ability to withstand hardship, count as factors in the evaluation of human capital only when they are recognized by the firm. In neoclassical theory, the firm is the place where human capital manifests its value by virtue of the scarcity of human capital resources on the labor market.

Thus the firm plays a key role in determining how the labor market will operate and whether it will remain stable. The firm is the agency that, over the long run, tends to bring factor prices into line with their marginal productivity. As an economically rational actor, the firm will behave in such a way as to determine the optimal quantities of various kinds of human capital required. Transmitted to the labor market, this demand for human capital will then set the conditions under which workers make their fundamental decisions about questions bearing on mobility. In the theory the firm functions as the agent whereby worker attributes are converted into capital. Thus it is the essential intermediary between worker attributes and goods and services, or, to state it another way, between the production of human capital and the consumption that structures the market.

A twofold externalization (or alienation in the Marxist sense) is therefore at work. Workers externalize their needs in the form of decisions affecting mobility, thereby producing human capital to which a value is attached by the firm. In attaching this value the firm becomes the agency of a second externalization by establishing an equivalence between human capital and the goods and services that it sells on the market. In quasi-Hegelian terminology the worker as subject is thus twice negated: once in his decisions to invest in human capital and a second time in the abstract value that becomes attached to his human capital when the latter is equated by the firm with a certain quantity of its product.

Thus in neoclassical theory, the firm, like the worker, plays a central role and yet is completely neglected as a concrete entity. This neglect is quite visible in the work of economist Fritz Machlup, who defines the firm as a "link in a 'causal' chain" or, again, as an "entity that reacts to changes in conditions (affecting prices and incomes, for example) by altering its relations to the suppliers of goods, labor, etc."[10]

How does it happen that the firm plays a central role in the theory and yet is ignored as a concrete actor? The neoclassical view is again summed up by Machlup: "The actors defined by the theory are only abstract constructs, ideal types, and care should be taken not to confuse them with actors in the real world, whose behavior, thoughts, and feelings may be quite different." Thus it is because of the requirements of theory that the firm is to be conceived, again in Machlup's words, as a mere "heuristic fiction, about whose concrete existence it is pointless to ask." It may be, however, that the neglect of the reality of the firm is not a requirement of theory as such but rather of the type of theory used by economists to explain how individuals interact. Human capital, the labor market, the firm: for neoclassical economists, all these are merely theoretical fictions that help us to understand how economically rational agents interact. Thus the firm in particular is reduced to a set of relations among independently existing economic actors, relations that can exist only because the firm makes them possible. It may seem that the firm plays a leading role as a rational profit-maximizing agent, but in fact this view is based on identifying the firm with the capital that it represents and thus on denying its existence as an autonomous object of theory.

It becomes clear that the economic theory of the labor market is a social theory and as such to be distinguished from a theory in the natural sciences. Furthermore it is a special kind of social theory, whose foundations may be challenged on grounds other than empirical falsification.

Not that the neoclassical theory of the labor market is invulnerable to empirical refutation. As we saw in the case of worker mobility, an abundance of empirical research challenges some of the fundamental tenets of the neoclassical view of the firm. The data show that the organization of production and the behavior of industrial managers influence the way the labor market operates. And once again economic theorists have responded to the challenges to the neoclassical view.[11] Their approach has been to modify the received theory by introducing new components of human capital that have value only in a particular firm or organization. For example, the notion of specific capital has been introduced to account for the influence of seniority on a worker's wage. Specific capital is the result of investments made by a worker in his employer's firm for which he happens to work. Defined in this way, specific capital is both an internal phenomenon and a market phenomenon. Other modifications have been made to the standard neoclassical theory in order to account for the influence of such factors as race, sex, and religion on worker pay. One way of doing this has been to introduce the idea of discriminatory preference on the part of the employer.[12] Interpreting wage discrimination as a consequence of employer preference has the effect of subsuming under the head of human capital worker attributes that at first sight have nothing to do with human capital as defined. Like the notion of specific capital, the notion of discriminatory preference has a dual status: it pertains to the internal structure of the firm and the value-assigning function of the labor market.

Attempts to integrate an ever larger number of structural variables into a market-based theory have recently been carried one step further in the form of a proposed microeconomic theory of the formation of hierarchies within the firm. The view taken in this line of research is that the internal organization of the firm serves as an alternative to the market when long-term labor contracts are used. It is a characteristic feature of such contracts that they do not establish the conditions of employment once and for all as the result of a single, negotiated agreement between two perfectly informed parties. Rather they set the stage for a series of transactions spread over an extended period. These transactions take place in unpredictable circumstances, and they may take on an unforeseeable strategic significance for one or more of the actors. A new capital good, information, plays a central role in these transactions and in fact constitutes a kind of secondary market. The internal organization of the firm must then be designed so as to optimize the production, circulation, and utilization of this new informational good, which mediates between the workers and the production process. Accordingly organizational practices may be analyzed as information-producing processes; informational capital then enters into the market alongside human capital. This brings us full circle: once again the role of the firm is central but only insofar as the firm is identified with capital—in other words, something other than itself.

Economists use the fundamental concepts of the neoclassical approach, capital and income, to construct theoretical models of the social factors that appear to have the greatest influence on the labor market. There is no question that in this way they have succeeded in constructing models that approximate reality fairly closely. But constructing adequate models is not the same as constructing an adequate theory. It is to this distinction that we turn next.

A.1.2 The Validity of the Market Concept and the Universality of Economic Theory

A.1.2.1 The Unity of the Market in Neoclassical Theory
In the most recent versions of the neoclassical approach, every social fact is treated as corresponding to a particular form of capital. Thus the increasingly complex relationship among the social actors—more succinctly, social reality—is treated largely in terms of the relations among specific forms of capital within the sphere of capital in general. As a result the idea of the market has lost some of its pristine simplicity since it is now taken for granted that exchange itself is a source of information and a factor that helps to shape organizations, which in turn affect the nature of exchange. Still it is beyond doubt that these recent contributions to the neoclassical

theory of the labor market do succeed in blunting earlier critiques of the tendency of economic theorists to rely on exogenous factors to explain away all anomalous results.

This has not been the only effect of these contributions, however. The key to recent theoretical advances has been to identify social structures with specific forms of capital. It follows that capital is at the same time identified with the specific social structures in which it is generated. But one of the strong points of traditional neoclassical theory was that its conceptual underpinnings were perfectly general, independent of the specific social structures found in any real society. This generality is diminished in more recent versions of the theory.

Neoclassical theories may take two possible directions. One is to retain the model of the perfectly competitive market, or, to put it another way, to restore full generality to the notion of capital. But then any empirically discernable structure in the market becomes a challenge to the fundamental soundness of the general theory. Each time reality is shown to depart from the predictions of theory, the effect is to consign theory to an ever more remote limbo of abstraction, where it becomes less and less useful as a practical tool. The alternative is to incorporate empirically identifiable collective structures into the framework of a systematic theory (based on a model of imperfect competition). This has the merit of preserving the theory's relevance to reality, but it tends to undermine its fundamental concepts from within.

The inability of the economic theory of the labor market to surmount these difficulties is the main reason for our decision not to rely on this theory as the frame of reference for our research. In our view comparative social analysis is impossible unless two conditions are met. First, the collective structures that occupy such an important place in any capitalist industrial society must be studied in and for themselves as independent theoretical objects. Such structures include the firm, the educational system, the occupational structure, and the system of professional and labor organizations. Second, these collective structures must not be studied merely one by one. It is important, rather, to study their relations to one another, for it is in these relations that one may discover phenomena of sufficient generality to permit comparison between one society and another. We believe we have shown that neoclassical economic theory is incapable of meeting both of these conditions simultaneously. Had we used neoclassical theory as our frame of reference, our empirical research would have been inherently limited and our ability to move toward more rigorous analysis at the theoretical level impeded.

Why is it exactly that, in dealing with the labor market, the neoclassical approach leads inevitably to one of two dead ends? The answer lies not in the ambition of neoclassical economists to provide a perfectly general theory but in the kind of generality they have tried to achieve and specifically in the use of the concept of human capital toward that end. Flexible as this concept may be in the hands of ingenious theorists, its definition is extremely rigid and reductive. Indeed it depends, in a way that is rarely made explicit, on a certain way of analyzing social time.

A variety of activities go into the production of human capital; education, apprenticeship, socialization by the family, experience in the workplace, and collective action are just a few. But the economic theory of the labor market reduces the time invested in each of these activities to a single kind of time, that which is embodied in human capital. Theorists can deal with this in two ways. Either they can use the concept of the market to effect the necessary unification of disparate experiences, in which case it becomes difficult to account for observed imperfections in the market. Or they can establish theoretical distinctions between time invested in one activity and time invested in another, in which case they will be able to account for imperfect competition but not for the way in which various activities interact. The market is in effect segmented—not so much that the usefulness of the notion of capital is destroyed altogether but enough so that its content is subtly undermined from within. Thus a fundamental question emerges from our critical examination of the neoclassical theory of the labor market: under what conditions is the labor market sufficiently unified to permit the useful introduction of the notion of human capital?

A.1.2.2 Marxist Theory: Commodities and Wage Labor

Like neoclassical theory, Marxist theory employs an abstract notion of time in its treatment of market exchange. Marx's celebrated dictum on this subject runs as follows: "That which determines the magnitude of the value of any article is the amount of labor socially necessary, or the labor-time socially necessary, for its production." In part this definition is offered in response to the need, felt by neoclassical as well as Marxist economists, for an invariant measure of value. But the definition in *Capital* is also a response to a quite different need: the need to make clear that, according to Marx, time acquires a social character when it is embodied in a commodity. The identification of time with the commodity is in some respects more direct in Marx than in neoclassical theory, because for Marx the identification is made whenever commodities are exchanged: "It is only by being exchanged," Marx tells us, "that the products of labor acquire, as values, one uniform social status, distinct from their varied forms of existence as objects of utility."[13]

In Marxist theory it is the "social relations of production" that determine how time in the abstract, invested in various ways in the production of labor power, relates to the value of that labor power and hence to wages. If neoclassical theory ran into difficulties because it could not readily deal with the complex relations between different forms of capital, does Marxist theory, with its concept of social relations of production, do better? Or does Marxist theory, in its most rigorous and cogent form, subsume the social relations of production under the head of capital to such an extent that they have no independent theoretical existence whatsoever?[14]

We examine these questions by considering once again worker mobility, the role of the firm, the importance of the labor process, and the organization of workers. Since we obviously cannot review the full range of Marxist-inspired work, we shall focus on a few recent contributions and attempt to relate them to what we take to be the scientific logic implicit in Marx's writings.

The importance of worker mobility as a factor in the social relations of production has been emphasized in the theoretical work of J. P. de Gaudemar.[15] De Gaudemar stresses the importance of worker mobility in the commodification of labor power. Mobility, he argues, is a characteristic of "the worker subject to the domination of capital and hence of the capitalist mode of production. In order for labor power to be traded as a commodity, the work force must be mobile."[16] The capitalist system accordingly tends to promote mobility in the work force.[17]

Here we see the same duality encountered in our analysis of the theory of human capital: on the one hand it is argued that mobility is an essential prerequisite in order for labor to become a commodity, while on the other hand the specific social forms that mobility may take, important as these may be, are dismissed as contingent and therefore irrelevant for theory.

A similar analysis underlies M. Aglietta's notion of "forced mobility."[18] "Forced mobility," Aglietta writes, "is a process that follows from the nature of the wage labor relation in a system in which accumulation is intensive." There are differences between Aglietta's notion of forced mobility and de Gaudemar's notion of perfect mobility, but in both cases the nature of the mobility in question is determined a priori by the nature of the system in which it unfolds. Either view may give rise to interesting comparative and historical research. But no matter which definition is preferred, neither is likely to lead toward a fundamentally new theory of the labor market or workplace relations.

The same kinds of problems crop up when Marxists try to decide how much theoretical importance should be attached to the labor process and the way it is organized. Again theorists confront a knotty problem of theory, not to say a logical dilemma, and no matter which horn of the dilemma they choose, the resulting theory comes into conflict with the facts. The dilemma is as follows. The quality of the labor process undoubtedly plays central role in Marx's work, where by "quality of the labor process" Marx means the concrete organization of production.[19] This hardly needs emphasizing since it is one of the most prominent features of Marx's writings. At the same time, however, Marx defines commodity production in its capitalist form as the "unity of useful labor and labor to create surplus-value."

By asserting the existence of such a unity, Marx seems to attach particular importance to the concrete labor process by establishing it on a footing of "conceptual equality" with the process by which surplus value is created—or, to put it another way, he establishes a theoretical tension between the two ideas. But to us the equation of the two concepts seems more illusory than real, since the definition of surplus value involves the idea that labor power is a commodity and thus based on a theoretical interpretation of the underlying nature of the movements of useful labor. De Gaudemar has made this point clearly: "The transition from productive labor to the productivity of labor is the same as the transition from abstract, general labor to concrete, useful labor. In the capitalist mode of production the latter corresponds to exploitation of the work force by capital."[20]

An exaggerated version of the same line of argument may be found in Aglietta's works, particularly in his book on the transformation of the American capitalist system from the turn of the century to the present.[21] He tells us:

Workers engaged in concrete production operations, are naturally heterogeneous in character. This is a question for the theory of the labor process. Labor power, as embodied in an individual, may naturally be applied to tasks that are either more or less complex. This is a question for the theory of wages and prices. It must be clearly understood, however, that neither of these questions touches on the theory of value in general. Both questions, and the theories proper to them, relate to specific transformations of value in general and to specific modifications of the fundamental laws of value to fit particular cases; but these specific laws do not replace the general laws from which they are derived.[22]

The position taken by almost all Marxist authors on the segmentation of the labor market is that segmentation is a contingent consequence of the interaction between the productive forces and the social structure. Not only a French writer like Aglietta but also Americans such as Edwards, Gordon, and Reich emphasize what they consider to be the functional, historically contingent, mechanistic nature of labor-market segmentation.[23] According to Aglietta, segmentation has an "immediate macroeconomic significance" in that it "affords firms a way of coping with uncertainty by enabling them to modify their wage structure and make flexible use of the work force."[24]

The logic that emerges from these remarks is severely reductionist. We see evidence of reductionism in the way Marxist theorists confront the facts and modify their theories in accordance with empirical results. There is no doubt that both Marxists and neoclassical economists could, if they so desired, provide "explanations" of our results. But providing explanations after the fact is not the same as producing fruitful problems for empirical research, problems with genuine theoretical standing. In order to answer the questions that interest us here, what we need are useful theories of the firm and of organizations in general as well as useful ways of thinking about the ways in which education and labor organization influence wages. We do not claim that empirical research by itself is enough to cast doubt on either Marxist or neoclassical theory. The kinds of questions we are raising can entail modifications to Marxist theory (or neoclassical or any other theory) only if they can be related to internal questions about the limits of that theory. Such questions have been raised within Marxism by authors concerned about the reductive nature of most Marxist theory to date.

A number of Marxist authors have begun to ask not merely about the forms of the productive relations but about the nature of the theory in terms of which those forms are to be imterpreted. In particular, Jean Mathiot, in a paper entitled "Wages and Their Reproduction," has questioned the theoretical status of a number of variables that Marxist theorists have hitherto regarded as concretely determined, most notably wages.[25] The theoretical question raised by Mathiot is the following: how to escape from the reductionist trap of "thinking of wages in terms of a theory of value fully worked out in the sphere of commodity exchange." His answer is to admit that "wages are related to capital other than by the subordination or subjection of labor to capital" and, furthermore, that "workers are a dynamic, driving force in the capitalist mode of production, a force that is not subordinate to some inner dynamic of capital."

The implications of this line of argument are by no means clear. It is possible to assert that productive relations are in some degree autonomous, only to go on to argue that they are ultimately determined by "the forms of capital or its contradictions—that is, in our view, by historical or national contingencies affecting the way the capitalist mode of production operates and reproduces itself. But it is equally possible to take a new approach to capital itself by incorporating into the theory other factors and social realities that are not held to be determined by it. Our empirical results suggest that the latter would be the wiser course.

We therefore feel that, for the time being, our results cannot be adequately comprehended within a Marxist framework because the currently dominant theory of productive relations is beset with internal and external contradictions. From this we draw a positive conclusion, however: our work may point the way to future improvements in Marxist theory.

A.1.3 Societal Analysis and Economic Theory

An important focus of our work has been the definition of several kinds of domain, which we defined as an overarching structure within which other structures (social structures, industrial organizations, and so forth) can interact with one another while retaining a considerable degree of autonomy. One question that needs to be asked, therefore, is how it is possible for the substructures of a domain to interact without undermining their autonomy. Part of the answer is surely that, within each substructure, realities external to that substructure are subject to interpretation; thus external structures can exert an influence without crystallizing as an integral part of the substructure within which interpretation is being carried out.

In contrast to economic theories, our approach therefore does not require that a sharp contrast be drawn between external and internal, general and specific. Rather each substructure (whether a firm, an educational system, or an occupational group) incorporates the general structure of the domain into its specific structure in the course of its formation. Thus we may well find traces of the overall interdependence of the system in each substructure, yet the autonomy of the substructure itself need not be called into question as a result. The idea of socialization then becomes crucial. In the course of socialization an actor will internalize the norms associated with the socialization process, and these norms then become effective beyond the limits of the substructure under whose auspices they were inculcated. With these preliminaries out of the way, we are now in a position to propose a theory of mobility fundamentally different from that of the economists. The economists argue that specific capital is associated with a particular substructure of the economy and leave the question of the relation of specific capital to the general structure in suspense. In contrast we have argued, using the idea of a domain in a crucial way, that there is nothing indeterminate about the relation between the norms established in a particular process of socialization and other social norms.

Thus whereas human capital and commodity approaches to the labor market are fundamentally unsuited to dealing with the relation of the general to the specific, our approach suggests a way of moving toward a new kind of theory. In this new theory the tendency of any society to integrate its various substructures plays a prominent part. Nevertheless the process of integration does not negate the autonomy of each substructure. Indeed we hold that the active autonomy of the various substructures generates the overall pattern of norms, which are then crystallized in each substructure.

This interdependence of the general and the specific distinguishes our domain-centered approach from market-based theories. Not that our approach is less concerned with achieving generality; we are looking for the invariant mechanisms through which social substructures interact to achieve a stable pattern, a pattern characteristic of a given society and not the result of chance. A general theory of this kind satisfies one prerequisite of empirical testing; its basic concepts are applicable across international boundaries.

Our basic concepts are not novel. A rigorous treatment of related ideas may be found in Michael Piore's work on the stratification of the labor market.[26] Piore's replacement of the idea of an internal market with the idea of a primary market for labor resembles our insistence that the general structure is determined by the interaction of specific substructures. Like us, Piore is loathe to argue that the effects of the latter can be felt only insofar as they are crystallized in the structure of capital itself—a concept so general as to obliterate the specificity of the various substructures. Thus, in effect, Piore agrees with us in seeing a unified domain rather than a market as the key to understanding work force stratification: the elaboration of such a theory was a response to evidence suggesting the existence of a balkanized labor market or, alternatively, fissures in the structure of capital. If the primary market is unified, the reason is that the associated processes of socialization are unified. These socialization processes are at once specific (in the sense that they are carried on within particular substructures governed by custom, formal rules, or certain patterns of apprenticeship) and general (in that they inculcate norms whose effects extend beyond the particular substructures in which they were acquired).

In a domain of this kind, no single rationality of the market governs the adjustment of supply to demand, nor do wage differentials behave as the market theory predicts.[27] Rather the supply-demand relationship involves the social, professional, and economic life of collective actors whose rationality is determined by the norms inculcated during socialization. Thus the important question to ask is not how workers and firms react to the laws of the market but rather how they conceive of the domain within which socialization takes place and how, in the light of their respective conceptions, they formulate their strategies.

Piore's model of labor market stratification could be analyzed in this light. What he calls the primary and secondary labor markets can be regarded, in our terminology, as domains, defined in concrete terms as consisting of aggregates of specific kinds of workers and specific types of jobs or firms. The primary and secondary labor markets (or domains) are not independent but subsumed within the larger structure of society as a whole; indeed the primary-secondary dichotomy extends its influence far beyond the bounds of the labor market as such. Piore's strata are not to be thought of as isolated market segments. They are unified in the following sense: a single principle of stratification, determined by qualifications and the manner in which they are acquired, governs both.

To sum up, then, we contend that the theoretical content implicit in our notion of domain and in what we are calling comparative social analysis is at bottom similar to Michael Piore's theory of labor-market stratification. Two further remarks will help to bolster this contention.

First, both our work and Piore's emphasizes the interaction between socialization and organization and the role of this interaction in shaping the behavior of the social actors. Second, both approaches start, theoretically as well as empirically, by accepting as real and important phenomena that economic theories have tried to explain away as anomalies.

To be more specific, both our work and Piore's seek to establish that the labor domain (to use the term we prefer to *market*) is unified, whereas neoclassical labor market theory has sought to demonstrate the existence of imperfect competition—that is, of disunity in the operation of the market. Another similarity is in the treatment of the question of the autonomy of labor relations. It is one thing to propose, as the most advanced Marxist theorists do, examining the question of autonomy within the framework of Marxist theory. It is quite another to treat this question in its own right as the basis of a new kind of theory, which is the course we are recommending.

Laying the groundwork for a new theory of the labor market is precisely what Michael Piore has accomplished in his work on the United States. We have followed his lead in identifying the factors that have an important influence on the stratification of the work force: education, organization, and forms of collective action. No analysis of the autonomy of labor relations is possible without taking into account not only these factors but also the principles that govern their interaction.

Many ambiguities remain to be cleared up regarding the definition of *domain*. In regard to our empirical work some of the problems are obvious: the work has had to be carried out by a number of different research teams, and there is as yet no general agreement as to what categories are appropriate. Doubtless there is also need for discussion of whether Piore's approach, concerned with labor market stratification in the United States, is compatible with the more "concrete" and institutional distinction between manual and intellectual labor that we have drawn for the purpose of comparing France and Germany. A full discussion of this question is beyond the scope of this book. We can do little more here than summarize the points at issue.

To begin, our claim that labor is in some sense autonomous with respect to capital would seem to beg the fundamental problem of economic theory: the problem of value. If one insists too dogmatically on autonomy, it becomes impossible to establish any connection between the theory of value and a theory of social action. Not that any currently available economic theory resolves this problem in a satisfactory way. The way the concept of capital is used in theoretical economics in effect establishes a one-to-one correspondence between the social structure and the value structure (each social actor is measured by the value of the capital he possesses). If such an immediate relationship between value and social structure is assumed, then no mediation between the two is possible. That is, no interrogation of one by the other can occur. One reason for introducing the notion of a domain is obviously to overcome this deficiency of economic theory. Only through further study of industrial organizations, industrial conflict, and the wage structure can we hope to develop the conceptual tools that will enable economists to understand the mediations involved and to make good use of them in new economic theories.

A.2 Actors, Organizations, and Society: Sociological Approaches

The implications of our work for sociology—especially those areas of sociology most closely related to our study; the sociology of labor and organizational sociology—are generally the same as those for economic theory. In particular there is the same question of the relation between the general and the specific (or, in the case of organization theory, between the interior and the exterior of an organization) that concerned us in our critique of economic theory.

The general and the specific, the interior and the exterior, the actor and the system, the individual and the social structure: all of these classical distinctions are usually taken to indicate that a sharp contrast exists between the two terms of each dichotomy. Our work questions whether this assumption is warranted. It further questions whether it is wise for sociology to specialize its inquiries as much as has been common in recent years. Specialization, we think, tends to obscure the reality of phenomena whose essence lies precisely in the fact that they cut across intradisciplinary boundaries.

A further question has to do with the level at which sociological analysis should be carried out. At first sight this may appear to be a different question from that of how boundaries should be drawn within the discipline. But in fact these questions are closely related in that both revolve around the nature of the paradigms that govern research within each subdiscipline.

A.2.1 The Sociology of Work

The sociology of work developed (particularly in France) during the 1950s in reaction to the scientific claims put forward by Taylorism and Fordism, according to which there is invariably one best way to organize a firm, and the human relations school of labor relations popular in England and the United States, according to which the firm should be viewed as a social system consisting of two organizations, one formal and the other informal.

Sociologists such as Georges Friedmann in France and H. Popitz in Germany argued that in order to understand the relationship between work and technology, it is necessary to "look at what happens before human relations are instituted" within the firm.[28] The firm, it was stated, "is primarily a place of work and only secondarily a place in which informal groups are constituted.[29] Alert to the effects of technological progress on human labor, sociologists influenced by Friedmann viewed the work situation as the best place for studying not only changes in the nature of work and the qualifications of the work force but also worker attitudes and the labor movement. Technology (or "technological progress"), analyzed as an exogenous factor influencing the structure of the work process, was generally adduced as the reason for all change. The analysis of the firm was reductionist in two ways. First, the firm was conceived of solely in terms of its technology and organization. Second, the organizational structure of the firm was considered in isolation from the social and economic system. The latter were said to constitute the firm's environment. More than that, they defined what was internal.

In linking changes in the work process to changes in technology, the sociology of work takes its inspiration from Marx (see Book I of *Capital*), but it neglects the effects of the economic system within which those changes take place, regarding technology as an exogenous factor, a universal phenomenon like the market in neoclassical economics. In the latter the firm is treated as a black box that reacts to market forces, whereas in the sociology of work, it is taken to be the place, evidently neutral in its effects, where the work situation happens to be located. In neither approach is the active role of the industrial organization taken into account, whether as a contributor to the structure of the labor market or to the nature of the work situation, or as an institution capable of influencing the relations between its inside and the outside world.

Because the sociology of work neglects the firm and the way in which it shapes its environment and is shaped by it, it has always been vulnerable to the charge of technological determinism. Technology is the only factor, according to this paradigm, capable of influencing the nature of work and the characteristics of workers.

Throughout the 1950s and 1960s therefore, the key question (still with us today) was, "How does the qualification of the work force change with changes in technology?" This question provides the background for one of the most important pieces of work done during this period, Alain Touraine's study of Renault, which traced the effects of changes in machine tools on the nature of the work and the work force.[30] This classic work marks a first turn away from the technological determinism of the sociological literature.

Taking the view that it is out of keeping with a genuinely sociological approach to attempt to relate the social behavior of workers directly to their material conditions, Touraine introduced two new ideas: the idea of the work system (or production system) and the idea of working-class consciousness. These ideas mark a considerable advance over the specious objectivity of the work situation. In particular they take account of the worker's desire to exert control over his work and of the fact that the implementation of a particular technology by a firm is a social action.

Touraine was motivated by a desire to move toward what he calls the "sociology of action." His notion of working-class consciousness is really a corollary to his broader idea of a historical system of action. The critical force of his work opened the way to a great deal of new research, of which the common denominator was to reject the idea of the work situation (and the technological determinism associated with it) along with the idea of the firm as a relatively closed social system.

The interesting approach taken by John Goldthorpe and his collaborators in the area sometimes referred to as industrial sociology, primarily associated with work done in Great Britain, amounts in effect to yet another critique of the power of the work situation to explain worker attitudes and behavior.[31] According to Goldthorpe, "affluent workers" in the automobile industry, while devoted to their firms, take a purely instrumental attitude toward their work. In other words they are interested primarily in earning enough to share in the benefits of the affluent society.[32] This economistic behavior is reminiscent of the behavior of the farm workers studied by Touraine.[33] In both cases it reflects diminished worker involvement in professionalism and accentuation of the economic rewards of work.

The way these workers see their position in the wider society influences the significance they attach to their job and to their work. Notwithstanding the views of Blauner and others, the instrumental attitude taken by these workers is not due in any direct way to automation or other technological characteristics of their work situation but rather to factors associated with their life outside work.[34] The point, however, is not to replace one kind of determinism with another, technology by mass consumerism or leisure activities. This objection has in fact been raised on occasion against Goldthorpe himself and other members of the Cambridge group, though they are always careful to relate the work situation to worker expectations concerning nonworking life.[35] Such expectations, it might be thought, are determined by factors both inside and outside the firm. If so, then Goldthorpe's work is similar to the work done in the 1960s of the so-called Chicago school associated with Everett Hugues and Howard S. Becker.[36] Focusing mainly on the study of occupations and professions (these terms are used in England and the United States) rather than on organizations, this work revolves around the analysis of careers. A career consists of a series of events (both positive and negative in connotation) related to membership in or entry into a particular professional or occupational group. Socialization is an important part of any career.[37]

The study of careers is in fact based on the study of socialization, but socialization is not conceived as a one-dimensional learning process. The members of an organization define the social reality in which they are implicated while being defined by that reality.[38] In other words the experience of the actors contributes to the structure of the system, whether an occupation or an organization, and in turn the structure of the system helps to shape the ideas and behavior of the actors. The work of the Chicago school did not, however, fully integrate the consequences of the interaction of socialization and organization because that work concentrated mainly on occupational socialization, both as a subjective experience and as the basis of an occupational culture. Our own work has followed the trail blazed by the Chicago school and by Alain Touraine, although we have paid no attention to either the subjective aspects of career, which interested the Chicago sociologists, or the definition of the situation by the actors, which interested Goldthorpe. In our view these are subsidiary to the main point. What Touraine calls the worker's project is not based on individual expectations or ideas but on the demands that workers make of thier jobs. These demands reflect the way that workers interpret their jobs as social relations. Accordingly it is just as relevant to consider careers and patterns of mobility and socialization, or again, the organization of the labor process, as it is to focus on ideas and expectations.

Our comparative approach focuses primarily on the origins of workers' ideas. We want to explain not merely how they define the situation but also why. We want to know the source of cultural norms and values, the grounds for choosing one strategy over another. Of primary interest to us is the set of processes that shape the subjective representations and behavior studied by other analysts.

There is nothing haphazard about these processes. By taking a comparative approach, we have been able to show how they are organized. We have clarified the logic underlying this organization and the social relations on which it is based. Our results in this regard have led us to question the sociology of work paradigm and to try to set our work in the context of more recent paradigms, which, however deeply indebted they may be to the sociology of work, have nevertheless in large part supplanted it.

How do socialization and organizations interact? What kinds of social relations are affected by this interaction? What is the role of the firm in initiating and shaping this process? These are the kinds of questions we want to raise. Our work has shown that sociology of work paradigm has no answers to these questions and that the new approach we have outlined does.

We have shown that neither the work situation itself nor technology (which in the classical work sociology paradigm is the major determinant of the work situation) can by themselves account for the organization of production, changes in the skill levels of the work force, or the behavior of workers. In looking at plants using comparable technology in two different countries, we found significant differences in a number of important respects. These were negative factual findings, useful as criticism but insufficient in the absence of a positive theoretical interpretation.

For this it was necessary to examine how socialization and organizations interact in what we may call the social construction of the actors in the social system and also to study the active role of the firm. Where earlier analysts saw universal phenomena, our research showed specific differences between the two societies we studied. We were able to identify structural factors that account for the observed variations.[39] One was the way the system of occupational training is related to the firm. This affects the social construction of the actors in each society and shapes the domains within which social relations develop.

Furthermore we have rejected the view that the firm is a black box responding to market forces or, alternatively, a neutral zone in which the work situation is shaped by an exogenous factor, technology, or again, significant only insofar as it is interpreted, or defined, by the workers in relation to their place in the system of production. All of these approaches distinguish between the inside of the firm and outside forces that structure it, subjectively or objectively. By contrast, in our approach we have been critical of the distinction between the firm and its boundaries. In fact the identity of the firm and its capacity to act autonomously are due to nothing other than its capacity to manipulate the inside and outside relations in response to social forces. Looking at the firm in the light of the interaction between socialization and organizations expands the sociology of work paradigm. Rather than look at the work situation in isolation from the rest of society, we socialize the idea; in other words we regard the work situation as a social construct whose structure depends on the social processes that shape the work domain and the organization of production.

This accounts for our interest in education and occupational training (as constituents of worker mobility) and in the organization of the production process, for it is the interaction of these that shapes the collective identity of the social actors and structures the work and skill domains.

A question arises. What is the relationship between macrosocial phenomena and microsocial phenomena? Recent research, much of it Marxist in inspiration, has reacted against the reductionism of classical work sociology and structural-functional approaches to the study of organizations and occupational groups by focusing attention on mobility and even by investigating the actors' own interpretations of their situations in the light of their previous experience and future plans.[40] This research, which harks back to the work of the Chicago school in the 1960s and, on this point at any rate, to the work of Pierre Naville, has attempted to treat changes in the division of labor and the skill levels of the work force synchronically and diachronically.[41] Since our own work is based on the study of mobility, socialization, and organization, we cannot help but feel some sympathy for this line of inquiry. But caution is in order. In interpreting their results, some of the writers we have in mind have tried to relate individual fates to what they call occupational systems, which in turn are supposed to shape collective fates (of which the fates of individuals are merely variants) in accordance with the logic of production and of social reproduction. Such an interpretation runs the risk, it seems to us, of falling into the same trap as the structural-functionalists these writers have criticized. By treating organizations as social systems to which individuals adapt through their assigned roles and associated norms, the functionalists reduce the theory of organizations to a special case of their general theory of society. Phenomena observed at the microsocial level are interpreted directly in macrosocial terms. The defect of this procedure is that it neglects, or denies, what goes on at intermediate levels, within the organization, say, or the occupational group (a weakness also found in some marxist approaches). To return to the question of individual and collective fates, if it is argued that these are shaped by all-embracing social systems, then the function of such subsystems as individual firms is reduced to that of bolstering the logic of the dominant system or of transmitting that logic to the individual actors. The workers are determined by the industrial system; their only identity as individuals subsists in the "margin of liberty" left them to depart from the "collective fate" of the group to which they belong, One small escape remains in this otherwise rigid determinism: some weight is given to the way individuals interpret their situation (reminiscent of the approach taken by Goldthorpe and Karpik). But this brings up a difficulty of another kind.

Is it in fact consistent to argue on the one hand that individual actors "help to shape the systems that organize their actions" while at the same time arguing that the dominant system ultimately organizes the fate of all? Perhaps, but only if one is willing to give up the rigorous dichotomy between actors and system. The same dilemma comes up in debates within the sociology of organizations and, more generally, between sociologists wedded to an individualist (or "atomistic") paradigm and those who defend a structuralist (or "totalistic") paradigm. As long as one remains dogmatically in favor of one or the other, this debate can never be resolved.

We have tried to sidestep this futile discussion by suggesting not so much a theory as a method of analysis whereby the social construction of the actors can be combined with, or related to, the social construction of their spheres of action. In this way we hope not to have forgotten the difference between microsocial analysis and macrosocial analysis even as we concentrate our attention on observations made at the intermediate level. It is here, we believe, that the interaction between socialization and organization takes place and the underlying social relations are revealed.

A.2.2 The Sociology of Organizations

Within the sociology of organizations we find the same kinds of debates over sociological method as in other areas of sociology. As Michel Crozier and Erhard Friedberg point out in their book *Actors and Systems*, most theories of the organization have run into difficulty over the problem of the relationship between the individual and the organization and between the organization and its environment. Various attempts have been made to overcome these problems in the context of individualist and structuralist paradigms.

We are particularly interested in two questions. First, how does the sociology of organizations deal with the relations between an organization and its members, or, as Crozier and Friedberg would put it, what is the appropriate way to analyze the relations between the actors and the system within which they act (by system they mean something broader than an organization)?[42] Second, how should the relations between an organization and its environment be analyzed, to what extend may society be regarded as the environment of an organization?

We will be concerned not with organizations in general but with the subset of all organizations composed of the firms we actually studied, which we propose to treat as special cases. Still we shall define the notion of an organization more broadly than is common in classical organization theory.

A. 2.2.1 Individuals and Organizations

When the sociology of organizations first began, its practitioners were divided between two diametrically opposed schools of thought. One emphasized the individual in the organization at the expense of analyzing the internal structure of the organization as such. The other emphasized the organizational structure at the expense of the actors.

The first group of writers was reacting against Taylorism and its call to scientific study of the organization, though Taylor's interest in improving the economic efficiency of business remained a goal. The human relations movement and its various derivatives accordingly held that one of the best ways for an organization to promote efficiency was to meet its workers' psychological needs. The theorists of human relations set about determining the hierarchy of human needs and the way one need interacts with another in order to help organizations achieve the goal of satisfying their workers, which it was held could be done regardless of the technology employed. Implicit in the whole approach was the hypothesis that, ideally, there should be a congruence between the psychological needs of individuals and the structure of the organization. Other theories followed the lead of economics in suggesting the existence of an equilibrium between the contributions made by individuals to the organization and the rewards received in return from the organization. Any imbalance between contributions and rewards, it was argued, is injurious to one party or the other. In keeping with liberal ideology, the argument was that "what's good for the firm is good for the workers," since the interests of both parties are supposed to be compatible.

All of these approaches may be interpreted as variations on a common theme: individual self-interest (as measured not by monetary rewards but rather by psychological fulfillment). Thus the relationship between the individual and the organization was conceived of in isolation from any kind of social relation. Individual and organization were sharply differentiated. Each was endowed with its own rationality and allowed to negotiate or bargain with the other in the open market. No attention was paid to the effects of organization or to the underlying social relations.

In order to fill this void a group of American researchers, especially A. S. Tannenbaum and S. E. Seashore at Ann Arbor, began treating the organization as an "integrated system of interdependent elements" rather than an abstract, undifferentiated entity.[43] Critical of the direct, almost mechanical link between satisfaction and productivity in earlier theories, these researchers showed that in fact many other factors were involved in productivity, including the nature of the system of control and hierarchy characteristic of the organization. It became clear that the behavior of individual members of an organization could be understood onlu by analyzing the organization as a whole (still viewed as autonomous, however). This marked an advance over the psychologism of earlier theories but still suffered from an oversimplified concept of the individual actor, who was seen as autonomous and rational.

Other writers tried to overcome this limitation by focusing on interpersonal relations, using microgroups as the elementary unit of analysis. The theories they proposed took interactions among the actors into account but neglected organizational phenomena as such. As Crozier and Friedberg rightly note, the interactionists assume that the organization functions perfectly, and the ethnomethodologists see right through it.[44] The former emphasize the strategies of the various actors and the mutual adjustments they make to accommodate one another, implicitly making use of a kind of market model based on symbolic exchange. The latter (structuralists after a fashion) use phenomenological methods to find the same relations of power and domination at the microsocial level as are observed at the macrosocial level.

Neither interactionists nor ethnomethodologists pay any attention to the interaction between organization and socialization, which is a key feature of our approach. The space in which the actors relate to one another is unstructured, and there is no mediation between the power that dominates the system as a whole and its reproduction in the microgroups. In addition to interactionism and ethnomethodology, there are two other main approaches to the theory of organizations, both deriving from structural functionalism: the theory of organizations as social systems and the so-called structural contingency theory of the organization.

The theory of the organization as a social system was first proposed by Talcott Parsons, for whom it was merely a special case of his general theory of social systems. This theory here was intended as an answer to a question first raised by Thomas Hobbes in the seventeenth century: how can individual motivations be reconciled with the social order? The Parsonian theory in fact recasts Hobbes's question: How, asks Parsons, can the personality system of the individual be integrated into the social system? We shall not review the content of Parsons's theory here, for it is already well known, nor shall we repeat the criticisms that have frequently been leveled against it. But we do want to indicate how we depart from Parsons's approach in our theoretical and empirical work.

To do this we must say a word or two about Parsons's theory. In this theory what Parsons calls the value system plays a multiple role. It provides, a normative orientation for action and for the system of roles and role expectations that defines the position of the actors in each subsystem. It also regulates the exchanges between the actors and the subsystems of the social system. Hence once the social system and its dominant system of values is known, the actors are in a sense given. The relation between the actors and the system is no longer problematic; it is completely determined. The actors are dependent on the social system, in which the real independent variable is the system of values.

By contrast, in our approach a key question is how the actors are socially constructed along with their spheres of action. Rather than regard the value system as the independent variable in our analysis, we regard it, along with the whole system of symbolic and cultural production, as a social construct and therefore look for the processes that contribute to it.

Our approach also differs from other approaches derived from Parsons's in one degree or another, or having affinities with his work, especially the approach that derives from the political sociology of negotiations and decision making and is commonly associated with the theory of industrial relations.[45] The latter theory is, according to Alessandro Pizzorno, derived in part from Durkheim's *Division of Labor in Society*.[46] It is based on the contention that "the social order is made secure not by integration within the framework of a system of values but rather by working representative institutions."[47] For Durkheim, representative institutions are a way of eliminating pathological forms of the division of labor. Society is not unified by a value system or a dominant authority; rather it organizes itself and evolves pragmatically in response to negotiations, or transactions, among its constituent groups. The equilibrium of the social system (or what Parsons calls latent pattern maintenance) is ensured by collective contracts or laws that enable the society to achieve some measure of stability and cohesiveness while allowing society to adapt to changes in its environment.

Touraine is probably right, therefore, in his belief that the theory of industrial relations is the expression of a liberal ideology in which the idealism of a value-centered theory has been replaced by pragmatic ratio-nalism and a philosophy of social change. Society is seen as a political marketplace in which the social actors haggle with one another over the slicing of the pie. Accordingly decision theory and strategic analysis take precedence over the theory of systemic needs and functions, which was deliberately intended to be more abstract, in keeping with a natural-scientific model of what science is or should be about. But the new theory is no keener than Parsons was to look into the underlying processes that shape the collective identities of the actors and their relations to one another. Neither approach considers the time dimension, so important in the social construction of social actors, as it relates to the interaction between socialization and organization. Both theories claim a specious generality and are therefore not particularly useful for comparative work.

The second body of work, commonly referred to as structural contin-gency theory, also derives from structural-functional sociology, which is more concerned with the laws that govern the way a system works than with the underlying processes that shape the social relations among the actors in that system. As the name implies, the theory is structural in orientation and treats the question considered here—that of the relation between the organization and the individuals who make it up—with benign neglect, though it does pay heed to the relationship between the organization and its environment. In our view, however, the two questions are logically related, and neither can be fully treated in isolation. Structural contingency theory enjoyed its heyday in the 1960s primarily in the English-speaking countries, where it developed as a reaction against theories that concentrated too intently on what goes on inside the organization.[48] The proponents of structural contingency theories argued that what goes on inside the organization can be understood only by studying the relations between inside and outside. The relationship between the organization and its environment, they argued, affects not only the internal structure of the organization but also its performance, and therefore its capacity to survive in a competitive world.

Central to the structural contingency approach is a distinction between the complex organization (or formal organization) and the social organization, a less formalized type of organization such as the family. Complex organizations were compared in order to discover possible relations between contextual variables and so-called structural variables, of which size and technology are typical. With these results in hand, a number of sociologists proposed new interpretations of Max Weber's model of bureaucracy, forgetting that Weber did not believe that organizations were determined solely by their formal-rational structure. For Weber the organization was a political system in which the divergent interests of various pressure groups could be expressed; hence power was an important aspect of organizational life.[49] But the structural contingency theorists, preferring more scientific quantitative methods to case studies, ignored all this and sought instead to determine the laws that relate organizational structure to performance.

The inherent formalism of the approach, however, prevents it from dealing with the question that concerns us here: the relationship between the organization and its members. Peter Blau's most recent work (along with the work of Pugh, Hickson, and other members of the Aston group) is a good example. For Blau the researcher must confront a stark alternative: study actors or study structures.[50] There is no room in his approach for studying the interactions between actors and structures or between socialization and organization.

Structural contingency theory has moved beyond the one best way of classical organization theory in one respect, however. By introducing technology as a contextual variable, it has been possible to argue that the optimal structure for an organization depends on the type of technology employed (Joan Woodward introduces three types, as we have seen: unit, batch, and process production technologies). This can lead to a kind of technological determinism,[51] though Woodward in her most recent work has introduced the system of control as a new variable that may alter the anticipated effects of a technology, thereby opening the way to an analysis of social factors affecting the introduction of a new technology.[52]

Similar comments apply to the work of Charles Perrow. Perrow introduces two additional variables: variability of raw materials and analyzability of the production process (that is, can it be programmed or not?). These he tends to regard as the primary determinants of the actors' behavior, as though their role were limited to making the structure of the organization compatible with the technology employed. On this view of the matter, good performance can be achieved by "maximizing the congruence between technology and structure."[53]

Let us defer until later our comments on the limitations of this approach in dealing with the relations between organizations and society. For the time being it suffices to say that the structural contingency theorists tend to reify both the concept of an organization and the concept of a technology by neglecting the extent to which both are social constructs and by overlooking the way in which socialization and organization interact to shape the collective identity of, and the social relations between, the various actors in the system. Our results have provided empirical support for the contention that the usefulness of structural contingency theories is limited. In particular, we have shown that these theories are not as general as they claim to be. Formalization, centralization, and functional specialization within an organization (to use some of the variables favored by structural contingency theorists) vary in meaning depending on the context. Their significance emerges only after they have been related to the specific groups of actors and types of social relations found within the organization. Organizational structures, in other words, are never culture free.[54] In our work, when we looked at organizations of comparable size using the same technology in two different countries, we found different hierarchical structures. More than that, we found that these differences could be explained by differences in the ways the social actors and their domains of interaction were shaped. But these kinds of differences (as well as differences in the nature of the supervisory structure) cannot be reduced to simple quantitative measures; interpretation is required.

In other words one cannot study variations in organizational structure in relation to the social environment without considering how social relations are shaped in a society. This entails a reformulation of the question of the relationship between the actors and the system or between the organization and society.[55]

A.2.2.2 Organizations and Society

According to the structural contingency theorists, the adaptation of the organization to its environment can be measured by its performance. In this respect the contribution of Pugh, Hickson, and the Aston group has clearly been important. They argue that many environmental factors influence the performance of an organization, and therefore it is not enough to treat only a few variables such as size and technology. Still they continue to view the environment in isolation from the organization; it is, by definition, external. To this it is not enough to respond, as John Child does, by arguing that it is wrong to view the relations between organization and environment as unilateral; the organization influences its environment just as much as the environment influences the organization.[56] The very concept of environment must be questioned. This has been attempted recently by a number of authors, who, however, modify the boundaries of the organization without proposing a fundamentally new view.

Among these recent efforts we include interorganizational analysis, network analysis, and, most recent of all, ecological analysis. Each of these represents an advance. Organization theory now considers complex interorganizational relations, power relations, coalitions, and even class relations and dialectical interactions (treated in the substantial body of work produced by Marxist-influenced theorists in the United States).[57] None of this work, however, treats the processes by which society shapes the organization and the organization (in part at any rate) shapes society. Weber's insight—that organizations are rooted in the social structure and an integral part of society—has never really been developed. Nor has Schumpeter's analysis, in part derived from Weber, in *Capitalism, Socialism and Democracy*. Mention should be made, however, of Arthur Stinchcombe's essay, which moves from a historical analysis of organizational development to an examination of the social conditions under which new forms of organization are likely to emerge. Stinchcombe argues that once a new form of organization has emerged in response to particular social conditions, it will tend to endure even after those conditions have disappeared.[58] Interesting as his essay is, it smacks somewhat of evolutionism a la Darwin. A similar remark can be made about recent ecological theories of the organization.[59]

We are not the only investigators to undertake international comparisons in order to answer questions about the relationship of the organization to society. Generally, however, the approach taken has been quite different from ours. The comparative work done by members of the Aston group under the leadership of Pugh and Hickson, for example, is actually just an extension of the structural contingency model.

It is hardly surprising that this research has led to the conclusion that the laws of organizational structure are culture free. The variables used to describe both internal structure and external factors are based on concepts so general as to make any true test of cultural effects impossible.

Paradoxically the paradigm within which this comparative work was conceived is based on a microsocial concept of organizational rationality, and yet it claims to be generally valid, irrespective of differences between one society or culture and another. The culture-free thesis leads logically to the theory of convergence mentioned in the introduction. Specific national variations from the norm are viewed as mere residues, ultimately to be smoothed over by the logic of industrialization.[60]

Since the structural and contextual variables used have been thoroughly desocialized, it should come as no surprise that the research leads to the conclusion that the predictions of structural contingency theory are quite generally valid. It may be closer to the truth to say that the research points up the formalism inherent in the model.[61]

Does it then follow that culture must be introduced as the only variable capable of explaining the residual differences turned up by some structural contingency theorists? Michel Crozier, in his 1963 book *The Bureaucratic Phenomenon*, gave a somewhat different and more convincing interpretation of the influence of culture. Crozier argues that the mechanisms of social control, as manifested within the organization, vary from one society to another. These mechanisms, he says, "are closely related to the values and patterns of social relations typical of each different society."[62] The organization is closely modeled on other social institutions. Crozier's approach marks a considerable advance over structural contingency theory in that it suggests the existence of a close connection between the organization and society. But it takes no account of the underlying social processes. In *The Bureaucratic Phenomenon*, at any rate, Crozier detected overtones of French-style organization in French social institutions.[63] But more recently he has acknowledged that classical institutional analysis and culturalist approaches are limited because they "are based solely on rather vague notions of values."[64] He has therefore turned his research to the study of the processes of integration found in every society, an approach most fully developed in *Actors and Systems* (written in collaboration with Erhard Friedberg).[65]

We want to treat this approach in some detail because it deals with a number of the questions that our own work was designed to answer.

Trying to tie together the wide variety of strategies observed in a whole series of empirical studies, Crozier and Friedberg emphasize not the diversity of particular strategies but the stability of what they call systems of action. Strategic analysis is "one side of the coin"; culture is the other.[66] But the notion of culture Crozier and Friedberg used is somewhat different from our own.

Classically, it is argued, culturalists have defined culture in terms of "values and norms which, in the final analysis, direct and shape observed behavior." Crozier and Friedberg reject this notion in favor of the idea that culture is an instrument or a capacity acquired through experience. Because culture is a capacity "constructed in and through action, it is inseparable from the structures" within which it is acquired. In other words, it is relational capital. As a social construct, culture makes it possible to relate the strategies of the actors to structural constraints on those strategies. Furthermore there are specific relations to be discovered among "modes of collective action, modes of institutional development, and cultural contexts."[67]

The notion of culture as capacity is no doubt a useful contribution to the analysis of socialization in relation to organization; the capacities of the actors are relational as well as organizational, individual, or collective. But what is the connection between an actor's strategic capacity to relate to other actors in the context of some organizational game and what the authors call a social capacity, presumably an attribute of society at large? In other words is the idea of culture as capacity still relevant when analyzing the relations between (national) cultures and organizations? Not that Crozier has not considered this objection:[68] he discusses it in at least one article, where he argues that the organizational capacity revealed by his type of research is not equivalent to a social capacity.[69] But considering the objection is not the same as disposing of it, and we do not believe that he has done so. Nor has he given, in our view, a satisfactory account of the connection between processes of integration at the microsocial level and the same processes at the macrosocial level.

In fact Crozier and Friedberg are critical of work that extrapolates unreasonably from microsocial analysis to macrosocial analysis, based on the notion that there is a homology between organizational structures and institutional structures. But they do not seem to have resolved "the problem of the interaction between organization and society" themselves, even if they apparently believe that further research into what they call "concrete systems of action" will contribute to doing so.[70]

We are not so sure. We wish to raise several objections to this line of research, objections that derive largely from our own work. First, Crozier and Friedberg seem to be interested mainly in what they called organized action rather than in organizations. Similarly they treat systems of action rather than actors. The focus of their theory is on an intermediate level of analysis, directed toward what they call concrete systems of action. These are said to act as mediators between social control in society as a whole and social control as it operates in organizations or groups. Doubtless this intermediate level of analysis is all too often neglected, but does that fact by itself guarantee that it is the key to linking microsocial to macrosocial processes? We are inclined to doubt it, particularly since we think that the nature and significance of social control change as one moves from one level to another. Indeed we cannot even begin to speak of significance until we have some category of actor in mind, and it may be asked whether the same categories of actors exist on the macrosocial level as on the microsocial.

The truth of the matter is that the concepts of actor and action are themselves responsible for the limitations of the Crozier-Friedberg approach and the difficulty (which they acknowledge) of treating the interaction between organization and society. "The actor exists only within the system," they tell us, "and the system exists only through the actor."[71] In fact, however, both actor and system exist for Crozier and Friedberg only to the extent that they wield power. In strategic analysis (as Crozier and Friedberg call their theory) power is in a sense the functional equivalent of self-interest in the economic model.[72] It is power that determines an actor's capacity to pursue a winning strategy and to structure his field of action, to acquire resources and cope with constraints, and to widen his margin of liberty. No account is taken of the sociological identity of the actors, their social relations, or the particular features of the domains within which collective action is carried out. The terms of the analysis are abstract and general—game, strategy, power—and the specific identities of the actors are lost. For Crozier and Friedberg it is more important to uncover the games the actors are playing and the strategies they are pursuing than to understand who they are. Pushing the point somewhat, we might say that it is the games and strategies that give shape to the actors rather than the other way around.[73]

The actors have only an immediate existence, in and through the action that, so far as the theory is concerned, constitutes their essence. Crozier and

Friedberg do not ask where power comes from or why the stakes of the game are what they are, any more than they ask about how the actors are socially constructed. "The actor sees his opportunity in the situation according to his capacity to grasp what the situation is, and acts accordingly." In other words, "opportunity makes the thief.[74]

Our approach differs from that of Crozier and Friedberg essentially in this: time is an important feature in our analysis of socialization and organization. It plays a part in determining how stable the identity of an actor is and what the nature of his domain of action will be. For Crozier and Friedberg, on the other hand, time is at best one more opportunity of which the actor may take advantage if he has the capacity to do so. Thus it acts indirectly as an influence on the choice of strategy or game.

The way in which Crozier and Friedberg conceptualize the actor and his action is not without influence on their view of the way the organization interacts with society. Indeed it colors their whole idea of the relationship between the general and the particular. But to say this is merely to note that they, along with many other writers, from Mancur Olson to Albert Hirschman and Thomas Schelling, from Raymond Boudon to Jean-Daniel Reynaud, share the methodological individualism characteristic of much contemporary social science. Taking such a position is not without consequences, but it is beyond the scope of this book to go into this question in detail. Suffice to say that concerned as they are in their theories to emphasize that the actor is to some extent free and autonomous, the methodological individualists apparently feel the need to develop their arguments in such a way that the constraints of the macrosocial system operate externally. To do otherwise, they feel, would concede too much to determinism (or collectivism). Yet they acknowledge the existence of macrosocial phenomena, which the individual actor cannot avoid. These, they say, are due to the aggregation of a large number of independent decisions, or, as Crozier and Friedberg would put it, to the crystallization of strategic choices made independently by the various actors involved in a particular system.

In other words the microdecisions of the actors engender macrophenomena at the system level—this, at any rate, is what Schelling argues, and his arguments have greatly influenced the work of Raymond Boudon, who has long evinced an interest in what he calls the perverse effects of individual decision making—that is, the "undesired effect of combining a great many uncoordinated individual actions."[75] Crozier and Friedberg believe that power relations constitute social structures. "Power," they say, "can only exist in a structured domain, the structure of which it helps to create." The structure not only imposes constraints on the exercise of power but also provides resources that can be converted into power by the actors. Standing between the microlevels and macrolevels of analysis is what Crozier and Friedberg call the "mode of regulation" of the system. This can be studied only by analyzing the concrete systems of action that form between the primary social group and the global social system. Here it is also worth mentioning the work of J.-D. Reynaud.[76] For Reynaud, the organization is the "institutionalization of a strategy." Conflict is analyzed in terms of relatively autonomous relations between occupational groups, whose behavior is governed by an internal logic that cannot be explained entirely in terms of characteristics of the society as a whole.[77]

Here, then, as in the cases considered previously, the externalization of the macrosocial is nothing more than a consequence of the methodology. The methodology requires an endogenous principle to explain the workings of the system of interaction, the strategic game, in which the various actors participate. There are two possibilities, which ultimately are the same. Either the analysis will revolve around the decision-making process and the relations between the actors in the system, rather than the processes by which the actors are themselves socially constructed.[78] Or it will try to reduce a social logic to a logic of action, in which the actors are finally conceptualized solely in terms of the games in which they participate or the strategies they adopt. In this case power relations take the place of social relations.

A.2.2.3 Comparative Social Analysis: From the Specific to the General

In the preceding section we raised the question of the relationship of the general to the specific or particular, a question that crops up in sociology whenever it becomes necessary to relate macrosocial and microsocial analysis. In this section we consider the work of Pierre Bourdieu and his followers, which in one sense constitutes a neo-Marxist interpretation of the relationship between the actor and the system.

Before taking up Bourdieu's views on this point, views not unlike those of the methodological individualists, we want to digress to show that on other, no less crucial points of theory, we are largely in agreement with the authors we have just finished criticizing and largely in disagreement with Bourdieu. What are these points of agreement? First, we too think that importance should be attached to the actors, the analysis of (concrete) systems of action, and above all the interaction between actors and systems. Taking this kind of approach enables sociologists to give due weight to both the freedom of the actors and the constraints inherent in the social structure. The structure itself is not viewed in a deterministic way; it is held to be a social construct. We share the methodological individualists' opposition to deterministic theories of every ilk, theories that tend to reduce actors to the role of mere structural supports. Our approach, though differently conceived from those we criticized in the previous section, tries to show, as they do, how both groups of actors and the domains within which they act are constructed simultaneously through the process of social interaction.

The criticisms leveled by Crozier and Friedberg at both classical organization theory and culturalist approaches to organizations are just and to the point, particularly in exposing residues of determinist thinking in the work they attack (some of it of structural-functionalist derivation and some of Marxist derivation). They are also right in pointing out the limitations of these approaches when it comes to conceptualizing cultural differences between individuals and groups, to say nothing of entire societies.

But we are bound to point out that we disagree with Crozier and Friedberg, and with Jean-Daniel Reynaud as well, when relating the general to the specific. Not that we disagree with their critiques of the classical hypothetico-deductive approach, which proceeds from the general to the particular. Like the authors mentioned, we too believe that one must begin with the analysis of the concrete and the particular. But our idea of how to go about empirical generalization is somewhat different from theirs.

Here we have put our finger on a key difference between our own work and that of the authors just mentioned. It is with this difference in mind that we mention Pierre Bourdieu (the jump probably calls for lengthier explanation than we are able to give here). Although Bourdieu's approach is further removed from ours than is the approach of the methodological individualists, his work is one of the most fruitful attempts to relate individual behavior (and interests) to social structures.[79]

Still, it is precisely the point at which we are in closest agreement with Bourdieu that is also the point of sharpest disagreement. We shall explain what we mean by this paradoxical statement by indicating how our work has led us to question Bourdieu's analysis of the relationship between the general and the particular, even though we have no better theory to offer in place of his. We must introduce one of Bourdieu's favorite and surely also most enigmatic ideas: that of the habitus.[80] For Bourdieu the object of analysis is not actors and systems but practices and structures, which may be either well or ill adapted to one another. Bourdieu's theory, to borrow Michel de Certeau's concise summary of it, "aims to explain the degree of adaptation of practices to structures by looking at how the former originate."[81]

The idea of habitus is introduced to facilitate the transition from practices to structures. It explains why the practices of agents (or social subjects—Bourdieu avoids the term *actor*) are well or ill adapted to the surrounding structures.[82] Despite the assertions of certain of Bourdieu's critics, the habitus does not simply reproduce (mechanically) the structures of domination in the society.[83] In fact Bourdieu frequently alludes to the creative, innovative possibilities inherent in the habitus: "The habitus is a principle of invention produced by history and yet relatively detached from its historical roots.[84] To the extent that use of the notion of habitus implies that the social actors are relatively free to decide on their own course of action in the context established by surrounding social structures, we have no quarrel with it. Where we differ with Bourdieu is over his conceptualization of the relationship between the habitus and social structures.

In Bourdieu's theory it is as though the determinacy of structures (or as he would say, their "necessity") shapes each individual by the habitus: "The collective is deposited in each individual in the form of 'enduring dispositions' (to act in one way or another) or 'mental structures.'"[85] Thus although Bourdieu rejects the notion that the habitus is immediately determined by the situation, he nevertheless argues that it must change in response to changes in the situation and that these changes eventually produce a lasting transformation of the system. It is hard to resist interpreting the habitus as a principle of stability that opposes the natural tendency of social structures to change and vary with time.[86] Bourdieu's insistence on the generative qualities of the habitus seems somewhat excessive in the light of his contention that the habitus "defines the perception of the situation that determines it."[87] More than that, what is particularly troubling in the light of our own work is that the relationship between habitus and structures is implicitly one of externality. As Bourdieu puts it, "The 'situation' is ... the necessary condition for the realization of the habitus."[88] This assertion is not without affinities to Crozier and Friedberg's idea that there is a relationship between capacities and opportunities. Another similarity between Bourdieu's work and Crozier's is Bourdieu's argument that the strategies that generate the habits are not necessarily conscious.[89] Bourdieu is no more interested than Crozier and Friedberg in the social construction of the actors. What concerns him primarily is the genesis of practices, just as Crozier and Friedberg are interested mainly in the origins of systems of action or social games.

Despite these superficial similarities, however, the underlying logic of Bourdieu's approach is quite different from that of Crozier and Friedberg.[90] In Bourdieu's work it as though collective, macrosocial phenomena are the decisive influences in shaping what happens at the microsocial and individual level. In Crozier and Friedberg's work it is just the opposite: the macrosocial is apparently constructed on foundations laid down by microsocial processes. For Bourdieu it is the social structure that predominates; for Crozier and Friedberg it is social relations.[91]

Each approach therefore invokes its own frame of reference, its own conception of the relationship between the general and the particular. Bourdieu deciphers the meaning of individual strategies or practices by referring to general criteria. Crozier and Friedberg, on the other hand, prefer to understand the structure of social action in terms of the particular and concrete.

Our own analysis is couched in terms different drom both of these. It cannot be reduced to either. The terms in which we conceive of the relationship between the general and particular are unlike those used by either Bourdieu or Crozier. We attempt to start with the particular and work toward a description of the general, but in doing so we try always to keep the particular in view. Indeed we find much that is general inherent in the particular and much specificity inherent in any general description. To rephrase this in a less abstract way, perhaps we should say that in our approach the actors and domains enter into the construction of the general without losing any of their specificity. Our previous critique of overly general approaches was meant as an indictment of theories that pay too little attention to the specific, particular characteristics of any situation. We were thinking mainly of purely formal and abstract theories, largely unsuited to describing concrete social realities. This is not the case with either Bourdieu's or Crozier's theory; neither is formalistic. The limitations of both approaches are due to the fact that they tend to work toward generality (or totality) in ways that leave out what is specific. Thus Bourdieu's science of practices and Crozier and Friedberg's theory of organized action can avoid treating the nature of the specific social relations that obtain between actors in different societies. When international comparison is carried out for heuristic purposes using either of these theories as a frame of reference, the result is likely to be a demonstration that the concepts used in the theories are general in nature. There will be no attempt to show, as we have tried to do, that general similarities sometimes conceal specific differences, invariants that underlie the particular social processes that shape the general pattern.[92] It bears repeating, however, that although our comparative approach has enabled us to point up differences between our way of looking at the problem and that of these other theorists, we have yet to provide an adequate theoretical account of our results. These remarks should be regarded merely as outlining a problem area. Further research will be required before we can hope to shed much more light on it.

A.3 Relations between Occupational Groups

Now that we have discussed economics and sociology, we should turn next to labor law, which we propose to view in its broad social context rather than in narrow legalistic terms. In France it was no easy task, either in law or in fact, to win recognition of the right of workers to organize.[93] Not so long ago the very idea of a collective contract was considered a legal aberration. The same was true even more recently of the idea that a contract might include a clause obliging one or both parties to enter into negotiations at a specified date. That facts make law can be seen clearly here.

In order to understand how this is so, sociologists began studying the relations between various occupational groups in order to understand what facts helped to shape modern labor law and work rules. The question we wish to raise is the following: what can we say in the light of our results about the work done by these sociologists, which in theory should account for specific national differences as well as set forth general laws?

A.3.1 The Sociology of Labor Relations

The first pioneering work in this area dealt with single countries. It tried to suggest what changes were necessary in order to make labor relations less unjust and less liable to conflict. Among those prominent in this kind of work were the Webbs in England, Perlman and the Wisconsin school in the United States, and Pierre Laroque in France.

The Webbs tried to show how collective bargaining could impose a common rule on the labor market and thus counter the tendency of employers to offer different wages in different industries, depending on the alleged capacity to pay within each branch, and to exploit competition among individual workers in search of employment. Unions, the Webbs suggested, could induce workers to accept the common rule by offering them incentives to join, mainly in the form of union-managed mutual insurance plans. This would promote an industrial democracy through which it would become possible to reestablish the competitive equilibrium of the labor market. Perlman and the Wisconsin school start from a fairly similar position. They stress that the function of the union movement is to combat the inherent individualism of American workers, an individualism made all the more invulnerable to change by the rampant ideology of "free labor in a system of free enterprise." Perlman differs with the Webbs on an important point, however: he argues that the goal of organization should be not to restore competitive equilibrium to the labor market but to strip employers of their prerogatives in matters of hiring and firing by establishing, through strikes and boycotts, a union monopoly in this area. For Perlman the aim is to change the rules of job allocation by promoting a form of class consciousness that he calls "job consciousness," based on a logic centered exclusively on workers and jobs and unconcerned with the economics of business and the labor market.

The works mentioned claim to be based on analyses of the situation in one country only. Perlman, for example, tries to show how any attempt by the labor movement in the United States to invoke Marxist ideology would prevent the development of a true class consciousness by arousing opposition within the working class itself. The only way to encourage the development of class consciousness, Perlman argues, is to stress job consciousness rather than Marxism. The Webbs' theory, on the other hand, is based on the idea that the trade union movement should complement the political activities of the Labour party, the aim of which should be to provide the support of law for the union effort to institutionalize the discipline of a common rule in the labor market.

The first systematic consideration of industrial relations in France can be found in Maxime Leroy's *La coutume ouvrière*. Leroy records the principles of union discipline, based on an analysis of union statutes. It was not until 1936 and the completion of Pierre Laroque's thesis that analysis of the problems involved in relations between employers and workers in France was extended beyond a purely legalistic framework. Still, this was a study of the labor situation in one country, a country dominated by a legalistic tradition and by the power of the state and by confidence that arbitration could resolve all labor conflicts.

A.3.2 General Theories of Industrialization

Behind all of this work looms the imperative of a response to Marx's challenge: there is no way to resolve the class conflict born of capitalism other than to destroy the capitalist system. This same imperative informs the earliest attempts to work out general theories of labor relations, which were made in the United States in the years following World War II. Leading the way were books by Clark Kerr and Abraham Siegel. In the early stages of their work these writers tried to develop a theory of industrial conflict valid for all capitalist countries. Through statistical analysis of the propensity to strike in various branches of industry in eleven different countries, they tried to show that the reasons for industrial conflict were relatively independent of specific national characteristics. They found that strikes were most common among miners and dockers, least common among railroad, retail, and agricultural workers. Accordingly they rejected purely economic theories of industrial conflict (which emphasized changes in the relative levels of wages and prices), arguing that workers are most likely to strike in industries where they form a homogeneous group isolated from the rest of the collectivity (these traits are particularly prominent among the miners). The work of Kerr and Siegel was one of the earliest attempts to put forward a systematic explanation of industrial conflict that took account of the relationship between, on the one hand, individuals and groups and, on the other hand, not just the firm but society as a whole. But the authors acknowledged that their research into the various branches of industry left a number of points unexplained and that the phenomena in question were complex and called for research into "a multiplicity of possible causes." [94]

In a second phase of their research the same two authors proposed a more general interpretation, which has been the starting point for many subsequent theories of industrial relations.[95] This time their study revolved not around strikes but around "the institutionalization of labor relations as a result of industrialization." Capital formation and mechanization provided the material basis for industrialization. But industrialization could not go forward without constant reformulation of the rules governing relations between employers and employees. The purpose of these rules is essentially to "structure the work force." This is a necessary feature of all industrial societies, whether capitalist or socialist in nature. But the necessary structure can be achieved in different ways; both the content of the rules and the way rules are written and promulgated may vary from one country to another. The goals are always the same, however: these concern methods of worker recruitment, training, job assignment, length of the working day, wage determination, job mobility, and workplace discipline. And according to the authors, they even include "ways of reducing the rebelliousness of individuals and groups ... and of producing philosophies, ideologies, and beliefs."

In their analysis of the causes of strikes, Kerr and Siegel had emphasized the social relations of workers both among themselves and with other groups in society. In their general theory of industrial relations they emphasized the way in which rules are hammered out in industrial societies through cooperation among workers, employers, and the state. The focus of attention has shifted from detailed observation of worker attitudes to general reflection on the way industrial society works. The analysis of actual actors takes a back seat to analysis of the "cooperation among actors."[96] It is argued that rules may be set in one of three ways: unilaterally, bilaterally, or pluralistically, the last involving the government in relations between employers and employees. "The traditional contrast between the abuses of capitalism and the labor movement is only a special case." A general theory cannot be "based on the reaction of the workers' movement but must study the whole range of rules governing the behavior of workers in relation to the labor process." We are told that the key factor in the way rules are formed is technological change, a necessity of industrialization. Technological change is historically linked to what are called industrialization elites. The actors in this theory are general and abstract, defined by the role they play in rule formation. Their freedom is tightly constrained by technology, which defines the production function and thus determines the possible combinations of labor and capital. The scale of production determines the possible content of each job, not only in the area of direct production but also in management and control. Relative factor prices then determine the possibilities of production, which in turn "closely determine job structures and classifications."[97] Changes in job structure are closely related to changes in technology, which also strongly influence training requirements and, more generally, the need for specific technical and scientific skills. The authors do admit that certain other factors exert some influence, in particular culture and ideology; the latter, they tell us, can, for example, "cause workers to favor a piecework system rather than allow foremen to choose the most practical and efficient method of remuneration." The relative length of in-school versus on-the-job training may vary to some extent from one country to another. "For the most part, however, the iron hand of technology tends to establish a relatively high degree of uniformity in job structures, wage differences, and technical training. This uniformity is accentuated by international and domestic flows of capital and specialized skills."

In this kind of theory the actors clearly play a secondary role. The authors do make one concession on this score. They distinguish among several types of industrialization elites on the basis of historical, social, and political criteria. Among the types identified are dynastic rulers, colonial administrators, middle-class entrepreneurs, revolutionary intellectuals, and nationalist leaders. Each of these ideal types corresponds to a strategy by which industrialization has been achieved historically. Workers can either adapt to or struggle against industrialization. If they accept it, the reason is that they hope to share in its benefits and raise their standard of living. If they reject it, the reason is that they want to prevent the destruction of their old craft guilds in favor of new work rules. Protest against industrialization takes different forms at different stages in the process. From individualistic responses such as absenteeism and sabotage, it moves on to more organized responses, including trade unions, arbitration and grievance procedures, and the formation of political parties. The more institutionalized the response, the more it is shaped by the nature of the industrial system within which it occurs and thereofre by the associated industrializing elites and political regimes. But John Dunlop, in his book *Industrial Relations Systems*, tells us that "the form of the rule does not change its essential character, which is to define the relations among the actors and regulate their work behavior in society."[98] The writers whose work we have been examining, particularly Dunlop in *Industrial Relations Systems*, also stress factors other than technology that help to shape industrial relations systems, such as ideology. The ideology of an industrial relations system, Dunlop writes, is the whole range of shared ideas by which the role and place of each actor in the system is defined. Ideology also shapes the actor's view of his role and the place of his fellow workers. For example, if employers took a very paternalistic attitude toward their workers while the workers felt that employers had no social role whatsoever, there would be no shared ideas that each group could use to legitimate the role of the other. A distinction should be made between the ideology of the industrial relations system and the ideology of the society as a whole. Since the former is a subsystem of the latter, however, there cannot fail to be a close relationship between the two.

On this view of the matter, the actors do have some role to play, but their behavior is shaped in large part by technological constraints (economic constraints are included under this head) and by the functional necessity to maintain some minimal level of ideological consensus. In the end this consensus can be based on only the one objective that all the actors share: to obtain a portion of the benefits of industrialization.

We begin from a different set of axioms. For us it is important to observe that the effects of technology vary from one country to another. In comparing two equally developed capitalist industrial societies, we found significant differences in job and wage structures and educational and training systems. We also found differences in the way production was organized and labor divided. Furthermore we found that these differences tend to remain fairly stable over time. We do not explain these observations in terms of ideological or cultural differences. Without denying the importance of social values, we were led by the logic of our approach to ask what the source of those values might be. In our view it is the social relations intrinsic to a given society and implicit in the educational system, organizations, and systems of industrial relations that give rise to different ideologies, and not the reverse. The authors whose work we have been considering take an ambiguous position on this point. Dunlop, for example, argues that "an industrial relations system creates an ideology" (pp. 380ff.) and so cannot be explained in ideological terms. Ideology, in the sense of a set of interpretations given by the actors in system of their roles, a product of the system, a product that helps to smooth its operation. It cannot explain the nature of the system.

The main difference, then, between their interpretation and ours is this: for them technological constraints determine the rules governing the operation of the system, whereas for us technology is one factor among others that helps to shape social relations. A technology can be used in different ways. Organizational effects modify technological effects, as can be seen in the fact that different firms using the same technology organize work in different ways. The possible forms of organization depend on the occupational structure, the various types of professional skills available in the job market. The attributes of workers are shaped in the schools, in occupational training, and on the job. Skills acquired by a worker before entering the labor market give him an identity and a degree of autonomy in his work on which the firm can capitalize. In turn, the willingness of firms to do this influences the occupational structure that will develop in the society as a whole. The interaction between socialization and organization determines the nature of industrial relations in the society, that is, the relations between workers and management, unions, the economic system, and society in general. Implicit in these industrial relations are three principles, to borrow Alain Touraine's terminology: a principle of identity, a principle of opposition, and a principle of totality. In a nutshell this means that the individual is defined by his productive contribution to society—that is, his social function—on which he bases his claims to certain benefits, as well as by his stance in regard to antagonistic groups—"more precisely, by obstacles that prevent workers from exerting control over their own work." Finally, the individual is also defined by the social sphere, the economic and political system, in which the social relation defined by the two prior principles is situated.[99]

The social construction of the worker is not unrelated to the social construction of the two other principal actors in the system, the employer and the state. What is important in each case is the relation the actor bears to the firm, in which all three kinds of social relations—educational, organizational, and industrial—are concretely embodied. We cannot hope to understand the system of industrial relations without first understanding how these various kinds of social relations interact.

A.3.3 General Theories of Exploitation

Generally Marxist theorists have been at pains to avoid attributing to technology and industrialization the important role bestowed on them by the authors whose work we have just been considering. For Marxists technology and industrialization are both merely aspects of capital accumulation. Capital, in turn, is defined essentially in terms of the social relation that it entails between the owners of capital and the proletariat, a relation of exploitation and domination that extends its influence throughout a capitalist society. What matters to Marxists is the social relations of productions and not their epiphenomenal manifestations.

One of the problems raised by this interpretation is that of the autonomy of industrial relations systems and of the relationship between the economic sphere and the political sphere. An example of the way this problem has been treated by some Marxists—a rather outrageous example—may be found in Vidal's work on power in the firm.[100] The Marxist theorist's position is delicate. He must find some way to give meaning to the notion that firms act without suggesting that this action is anything other than a contingent mediation of the influence of capital in the abstract and yet without denying that the action of the firm may be to some degree autonomous. In pure Marxist theory the allowable degree of autonomy is extremely limited, if not nil, with two exceptions. First, there may exist relations of domination and dependence between firms (subcontracting being the most visible of these). Second, since the firm is the place where the class struggle comes to a head, it is within the firm that capital runs up against obstacles to further accumulation and realization. Leaving these two exceptions aside, Vidal draws the following conclusion:

Because the firm is a product of the market and of the relations of production and exchange that are shaped by the market, it produces [corporate] power in the same way that the social formation produces political power.... Hence the problem of power within the firm, and of power as an issue in social conflict, can be approached within the same theoretical framework used to study power in the social formation.... [This latter power] is defined by the class relations that produce it, as they impinge on the sphere of the political. Only by studying class relations in general and the institutions that help to shape them can we hope to resolve the problem of power.

To take such a position is tantamount to denying that what goes on in the firm has any autonomy or indeed any importance (but for the two exceptional cases mentioned). Politics itself has little or no autonomy since it is determined by class relations, which are themselves a product of the relations of production, or perhaps one should say of the relation of production, that of capital to proletariat. Accordingly, "Unions are merely organizational embodiments of a social movement, and their power depends on the extent to which they are obliged to operate on the social and therefore on the political level. To the extent that they are so obliged ... they contribute to the destruction of the power [of capital]." Although it may be possible to study the "destruction of the power of capital" independently, the only reason to do so is presumably in order to understand changes in class relations based on changes in the conditions under which capital may be accumulated and realized. These conditions vary from one historical period to another and from one society to another. These variations may be interesting to study but cannot amount to anything other than mere contingencies. The fundamental fact is always the same: the iron law of accumulation reigns supreme and invariably reproduces the domination of labor by capital.

If one accepts such a view, differences in the management of labor relations between one country and another cannot be of anything more than historical, indeed anecdotal, interest. They are merely different ways of extracting surplus value, of managing capital, For a Marxist the management of the work force is just an aspect of the management of capital, understood in an economic sense and not in terms of a social relation. Capital is merely the sum of "dead labor" and living labor embodied in the product, or, to put the same point another way, the sum of constant capital and variable capital. The share of a capitalist's resources that will be devoted to constant as opposed to variable capital (the ratio between the two determining what Marx calls the "organic composition of capital") depends on the productivity of labor. As productivity goes up, wages go down because wages are determined by the "socially necessary labor-time"

required to produce substistence goods. Productivity in turn depends on
capital accumulation, which makes it possible to extend and intensify technological progress. Hence there is an inherent tendency in capitalism to
expand the sphere of wage labor to the maximum possible extent in order
to prevent the mass of constant capital from overwhelming the mass of
variable capital, since surplus value can be extracted only from living labor.
It therefore becomes necessary to integrate new social groups (children,
women, immigrants) into the work force, groups that previously belonged,
at least in part, to the sphere of domestic rather than capitalist production.
This results in a stratification of the work force and in wage differences
between different groups of workers. In reality this kind of segmentation
has always existed; capital has always expanded in this way, creating first a
scarcity of labor and then a "reserve army," as prosperity gives way to
recession: "Capital accumulation is always accompanied by an increase in
the ranks of the proletariat."[101]

Some Marxist writers have tried to explain the fact that real wages have
increased and that working conditions have improved as more and more
capital has been accumulated. They argue that these changes have been due
to the class struggle and to capitalist reactions to it. In the early stages of
the division of labor, workers were still allowed some autonomy. To reduce
this autonomy, Taylorist methods were employed "to define the nature of
each job and to insure that every movement would be carried out in a
prescribed order." Ford further reduced the worker's autonomy by introducing the assembly line. This, however, has the effect of uniting all
workers against management in a fight for better working conditions and
higher wages. Capital responded to this new state of affairs by turning to
automation. This freed the machine from all dependence on the limitations
of its human operator. Automation also allowed firms to be more flexible in
choosing where to locate their plants; it became possible "to move plants
away from large cities and to create an environment designed to take the
edge off conflict in the workplace."[102] The aim of this, we are told, was to
"overcome the resistance of the workers" by changing their working conditions as well as their environment outside the plant. To work toward this
goal capitalists introduced a number of institutional innovations: financial
insitutions capable of concentrating large amounts of capital, institutions
for managing the monetary system, and institutions of collective bargaining. Collective bargaining, according to this view, is a way of programming
increases in the nominal basic wage in order to make sure that it keeps pace
with changes in the sphere of consumption. Furthermore social welfare
systems have been established in order to make sure that the unemployed

continue to fulfill their role as consumers. "Collective bargaining takes place within a branch of industry, and firms band together in trade associations that reveal the true nature of the underlying class conflict.... The fact that all firms in a given branch of industry can be sure that the basic wage in each will be determined according to the same rules is a crucial factor in shaping the social conditions under which production is carried out" (p. 246). As Aglietta sees it, these new social forms (collective bargaining, welfare, unemployment insurance) establish a link between the abstract sphere of value (or commodity exchange, including the labor-power commodity) and the concrete sphere of activity. In other words the social structure and its consituent "forms effect a mediation between the sphere of value and the sphere of activity. Looked at in this way, the industrial relations system is no longer contingent. It is rather the structure through which the work force is managed. It enjoys a relative autonomy, relative because it is dominated by the laws of value but nonetheless real. In essence we have just summarized Michel Aglietta's approach to the study of what he calls the capitalist system for overcoming worker resistance.

What is wrong with this approach? Our work suggests a number of answers to this question. Aglietta argues that changes in the division of labor have historically been the result of efforts by workers to impede the "expanded reproduction of capital" and of efforts by capitalists to overcome worker resistance. Like him, we believe that the division of labor and the place of workers in the production process are important variables. These variables are greatly influenced, however, by the ways in which actors are socialized in one country or another and by the kinds of organization that result from each type of socialization. Different social forms may modify the effects of economic laws, but economic laws are never the sole or even the principal determinants of social forms. A country's educational system, for example, is shaped by noneconomic forces and cannot be explained by arguing that the schools are the organ whereby the system reproduces itself. The firm adapts to this system and attempts to exert influence over it in order to maximize its profits, but the desire to maximize profits is not what determines the evolution of the educational system. It has a life of its own and is run by its own personnel, ever watchful to prevent changes in its character. The way in which workers are socialized by the schools affects their place in the production process and therefore has important consequences for the nature of that process. The school thus interacts with the organization in ways that affect the system of industrial relations.

The latter system is therefore not fully described by saying that it involves the class struggle and attempts by capitalists to overcome worker resistance. Indeed worker resistance is one of the variables that need to be explained. The amount of such resistance varies from one society to another; the goals of workers, and the forms their organizations take, are not the same in all places.

The fact that we are inclined to accord priority to the actors over the system is unacceptable to Marxists, for whom capital accumulation is the all-important factor. We do not believe that either the system of production or the system of occupational training can be fully explained by invoking the alleged need to accumulate capital. Other social relations than that of capitalist to worker play a part. Workplace relations can be understood only in a wider context involving other, more complex social relations. In this respect we are closer to the strategic analysis of Crozier and Friedberg than we are to the Marxists.

A.3.4 Strategic Theories

Marxist writers like to deny the autonomy of industrial relations systems because in the capitalist mode of production, as they see it, the object of production is to produce exchange value in the form of commodities, and this purpose "informs every aspect and every phase of the labor process as well as the realization process."[103] By contrast, American economists of the industrial relations school regard the industrial relations system as a subsystem of society of importance equal to that of the economic subsystem. It is the industrial relations system, they say, that determines the rules governing worker mobility and wages, and it does this more or less independently of economic constraints to which firms may be subject (such as production costs, prices, and output targets). For the economists, these constraints are given, and firms adapt to them by determining how to use the labor factor. The problem for the firm is to administer the work force while making due allowance for internal as well as external constraints: what skills are available, what ideology predominates among the workers, how well are they organized, what is the size of the organization—all these are questions that firms must ask. "Each subsystem contributes to the overall operation of the system by carrying out the specific function for which it is responsible."[104] On this view of the matter, conflict plays a secondary role. It is "a superficial symptom of more fundamental features of the system, namely the way in which rules are elaborated and administered." If the industrial relations system is autonomous, it is because the actors who participate in it have the same basic goal: to keep the system of production working even if at times that underlying unity may be disturbed by temporary disagreement.

It is also possible, however, to treat conflict as being of primary importance, indeed as the underlying reason for the autonomy of occupational groups. The problem for the sociologist then becomes identifying the incompatible objectives of the various actors in the system.[105] No assumption is made that the fundamental conflict is that between labor and capital. Rather the object of analysis is condidered to be the "irreducible diversity of social relations involving dependency and/or conflict."[106] Elsewhere Reynaud tells that

labor conflicts involve concrete social groups, bound together by shared values and feelings of solidarity that cannot be called anything but class values and class feelings. It is imperative, however, to speak of class struggles in the plural. That the kinds of conflict are many cannot be explained merely by saying that, while there is but one underlying process, there are within that process many different 'situations.' In fact there are many objectives, many issues involved in the kinds of conflict in question here, and these cannot be specified in advance. It is this variety of objectives that is resonsible for the variety we observe in labor conflict. (ST, pp. 107–108)[107]

Doubtless it could be argued that by sticking this much to details, one loses sight of the essential. But the real question is whether the essential—whatever it may be: logic of accumulation or rational investment in human capital—really enables one to explain social change in all the places where it can be observed, within the factory as well as in society at large. If we concentrate on the essential can we ever hope to provide a specific theory of social change that is not merely an a posteriori modification of a core theory accepted as true a priori but later altered to fit whatever factual findings turn up? Is this not the case with the treatment of discrimination and informational capital in neoclassical economics or with Aglietta's theory of structural forms? Adam and Reynaud put it this way: "General economic, political, and cultural factors are too enduring and too far-reaching to explain in detail what happens in industrial conflict in each factory. The problem is not whether the general theories are valid; it is clear that their very generality makes them unfit to explain industrial relations in detail."[108] It is one thing to notice that there exist general constraints obscured by tradiional market analyses. It is another to erect those constraints into a rigidly deterministic theory, indeed a theory that cannot withstand scrutiny, given the wide variations that exist among countries, regions, industries, and firms. These variations indicate that other factors are at works, and unless we understand what those factors are, we cannot hope to obtain a unified comprehension of the whole system, with its abundant variety.

How, then, is this variety to be understood? For Adam and Reynaud the game theory paradigm provides the key. Labor conflict develops according to a logic of its own. To study it, one must resort to "dialectical analysis of the interactions among various strategies, each of which has a unique character and function. Strategy confronts strategy and in the process something new—a new structure—is created, even when what seems to be going on is a mere repetitive ritual" (PUF, p. 236). But social conflict is in fact an ongoing game. The results of one contest establish the preconditions of the next. Furthermore the game is mixed rather than purely competitive: "Some outcomes are preferable to others for both parties. If this assertion seems open to doubt, the following, related one will hot: Some outcomes will be rejected by both parties in favor of others" (PUF, p. 132). In social conflict, moreover, information is imperfect; the aim is not to maximize reward but merely to obtain improvement in the situation. Finally, the actors in the game are complex; there may be unstable alliances, or new players may appear on the scene. The stakes may vary during the course of the contest, and even the rules may change. The game is not fixed but floating. "Thus we move out of the sharply defined world of game theory and into the amorphous, fuzzy world of social processess" (PUF, p. 181).

The problem with this method of analysis is that although it takes social action for its object, it claims to be relatively independent of the characteristics of the actors. This is where we part company with the proponents of strategic analysis. They look upon conflict as a decision-making process involving actors obedient to different, not to say antagonistic, forms of rationality. But what they analyze is an activity: "In order to analyze and predict behavior in conflict (as well as the timing and extent of the conflict itself), it is reasonable to assume that the actors want something, that they have an objective and that they will cast about for the most efficient way to attain that objective, that is, in short, that they are rational (where by rational we mean a goal-directed activity employing means appropriate to the desired goal)" (PUF, p. 119).

This may strike one as reminiscent of Lionel Robbins's description of economic activity as one of finding the most appropriate use of scarce means to achieve diverse ends. But Adam and Reynaud draw a contrast between their view and that of the economists, a contrast they consider fundamental: "Under certain conditions it is permissible to speak of a unique form of economic rationality. But in speaking of social actors one must speak of forms of rationality in the plural.... This is not an unfortunate feature of the situation in one particular country, peculiar, say, to France and its divided society, even if that society typifies the general case. It is a fundamental social fact ... a characteristic of most societies (and most probably of all societies larger than a village or tribe that are not completely static)" (PUF, pp. 122–23). The authors' intention emerges clearly from the fact that they mention the pluralism of forms of rationality almost in the same breath with nonstatic societies. Conflict, they would argue, functions as an instrument of social change. Changing coalitions of actors, guided by various forms of rationality, enter into temporary compromises. It is the essence of this situation that nothing is stable—not the issues, not the actors, and not the outcome of their interaction. Take the work force, for example. At any moment its ranks may be swelled by an influx of new workers: immigrants, women, children, or others. This may upset any themporary compromise between workers and management. Social conflict must therefore be analyzed as an ongoing process within society. New objectives and new groups of social actors may emerge at any moment in a more or less contingent manner. The object of analysis is the process, the action. The actors engaged in this process at any moment may be "concrete social groups" (ST, p. 107), but still they are contingent. Adam and Reynaud do stress the importance of determining the characteristics of each group: "What each group asserts is not merely its own 'special interests' but also its intrinsic characteristics, its forms of cohesion, or again, to borrow Renaud Sainsaulieu's term, its identity" (ST, p. 103). Still, the actor plays a secondary role in the analysis: "The actors are usually complex.... We focus not on a man or a collectivity but rather on an action" (PUF, p. 119).

In contrast we do not believe that strategies and actions can be understood without studying the actors. Furthermore we believe that the characteristics of the actors in any society are largely predetermined and stable. As for workers, their place in the firm is explained by the interaction between socialization and organization, the kind of union organization they prefer, the kinds of alliance into which they are willing to enter with other groups, and their relations with their employer and their union. The firm too is shaped by the interaction between socialization and organization and in turn helps to shape the qualifications of its employees. It further affects the loyalty or hostility of its workers.

Accordingly, when explaining relations between different occupational groups, we rely largely on the identity of the actors, which we believe is determined prior to the action we are trying to explain. Socialization shapes action, in our view. It also shapes the rules that govern action, largely by influencing the nature of what we have called the collective action domain. In other words industrial action is shaped not internally but externally, and this is why it varies from one country to another. The actor cannot be reduced to his immediate action alone.

In our view the industrial relations system is not as autonomous as the strategic analysts think. To put it in a rather provocative way, the industrial relations system is incapable of explaining industrial relations because the effects of the educational system and the organizational system must also be taken into account. Before industrial relations can be studied, one must first study how the actors acquire the features of their identity that remain fairly stable over time and, further, how the collective action domain is shaped.

If, in theory, the number of possible strategies is infinite, the collective action domain winnows the number of genuine possibilities. This winnowing determines the shape of the actual industrial relations system. The fact that in a given country the same strategies are used repeatedly merely provides historical confirmation, but no explanation, of the fact that the actors in that country have their own specific identity and the pertinent domains their own determinate shape.

Notes

Chapter 1

1. Foremen are included in the white-collar category.

2. In section 3 of this chapter we will give a more detailed description of the various credentials and corresponding training levels in each country. In the first two sections the following terminology will be used: basic occupational training, which normally qualifies a worker for industry, up to a skilled position, culminates in the award of what we shall call the basic apprenticeship certificate. In France this is officially designated the Certificat d'aptitude professionnelle (CAP). Between this level of certification and a college degree is another level of certification, whcih we shall call intermediate-level occupational certification. For schooling below the college level, there are three kinds of diplomas in both countries. The highest level is the baccalauréat in France and the Abitur in Germany. [We shall refer to both as the baccalaureate—Trans.] The next lower degree is called the Mittle Reife in Germany and the Brevet d'études du premier cycle (BEPC) in France. The lowest-level diploma is called the Certificat d'études primaires (CEP) in France, The German counterpart is the Hauptschule graduate. The statistical basis of our information is contained in the two 1970 studies mentioned in the introduction.

3. In Germany there are four kinds of intermediate certificates. In ascending rank order, they are the professional school certificate, the foreman's certificate, the technician's certificate, and the graduate engineer's certificate (the so-called graduate engineers are engineers without college degrees).

4. In France intermediate-level occupational training leads to the award of one of several kinds of certification: brevets professionnels, brevets d'enseignement industriel, baccalauréats de techniciens, or diplômes de techniciens supérieurs.

5. "Capacity to structure" can also be used in connection with other variables, both individual and collective, such as experience, social background, and general educational level.

6. These results cannot be drawn directly from table 1.1 because we did not indicate the general educational level of workers holding occupational certification. By way of example, the 50 percent mentioned here are divided as follows: 41 percent have no occupational certification, 8.7 percent have a CAP (of the 31.2 percent), and 0.3 percent (of 1.9 percent) have intermediate-level professional certification.

7. In 1970 nearly 25 percent of workers without any school diploma or with nothing more than a CAP had attended secondary school. It is likely that a much higher percentage of w-c workers have attended secondary schools.

8. In contrast to France, the gap between w-c and b-c workers in Germany is considerable.

9. In the firms we studied we distinguished five categories of workers: (1) management personnel; (2) w-c workers not classed as management personnel but carrying out high-level technical or leadership functions (includes shop foreman, technical and maintenance foreman, and office supervisors, whom we shall refer to as supervisory staff); (3) other w-c workers who will be referred to as nonsupervisory staff; (4) skilled workers; and (5) unskilled workers.

10. In this subsection we shall be making extensive use of the 1972 study mentioned in the introduction (some of the tables contained in this study have been published; others have not).

11. These include petroleum refining, cement, basic chemicals, and metal production. Sectors of the first type include cotton, rubber, shoes, and foodstuffs. The last ratio in table 1.2 (6/3), calculated by using the figures for average seniority in row 1, yields 1.07 for sectors in which the work force is stable and 1.30 for sectors in which it is unstable (the overall industrial average is 1.20)

12. The average seniority ratio for all industry (column 3) is 1.54 , with extremes of 1.70 and 1.20 for the highest and lowest sectors, respectively. In Germany the corresponding figures are 1.28, 1.15, and 1.38. We find similar results when we compare the two countries by company size.

13. See table 1.1.

14. The difference in the percentage of workers who attended secondary school is even more marked when we compare industry with the tertiary sector in Germany (12 percent versus 37 percent. This enhances the uniqueness of German industry's position: industry employs mainly workers who have received a certain kind of occupational training after leaving school (see section 3 of this cahpter).

15. This identification is no doubt more marked in industry than in the tertiary sector, where the training of workers is more diversified.

16. In Germany students who fail to make this hurdle can hope to succeed in the system of occupational training.

17. J. P. Daubigney and J.-J. Silvestre, "Comparaison de hiérarchies des salaires entre l'Allemagne et la France," report prepared on behalf of the Centre d'Etudes des Revenus et des Coûts, mimeographed (Aix: Laboratoire d'economie et de sociologie du travail, December 1972); and J.-J. Silvestre, "Comparaison de structures de salaires et d'emplois entre les deux groupes d'entreprises," *Revue internationale du travail* (December 1974).

18. J. Bouteiller and J.-J. Silvestre, "Hiérarchie des salaires et structures d'emploi: comparaisons internationales," in *Questions sur le travail industriel* (GRESI, Ministry of Industry, Commerce, and Crafts, July 1977).

19. The percentage of workers classed as unskilled but nevertheless holding some kind of credential is smaller in the under-thirty-five age group (18 percent) than in the over-thirty-five group (26 percent). These older workers find that the skills they acquired when they received their training have become obsolete.

20. This difference is much less marked in Germany, which makes the fact that the relationship between age and qualification of workers is reversed when we move from Germany to France even more paradoxical.

21. The first figure in parentheses is the value of the index in France, the second its value in Germany.

22. One might equally employ the now standard distinction between primary and secondary sectors.

23. J. Bouteiller and J.-J. Silvestre, "Structures industrielles, marché du travail et différences de salaires. Le cas de la France et de l'Allemagne," *Les Annales de l'INSEE* (December 1974).

24. D. Marsden and C. Saunders, *Pay Inequalities in the European Community* (London: Butterworths, 1981).

25. The coefficient of variation of the average b-c worker's wage is 16.5 percent in France compared with only 7.5 percent in Germany.

26. These workers account for only 8 percent of the w-c work force in Germany compared with 33 percent of the b-c work force.

27. The group we earlier referred to as management personnel (see section 1 of this chapter).

28. In this group we can also include a fair proportion of workers holding intermediate-level credentials of relatively low level (such as brevet d' enseignement industriel and brevet professionnel).

29. The significance of this figure may not be fully apparent. Intermediate-and higher-level certifications are rare in sales and administrative departments in German industry, where the highest positions can be attained by workers equipped with no more than a clerical apprenticeship certificate. This suggests that the

number of technical employees having intermediate credentials is much higher than 42 percent.

30. In absolute terms foremen in the two countries have approximately equal seniority. But the proportion of foremen differs, as does the ratio of the average seniority of foremen to that of workers, which is higher in France.

31. The firms considered in study 2.

32. Here we encounter the effect of one of the fundamental differences between the two countries. The wage gap in France is wider overall and systematically wider at each step in the skill structure and hierarchy: skilled to unskilled workers (1.29–1.15), office employees to skilled workers (1.43–1.25), foremen to skilled workers (1.38–1.27), and management personnel to office employees (1.80–1.34).

33. See especially chapter 4, where we treat the social effect and the national effect.

34. This information is drawn from a study carried out by the Institut national des études démographiques (INED). The major results have been published in INED, *Population et l'Enseignement* (Paris: Presses universitaires de France, 1970).

35. In France, not only can students move from track 2 into track 3, but even students in track 1 have some chance of entering track 3. This is totally ruled out in Germany.

36. Occupational training is offered one day a week to youths who leave primary school at fourteen or fifteen without prusuing a full-time school program. It is not available to those enrolled in a full-time school or occupational training program.

37. Seven percent of those who graduate from elementary school enter a full-time occupational training program.

38. These pupils are generally those who failed to obtain an elementary school diploma. They come mainly from the most underprivileged classes.

39. We shall deal mainly with occupational training for industrial workers in the remainder of the book. Whenever we talk about training for w-c workers, explicit mention of the fact will be made.

40. Note, moreover, that in Germany large firms may be institutionally associated with small craft shops. Hence it can be assumed that nearly 50 percent of all apprentices are trained in medium to large firms.

41. If the number of students who have difficulty in secondary school amounts to 70 percent of the total, then we find that 40 percent continue in school beyond the age of sixteen by repeating one or more years, 12 percent go to work, and 18 percent (that is, 25 percent of this particular group) take up short-term occupational training. This 25 percent figure should be compared with the 72 percent of German youths who do not go on to college after completing secondary school but sign up for a worker or clerical apprenticeship program.

42. The numher of apprentices decreased during the period 1967–1972 while France was enjoying exceptionally high economic growth.

43. Generally referred to as in-house training, this is not limited to manual workers.

44. This heterogeneity is not incompatible with the fact that one finds a large number of youths from underprivileged social classes both in track 2 and among those prematurely eliminated from secondary schooling.

45. We defined this training earlier as being situated between basic apprenticeship and university training (which in France includes the so-called grandes écoles as well as the universities).

46. C. Baudelot and R. Establet, *L'école capitaliste en France* (Paris: Maspero, n.d.), pp. 213–214.

47. Based on the INED study cited above. Recall that in section 1 we noted that 58 percent of French supporting staff personnel working in offices attended secondary school, compared with only 28 percent in Germany.

48. Another difference whose significance is similar can be found by calculating the ratio of percentages of workers' children: the result is 0.72 for France compared with 0.56 for Germany.

49. These remarks are valid for the period 1950–1970, which interests us here. Recent changes in the French and German educational system may require some modifications in the details of our description, but we do not think that our general conclusions will require serious alteration.

50. Here we are mainly interested in scientific and technical training.

51. The point that there is only one hierarchy in France, and therefore only one educational elite, can be illustrated by the following anecdote. When the Barre government decided to upgrade French technical education, the only policy it could come up with was to make it easier for the best pupils in the technical high schools to enter the grandes écoles.

52. In Germany, when a child completes elementary school at age ten, the choice of his or her educational future is formally left to the parents. This is not the case in France.

53. Here we are using the unpublished results of a study carried out in 1973 by the Statistical Office of the European Economic Community (Common Market) concerning worker mobility in the period 1972–1973 (= "1973 work force study").

54. The study mentioned in n. 53 shows that in 1972–1973 47 percent of all job changes in France and 34 percent in Germany were made by workers who already held jobs in industry.

55. It was not possible to compare mobility of workers between the secondary and tertiary sectors by type of credential held. The indexes used here allow us only to make conjectures about such movements. However, the magnitude of the observed differences between the two countries lends credence to these conjectures.

56. The relative stability or instability of the work force is a matter for individual behavioral analysis as well as labor market analysis. The same dualism exists in the analysis of mobility between occupational categories.

57. We shall have more to say later about what we mean by forms of socialization. But the example of German apprenticeship shows that a form of socialization is characterized not only by the capacities that the workers subjected to it acquire but also by the kinds of social relations in which they become involved as a result of undergoing the form of socialization in question.

58. We were unable to gather systematic data about these various tendencies in France. The lack of such data is a characteristic feature of the system we are describing. Similarly the importance of seniority, about which we shall have more to say later, is another form of indirect proof of our contentions.

59. These results vary from industry to industry. In energy, chemicals, and the extractive industries, the differences are considerable. In metals they are not so pronounced. Caution is in order here, however, because the sample on which these figures are based is very small.

60. We shall have more to say later about this important difference, which can be related to the fact that many w-c workers as well as craftsmen hold the foreman's license, required in particular to train apprentices, In France most of the mobility between the wage-earning and non–wage-earning groups of the work force consists of movements back and forth from the category of independent craftsmen to that of skilled workers in industry.

61. Over a five-year period, the overall mobility rate in this area was 50 percent higher in France than in Germany.

62. These effects are all the more pronounced because it is mainly the most highly qualified workers who are likely to quit industrial jobs.

63. Here we are considering only workers who actually received come kind of certification at the end of their training. As for workers who took various kinds of refresher courses or enrolled in programs to upgrade their skills, the rates (observed between 1965 and 1970) are as follows: 18.8 percent of all workers in Germany compared with only 6 percent in France. The broadening of adult education in France since 1971 had undoubtedly reduced this difference. But we do not think that the recent changes in French law in this regard have had much of an impact on the percentage of workers holding professional credentials.

64. The acquistion of this level of certification often coincides with a worker's leaving the firm with which he began his career.

65. In German firms where we were able to gather data of this type, we found that, foremen aside, nearly 80 percent of those in low-to middle-management positions who had had some kind of occupational tranining during the course of their careers were working for a firm other than the one for which they were working when they began that training.

66. The absolute percentage figures are greatly influenced by the jobs structures in the two countries and by the distribution of types of credentials. On the other hand, one can draw significant conclusions by comparing the gap between the under-thirty-five and over-thirty-five groups in both places.

67. This 9 percent difference is very important; remember that the percentage of nonproductive workers among all workers with more than ten years' seniority is on the order of 25 percent.

68. In particular, see L. Mallet, *Les modalités d'accès aux emplois*, Bibliothèque du CEREQ, vol. 2 (1974); and the collective work, *L'accès aux emplois de la mobilité professionnelle*, Bibliothèque du CEREQ, no. 12 (1979).

69. In large industrial firms (those employing more than 1000 workers), the percentage of w-c workers is 33 percent in France and 26 percent in Germany. In small firms (fewer than 1000 employees), the figures are 19 percent and 17 percent, respectively. In branches where the work force is most stable (petroleum, chemicals, cement, metal fabrication), the percentages of w-c workers are 36.5 percent in France and 28 percent in Germany. The percentages of w-c workers are the same in both countries, 23 percent, in sectors where work-force turnover (particularly among b-c workers) is most rapid: textiles, shoes, rubber, foodstuffs.

70. This is not incompatible with the fact that the situation allows for upward mobility for some workers capable of adapting to its demands.

71. Around 75 percent of management personnel in French firms hold college degrees, compared with only 30 percent in Germany.

72. This does not rule out the need for looking at each dimension independently in order to bring out what is unique about each and what kinds of interaction may occur.

73. Here we are using the term *qualification* in a very broad sense. Included under this head are criteria governing access to jobs, technical competence, leadership ability, and ability to get along in specific kinds of shop floor organizational environments.

74. For example, table 1.9 shows that 77 percent of college graduates in Germany hold jobs outside industry, compared with only 45 percent in France.

75. As we are using the term *domain* or *span* here, it refers to the characteristic features revealed bu empirical investigation, in particular the continuities, discontinuities, and interactions we have been discussing throughout this chapter. We shall go into greater detail about the theoretical meaning of this term in subsequent chapters.

76. This is the sort of conclusion to which we might have been led had we chosen to construct a multivariate econometric model.

77. Education and experience are important determinants of the worker's professional status as manifested on the French labor market. It bears emphasizing that these are a priori objective characteristics, neutral with regard to occupational classification.

78. Here it is probably worth drawing a distinction between the German case, in which the influence of what is usually called social origin is modified by the force of occupational classifications, and the French case, in which social origin operates through variables such as educational achievement, which are presumably universalistic in character and less directly related to occupational factors.

Chapter 2

1. Existing theories, whether economic or sociological, were not very useful for explaining our results.

2. Interested readers may wish to consult our research note, which reports on the most important results of these monographic studies: M. Maurice, F. Sellier, and J.-J. Silvestre, "La production de la hiérarchie dans l'entreprise: recherche d'un effet sociétal, comparaison France-Allemagne" (Aix-en-Provence: LEST, 1977), esp. part 2, pp. 189–614.

3. Since some of the firms studied were quite large, having a number of different plants, research for the monographs was carried out in part at the corporate headquarters, in part at one or more of the affiliated plants.

4. Joan Woodward, ed., *Industrial Organization: Behavior and Control* (Oxford: Oxford University Press, 1970). See also Jean-Daniel Reynaud, "Conflits du travail, classes sociales et contrôle social," *Sociologie du travail* 1 (1980): 109; and Dominique Monjardet, "La variable technologie dans les études d'organisations," in *Nouvelles fomres d'organisation du travail* (Paris: Bibliothéque du CEREQ, 1976).

5. Joan Woodward, *Industrial Organization: Theory and Practice* (Oxford: Oxford University Press, 1965).

6. The second category (nonmanagement w-c workers, and clerical help) includes all w-c workers and technicians who do not give orders to other workers. Manage-

ment personnel includes supervisors, technicians, and w-c personnel who do exercise authority. Also included under this head are managers.

7. As the question of wage differences was at the beginning of our work.

8. Grouping positions in this way is justifiable, we think, since technical personnel can in large part substitute directly for productive personnel, and administrative personnel can substitute for management personnel in many of their economic and social management functions.

9. Although a large degree of contingency remained. Recent experiments with reorganizing systems of production, though limited in extent, show this quite clearly. There is no one best way to construct an automobile or a typewriter.

10. A number of students of German society have reached the same conclusion: that occupational training is an important issue for labor, management, and government. J.-D. Reynaud even suggests that it is the basis of what he calls the joint regulation system involving both labor and management, which he says is characteristic of industrial relations in Germany. See Reynaud, "Conflits du travail," p. 373.

11. Since the recent crisis, Germany, like other countries, has tried new forms of labor rationalization, particularly in conjunction with new technologies. Will this lead to a deskilling of the work force, as some German sociologists and labor leaders think, and will it undermine the current system of occupational training? It is too soon to say. It is worth noting, however, that there has in recent years been growing debate about the training system. There seems to be some sentiment in favor of reducing the practical portion of the training and increasing the theoretical or classroom portion. This has aroused opposition from industry, some businessmen apparently feeling that it would lead to a reduction in the qualification of the work force.

12. The history of occupational training in France shows that originally there was some hesitation whether training programs should be connected with industry or with the school system. Within a very short period, however, the school system obtained complete control over occupational training.

13. This is confirmed by the results of experiments at restructuring the work process that have been carried out in recent years in most of the industrialized countries. These experiments have frequently shown that work can be organized in different ways around the same technology. Also changes in organizational structure have in some cases led to changes in the technology itself.

14. To borrow from the results of a study carried out under the direction of J.-D. Reynaud, "Evolution de l'autorité dans l'entreprise industrielle," in *Entreprise et Personnel* (1971): 15–16 cited by Michel Brossard in "La structure de l'organisation du travail dans l'entreprise et les pouvoirs dans le système de relations indus-

trielles" (thesis, troisième cycle, in the Faculté des Sciences Economiques, Université d'Aix-Marseille II, 1977), p. 43.

15. These social conditions have often been seen as major obstacles to attempts to restructure the organization of work.

16. In relation to general education, which is considered to be the predominant, socially legitimate system.

17. Here we are partially reiterating an analysis of the work system previously published by us in "La production de la hiérarchie dans l'entreprise: recherche d'un effet sociétal. Comparaison France-Allemagne," *Revue française de sociologie* 20 (1979): 347.

18. Although there are in Germany 467 Lernberufe (trades for which there is an officially recognized apprenticeship, not all of them industrial trades), labor statistics make it possible to identify a core group of basic occupations around which other trades seem to be organized (these include lathe operators, tool and die makers, mechanics, and electronics technicians). For the most part these basic trades can be employed by any firm. See "Berufswege und Arbeitsmarkt" (Nürnberg: Institut fur Arbeitsmarkt und Berufsforschung, 1976), pp. 30–33.

19. In the 1960s, 68 percent of the students in a given age group enrolled in some kind of apprenticeship program, 53 percent of them in the industrial trades.

20. See Maurice, Sellier, and Silvestre, "Production de la hiérarchie."

21. Actually there are four complete crews in each production unit in order to allow for time off in each rotation cycle.

22. Polyvalence is not only found in connection with process production technology. It seems to be closely associated with the emphasis placed on apprenticeship and skill development. It concerns both skilled and semiskilled workers (or angelernte Arbeiter as they are called in Germany, that is, workers who have opted for the two-year-apprenticeship program and who are found mainly in plants using line production technology).

23. The German firm described here was established in 1957.

24. Serge Mosovici, in his *Essai sur l'histoire humaine de la nature* (Paris: Flammaion, 1963), pp. 429–436, has used the work of historians of science and technology to demonstrate the existence of profound differences between chemical engineers and mechanical engineers. The chemical engineer is more a scientist interested in applied science and research and development. By contrast, mechanical engineering is a profession that developed out of the skilled crafts.

25. Duncan Gallie, *In Search of the New Working Class: Automation and Social Integration within the Capitalist Enterprise* (Cambridge: Cambridge University Press, 1978), p. 100.

26. A study carried out along the same lines as our own, done in England shortly after we did our work, turned up significant differences in the organization and operation of similar firms (especially in petrochemicals) in Germany, England, and France. See M. Maurice, A. Sorge, and M. Warner, "Societal Differences in Organizing Manufacturing Units: A Comparison of France, West Germany, and Great Britain," *Organization Studies* 1 (1980).

27. Gallie, *In Search of the New Working Class*, pp. 98—99, discusses this in connection with French and British petroleum refineries in the period after 1960.

28. Other observations made in the same plant confirm this point.

29. The limitations imposed on our research did not allow us to measure the relative productivity of various categories of worker. Still we can conjecture that, assuming comparable overall productivity levels, the specific productivity of b-c workers in German firms is higher than that of their French counterparts. The difference is compensated by the larger number of supervisors in France, particularly direct and indirect production supervisors. Here, indirect production supervisors mainly work for techincal departments that do production design and planning.

30. Since the 1975—1976 crisis, German firms in some branches where rationalization is particularly important have been employing more semiskilled workers. This development has provoked reactions on the part of the unions. It has not always been welcomed enthusiastically by supervisory personnel and even some officials of the chambers of commerce and industry, who see it as a potential threat to the enhancement of the general level of qualification in the work force.

31. The technology used in France and Germany is quite similar. Tooling must be changed with each new series. The delivery deadlines laid down by auto manufacturers are very short. Two kinds of jobs require the most skill: adjustment of machinery after new tooling has been installed and quality control at each stage of production to ensure compliance with government-imposed auto safety standards.

32. German shift leaders have more responsibility and more autonomy than their French counterparts. They decide where to assign assembly line workers, supervise retooling, and fill in for the Meister on Saturday overtime shifts or when the Meister is absent.

33. Recall that the coefficients are used to scale up the minimum wages fixed by collective bargaining (at the national or, in some cases, regional level) for each category of job (production worker, w-c worker, technician, foreman, engineer, and manager).

34. A report on working conditions prepared in 1971 by a committee of the CNPF (the leading French business organization) drew this parallel, pointing out the tendency toward "bureaucratization" of industry resulting from the application of the French classificational system (which was first adopted in 1945 and is known as

the Parodi system). See J.-D. Reynaud, *Les syndicats en France* (Paris: Editions du Seuil, 1975), 2: 206–207.

35. Ibid., p. 221. The assignment of coefficients is as important a factor in the firm's organization as the number of employees. No modification may be made to the organization chart without the express consent of top management. Any proposal to change coefficients or job descriptions must be approved by the board of directors.

36. More recently some petrochemical firms have tried to encourage polyvalence in order to overcome certain maintenance problems. French firms have relied on subcontractors to do this work more commonly than their British and German counterparts, even when the companies in question were all subsidiaries of the same multinational. But certain problems associated with subcontracting have led some French firms to resort to polyvalence in the hope of more effectively integrating production and maintenance work. See Raymond Galle, "La socialisation du travail dans les installation sutomatisés à feu continu: le cas du raffinage pétrolier" (Aix-en-Provence: 1980) Laboratoire d'Economie et de Sociologie du Travail, (submitted as a thesis to the Université d'Aix-Marseille II).

37. This firm administers psychological tests to newly hired workers in order to assess their potential.

38. They were awarded a coefficient of 185, which gave them the right to participate in the management retirement fund, a right frequently coveted by skilled workers.

39. This opinion was offered when the interviewer asked whether it was possible for polyvalent workers to become shift leaders.

40. Proof by contradiction of an opinion widespread among polyvalent workers themselves. As one CGT delegate told the interviewer, polyvalent workers want "a guarantee that they will be assigned work in keeping with their qualifications, whereas now they can actually be assigned to any operator's job."

41. Status groups can create solidarity of this kind. It is no accident that the most powerful unions in France are in the government bureaucracy and in firms where workers are protected by the state.

42. This introduces two new echelons into the organizational structure of the shop, situated between the shift leader and the assembly line workers.

43. In the French case the parent firm was a tire manufacturer. In the German case it was a large metals conglomerate. In both cases the hubs were destined for major automobile manufacturers.

44. An experiment with hiring men who held the CAP proved a failure. "We were soon forced to assign them to tool and die making or maintenance jobs. It is more

and more common for workers who have the machinist's CAP not to be satisfied with working in their trade in the shop or even with becoming tool-and-die makers. They all want to be sales engineers."

45. Two shop supervisors and four foremen were promoted from semiskilled worker to head mechanic, chief mechanic, foreman, and finally (in two cases) to shop supervisors. Access to supervisory positions follows a different course in French and German firms.

46. We observed three companies most closely: two in France, one employing 2086 workers, the other 3797, and one in Germany, employing 1695 workers. Within these companies we compared plants of approximately the same size, each employing about 1000 workers. These companies were subsidiaries of large industrial conglomerates, employing about 45,000 workers in the French case and 60,000 in the German case.

47. It was probably all of these requirements taken together that induced these companies, French and German, to train part of their own work force themselves, which required setting up an in-house apprenticeship program more common in Germany than in France.

48. Here *qualification* is used in a sense somewhat different from the formal one, which relates to the criteria on which the system of classification is based. Something closer to "professional status" is meant.

49. It may be assumed, however, that the skill factor influences worker strategies. For example, in the tobacco plants studied by Michel Crozier, is it not the skill factor that determines the position of the maintenance workers in relation to the production workers and the chief engineer?

50. The skill factor and the work domain react to one another. The skills of the workers help to shape the work domain, which in turn helps to shape skills.

51. Master workers were found previously in industries that used highly skilled labor. However, recently, in connection with efforts to upgrade the status of manual labor, the idea of the master worker has been revived in order to provide a goal that a worker who amasses considerable seniority may hope to attain, even if he cannot count on moving up to the rank of foreman, w-c employee, or technician. It seems likely that these recent measures will make the status of master worker more common than in the past.

52. In another plant recently brought by merger under the same corporate management as the plant described here (which as yet has no master workers), even skilled workers are not allowed to run numerically controlled machine tools. As one production manager told us, "I can't trust a man who is not competent to run a numerically controlled machine that costs a couple of hundred thousand dollars. These machines are really operated by the foreman in conjunction with a technician under the supervision of a young engineer."

53. Again this was no isolated initiative. The chief industrial engineer in this company told us that "the idea of using 'demonstrators' is spreading like wildfire in France, particularly in the heavy machinery business." If this particular plant led the way, the productivity gains achieved (men-machines) persuaded others within the same company to follow suit.

54. The chief industrial engineer tole us that seven to eight years were needed to identify such men.

55. Very large-scale machine tools that cost about $5000 per hour to run. This company owns a dozen machines of this type, in some cases the only ones in France.

56. Still more explicitly, one production executive told us that "a demonstrator is a kind of commando we can send in to cut time requirements by 30 to 40 percent."

57. Executives admit that this exists and say that it has to do in part with the ambiguous nature of the relationship between demonstrators and supervisors.

58. Constituting a kind of shop work bonus, one way of responding to the downgrading of manual labor.

59. The Technical Planning Department (which is under the supervision of a product group manager) calculates the amount of time allocated for each type of job and schedules the use of each machine. A computer is used to figure out the optimal scheduling for each facility.

60. The foremen, after negotiating with the production manager sign a compact committing themselves to meet the deadlines and the to adhere to the planned schedule. This document is the final arbiter in case of dispute or delay. If deadlines are not met, the demonstrators are sent in rather than changing the schedule by the required hierarchical channels. Where large-scale machine tools are not involved, subcontracting is sometimes preferred, which is rarely the case in Germany.

61. In companies organized as Gemeinschaftsbehandlungen (GmbH, or limited partnerships), there are usually three managing executives, one of whom is the Geschäftsführer technik (equivalent to the vice-president in charge of production).

62. A timekeeper from the technical planning department is assigned to each shop, and in many cases he is authorized to mark a particular worker down as requiring extra time to do a given job (with the consent of the shop foreman). This allows the issue to be treated at the shop level rather than passed along through hierarchical channels as in French firms.

63. Peter Lawrence, in *Managers and Management in West Germany*. (New York: St. Martin's Press, 1980), p. 144, shows how technical functions ancillary to production tend to become "integrated into the production hierarchy": those in charge of the technical departments usually report to production executives rather than to the vice-president for engineering.

64. Information on this subject is provided in the next chapter.

65. The other element is the high value placed on training (Bildung).

66. The principle is "to each according to his work, or his productivity." This is defended by the unions themselves and is not without influence on the way they look at wage policies, as is shown by the following statement of M. Loderer, president of I. G. Metall: "There is nothing wrong with bringing those at the bottom of the scale along a little faster than the rest, but complete equality is out of the question: we remain firmly committed to the Leistungsprinzip" (interview with Paul Fabra in *Le Monde*, 23–24 April 1978, p. 21).

67. It is hard to get accurate information on this subject from the firms. In part, subcontracting involves a portion of the work force, the need for which varies with the changing requirements of the firm. But subcontracted workers also have a different status within the firm from that of regular workers, and this is sometimes used to keep down labor costs by avoiding raises and social benefits that must be paid to regular workers. According to an executive in one French petrochemical firm, the number of temporary and subcontracted workers employed (in 1975) was around 250, almost equal to the number of regular employees.

68. Gallie's comparative study, *In Search*, provides further information on the subject of maintenance organization in English and French oil refineries (see pp. 110, 233, 310).

69. A recent comparative study of French and German machine building pointed out that German firms were less likely than French firms to resort to subcontracting. Can this be regarded as an effect of the greater value attached to production in German firms and of the greater cooperation one finds among technical and manufacturing departments in Germany? See Jacques Perrin and Bernard Real, *L'industrie des biens d'équipement mécanique et l'engineering en France et en Allemagne de l'Ouest* (Grenoble: IREP, 1976), 2: 256.

70. Lawrence, *Managers and Management*, p. 144, points out that it has recently become common in German firms to have both manufacturing and maintenance under the supervision of a single manager, the production manager, who supervises the shop supervisors and the maintenance supervisors.

71. One maintenance technician told us during an interview, "The fellows in production think they're superior because they produce and therefore make the money that is used to pay the rest of us." It should be noted, however, that the recent trend toward replacing chemical engineers who are college graduates with nonuniversity-trained graduate engineers should, according to those we interviewed, help to reduce tensions between manufacturing and maintenance departments because the men in charge of both will then have similar training.

72. The Prokurist is legally invested with the authority to sign fairly significant

contracts. The title is sometimes awarded as an honorific to certain high-level managers. It carries with it financial benefits upon retirement.

73. For example, in the two firms most comparable in terms of size and type of production, maintenance supervisors accounted for 46 percent of all supervisors in the German firm and for only 16 percent in the French firm. By contrast, production supervisors accounted for 41 percent of the total in France and 28 percent in Germany.

74. In the period just prior to our study, he was providing advanced training to around 150 engineers and technicians and was planning a new training program for skilled workers in the department.

75. The kinds of cooperation between manufacturing and maintenance described here for one petrochemical plant are also found in the metals processing plants we studied, though in somewhat different forms. In particular, the maintenance departments in these firms helped to prepare tooling and to upgrade existing machinery.

76. Some firms have tried to foster worker polyvalence in order to enable workers to do routine maintenance and repair breakdowns right in the production shop.

77. Besides our own observations in German firms (confirmed by the IREP study cited in n. 69, in the case of the machine building industry), Duncan Gallie claims that his studies of oil refineries in France and England show that maintenance is more efficient in the French firms. He explains this, however, by arguing that French management controls maintenance work more closely than it is possible for English management to do, given the work rules laid down by British craft unions. This suggests that craft unionism in England has impeded the use of subcontracting, which French unions are relatively powerless to prevent.

78. Stoppages are costly in capital-intensive industries in which technology rapidly becomes obsolete.

79. In reality the maintenance manager is more uder the control of corporate headquarters than of the plant manager.

80. Previously there were often too many maintenance personnel. The new organization shifts the burden onto the subcontractor.

81. Echoes of these conflicts are frequently heard at union meetings. As one unionized employee of this firm told us, "At informational meetings for all personnel you have to be very careful when you mention either maintenance or production, because you get the feeling that one false step can arouse two hostile armies!"

82. See especially the representative article by Clark Kerr, John T. Dunlop, Frederick Harbison, and Charles A. Meyers, "Industrialism and World Society: The Road to Similarity," *Harvard Business Review* (January–February 1961).

83. Job access is not determined solely by formal rules laid down by collective bargaining agreements or specified in terms of credentials. Labor management and training policies also play a part.

84. *Achievement*, as the term is used in English, has a rather similar connotation [authors' note].

85. We shall have more to say later about the recent reform in the training of graduate engineers. On this subject see lalso chapter 1.

86. See especially Weltz, Schmidt, and Sass, *Facharbeiter im Industriebetrieb* (Frankfurt, 1974) and Gunther Bechtle, "Organizzazion e produttività nella Republica Federale Tedesca," *Industria e Sindicato* 22 (1980): 15.

87. The rate of social reproduction of skilled workers in Germany is higher than that of their French counterparts: 61 percent of German skilled workers are children of skilled workers, compared with 46.7 percent in France.

88. This is a general characteristic of professionalization. Every profession tends to reproduce itself, especially by exerting control over the admission of new members.

89. This at what emerges from Weltz, Schmidt, and Sass, *Facharbeiter im Industriebetrieb*.

90. This form of apprenticeship, which has been growing in importance, is organized nationally by the chambers of commerce and industry. The program lasts two years rather than the three and a half years required for a regular certification in a skill.

91. The idea of a career for industrial workers has recently taken on the allure of significant social advance, as is shown by the terms of the labor contract signed by the Renault Motor Co. in June 1980, which explicitly provide for regular career advances for what are called production agents—actually semiskilled workers. We shall have more to say about this later.

92. In the next chapter we shall explain the procedures for moving from one wage group to another and, more generally, the way in which the pay system is administered.

93. Labor contracts require the consent of the company council whenever a worker's wage group is reclassified.

94. This is the most common situation, traditionally associated with the metal trades.

95. However, the possession of a Meister's certificate does not automatically entitle the holder to a job as foreman. As long as no such job is available, certificate holders are merely listed as eligible for promotion to foreman.

96. This type of Meister, also known as an Industrie-Meister, is found mainly in line production firms and firms engaged in transport, in which technical demands are not high. They do not supervise skilled workers.

97. This was encountered in the heavy machinery plant using unit production technology.

98. Lawrence, *Managers and Management*, p. 52, has noted that German firms tend to incorporate specialized technical knowledge into the line of authority itself (in the assistants, for example), which tends to limit the proliferation of staff positions and resulting line-staff conflicts.

99. The German firm is both a technical production unit and an administrative unit. The term *Betrieb*, which means production unit or plant, may designate a single shop or the entire company, which shows what a high value is attached to production. In Germany *plant*, as distinct from *firm*, commonly refers to a fairly autonomous production unit. Perhaps this is why technical and engineering departments seem to be subordinate to production.

100. Lawrence, among others, has shown in *Managers and Management*.

101. To become a Meister one must be at least twenty-five years of age.

102. At the end of the last century, craft apprenticeship was established by law as virtually the only kind of nonuniversity professional training. In 1955 of 790,000 apprentices in the industrial trades, only 34 percent came under the chambers of industry, the others being supervised by the council of trades. The role of master craftsmen (Handwerksmeister) in training apprentices was still very important, as most apprentices were trained in small to medium firms.

103. Steelworkers in the Ruhr used to choose the most highly regarded Meister to train their sons; our example occurred in 1974.

104. German industrial society has sometimes been called a civilization of the Meister. Though this is putting the case rather too strongly, it does indicate the central position of the Meister in the German productive system.

105. This observation is confirmed by Lawrence, *Managers and Management*, pp. 159–161.

106. Lawrence, in ibid., p. 160, notes that decisions to buy machinery are frequently made by line production managers rather than staff specialists. He also notes that shop supervisors sometimes attend machinery shows in the company of their Meister.

107. In unit production heavy equipment manufacturing plants, customer relations are quite important. The sales department will often call on the services of production officials—shop supervisors and foremen—for advice about technical questions regarding the treatment of metals or welding, for example.

108. Especially in France in technical departments that have their own internal hierarchy, and even more commonly in Great Britain, where there is a sharper dividing line between line and staff functions. See Maurice, Sorge, and Warner, "Societal Differences."

109. Although graduate engineers can fill other positions in the firm, particularly in the technical and design departments. Conversely we find some university-trained engineers in production units, more commonly in chemicals than in metallurgy.

110. There have recently been important changes in this training, suggesting to some German observes that the end of the graduate engineer is at hand. Cf. Lutz and Kammerer, *Das Ende des graduierten Ingenieurs?* (Frankfurt: EVA, 1975). This study focuses on the new graduate engineer's course, which tends to integrate the Ingenieurschule into the university more than in the past by emphasizing theoretical work at the expense of practical on-the-job training. According to the authors, this practice risks destroying the uniqueness of the graduate engineer's position in the German training system entailing changes in the way graduate engineers fit into the industrial work system.

111. In the early nineteenth century the German engineer was classed with craftsmen and technicians of modest social background. In many cases the engineer's technical training was merely a variant of craft skill decked out with esoteric scientific ornament. Wilhelm II, in response to the growing needs of industry, established schools of engineering within the universities despite the prejudice of the bourgeoisie at the time. See Organization for Economic Cooperation and Development, *Le rôle des diplômes dans l'enseignement et la vie professionnelle* (Paris: OECD, 1977), pp. 163–164; and Hortleder, *Ingenieure in der industriegesellschaft* (Frankfurt: Suhrkamp, 1973).

112. Cf. Lutz and Kammerer, *Das Ende.*

113. See ibid. and Claus Oppelt, *Ingenieure im Beruf* (Berlin: Max Planck Institut für Bildungsforschung, 1976).

114. Except in the chemical industry, in which university-trained engineers (some with doctorates) frequently hold high-level positions.

115. Since the training of graduate engineers is today more integrated into the university system than in the past, students increasingly do a worker's apprenticeship upon finishing secondary school and before entering a Fachhochschule to obtain a graduate engineer's degree. They feel their chances of finding a job are better this way than if they went to a Technische Universitat.

116. The fact that more time is devoted to technical tasks than to personnel administration does not mean that middle-level supervisors in Germany play no administrative role. This will be described presently in greater detail.

117. In this respect the VDI (Association of Chemical Engineers) plays an active

role in maintaining its members' income at a high level. University-trained engineers (and those holding the doctorate) almost automatically have the status of Leithende Angestellte (high-level management), whereas graduate engineers are divided between Leitende Angestellte and the lesser AT , or noncontract status.

118. When the firm was established these positions were filled mainly by university-trained chemists. In the past few years, however, the tendency has been to replace these with graduate engineers. Now that the real problems of chemistry have been solved, the graduate engineers are best suited to making improvements in the production process and streamlining the maintenance operation.

119. The flexibility of the system and social relations within it can be seen in the overlap of functions at all levels in the line of authority.

120. In this respect decision making is done according to a system similar to that used in Japanese firms (the Ringi system), though the Japanese system is more formalized and more generalized than the German. There is reason to believe that in Germany comanagement has fostered collegial decision making.

121. German works councils assume part of the burden of personnel management, these departments often being much smaller than their French counterparts.

122. This carries with it the title Industriekaufmann.

123. A degree in business economics.

124. A number of formulas are under discussion.

125. Among the required courses are business economics, macroeconomic and microeconomic analysis, and mathematics and statistics, personnel management, marketing, finance, and production courses are optional.

126. Most of the time-study specialists have received the REFA training, which will be described subsequently.

127. It is probably the fact that economic considerations are generally evaluated in conjunction with technological considerations that has led some observers to think that technology takes precedence over economics in the minds of German managers. Lawrence, *Managers and Management*, pp. 105–106, goes so far as to speak of a certain diseconomy in German firms. He argues that German managers think first of product quality and production technology and only secondarily of economic performance.

128. W-c employees have a certain prestige. Originally they were referred to as Privatbeamter (functionaries of private industry).

129. Which may explain why the proportion of supervisory personnel, particularly in administration and sales (and especially in unit production heavy equipment manufacturers, where these functions are highly developed), is frequently higher in Germany than in France.

130. The tube manufacturer, which operates several plants, runs a training center for supervisory personnel. At the time of our study, prospective shift leaders were sent to this center for nine-month residential courses. Planning was underway, however, to make the system more flexible in order to allow access to a larger number of candidates.

131. The rigidity of the French classificational system contributes to this compartmentalization. Production workers and maintenance workers do not have the same coefficients, to take one example. By contrast, in German firms, it is easier for workers to move from one department to another in response to changing requirements. As far as management is concerned, the ease with which a worker can make such transitions, his availability (Einsatzbreite), is important in evaluating his worth. See Lawrence, *Managers and Management*, p. 134.

132. In large firms like Renault, there are special personnel assistants whose job is to help management determine the potential of production workers. These assistants act as liaison between the personnel office and shop floor management without actually playing a supervisory role. Here, too, training generally follows promotion decisions. Once a worker is determined to have potential and is assigned to a new post, training may be offered to him. See Philippe Tresse, "La question des ressources humaines à la Regie Renault."

133. See document no. 23–7, *Les emplois d'ouvriers qualifiés de fabrication dans la mécanique* (April 1975). The author of this report notes that "the dynamics of machine-shop skill lead the skilled worker to abandon the production ship rather than remain there" (p. 146).

134. Ibid., pp. 193–94.

135. Remember how demonstrators and master workers are chosen in plants manufacturing heavy equipment. These constitute a kind of worker elite, whose long experience affords considerable skill and warrants a high level of responsibility.

136. Personnel managers and other supervisors often argue that on-the-job training is necessary regardless of the type of firm. As the personnel manger in one tube plant put it, "This is a trade that can't be learned just anywhere. There aren't many machines like ours around. The men we train stay here because they can't find the same kind of work anywhere else." The same argument was made by the personnel manager in the automobile wheel factory.

137. To date the credential most commonly held by foremen was either the CAP or the CEP, in about equal numbers. This lack of any marked preference shows how little importance firms attach to this kind of credential.

138. The fact that morale among foremen has been low in recent years has led some companies to take a fresh look at the job of foreman. The most common approach has been to accentuate the foreman's coordinating role rather than the

old stereotype of the "NCO of industry." See Xavier de Baurepaire and Herve de Saint-Germain, *Les nouvelles fonctions de la maîtrise* (Paris: Editions d'organisation, 1977).

139. Nonetechnical work took up 70 to 80 percent of their time.

140. Some firms provide foremen's assistants to relieve the foreman of part of the administrative burden and in some cases to take over part of his technical role as well.

141. This idea was introduced in a broader context by A. Touranie and C. Durand in their work on foremen. It is the basis of their theory of the countervailing power of the foreman as a buffer between the firm and its employees. See C. Durand and A. Touraine, "Le rôle compensateur des agents de maîtrise," *Sociologie du travail* (April–June 1970).

142. One of the most common complaints of French foremen is that they are bypassed by union delegates, who negotiate directly with management. On this point see J.-D. Reynaud, "Evolution récente en matière de représentation du personnel et de droit syndical," *Personnel* (1979).

143. In one of the firms we studied, the personnel manager argued that centralized social management was justified as a way of protecting the front-line managers: "You've got to protect the foremen against being shot."

144. The status of the Meister in the German firm is such as to set him apart from ordinary skilled workers. Still, though his status that of w-c worker, the Meister operates in the same skill domain as the Facharbeiter. Status differentiation occurs within a context of homogeneous professional identity. And in the end the authority of the Meister rests more on his professional qualifications than on his position in the hierarchy.

145. Lawrence, *Managers and Management*, pp. 152–61, argues that this has not afflicted the German Meister. On the basis of recent studies Lawrence concludes that the status of the Meister remains high and that there is no lack of candidates for the job of foreman as there is in other countries (p. 156).

146. The recent development of human resources management techniques has led to the systematic gathering of data on employees by the foremen, data that are then passed on to the personnel department and often kept in computerized data banks. Until now the management of this kind of information has been within the purview of the foreman, and this new development tends once again to bypass his traditional role.

147. By way of compensation for this loss of responsibility and autonomy, some companies offer shop foremen about 10 percent higher pay than technicians and maintenance foremen—in essence, foremen are paid a bonus for wielding authority on the shop floor.

148. It is sometimes forgotten that Fayol's emphasis on the unity of command principle stood in the way of acceptance in France of Taylor's idea of functionalizing authority on the shop floor. In this respect Fayol's influence on French management slowed the spread of Taylorism or modified its content. Fayol wanted both to strengthen the foremen and to retain unified command, and thus his ideas played a part in increasing the number of foremen in French firms while turning the foreman into an authoritarian overseer and thus reducing his competence to the level of the ordinary semiskilled worker.

149. Cited by Beaupaire and Saint-German, *Les nouvelles fonctions de la maîtrise,* pp. 72–73.

150. Frederick H. Harbison and Eugene W. Burgess, "Modern Management in Western Europe," *American Journal of Sociology* 60 (1954): 15–23; see also Burgess, "Management in France," in F. H. Harbison and C. A. Myers, eds., *Management in the Industrial World* (New York: McGrow-Hill, 1959); chap. 110 Harbison himself observed in 1955 that the span of control of the German Meister was higher than that of the American foreman in steel plants of comparable size and type of production. The ratio of foreman to workers averaged one to forty in Germany and one to fifteen in the United States. See F. H. Harbison, F. H. Cassel, E. Kochling, and H. C. Richmann, "Steel Management on Two Continents," *Management Science* 2(1955): 31–39.

151. In American firms the foreman is regarded as belonging to the first echelon of management.

152. Our point in mentioning this is more than one of mere historical interest. This school of thought has gained considerable influence in Europe (including Eastern Europe) and until recently has dominated a number of debates on the resources development.

153. This is a central question in the work of Raymond Boudon (and a number of other authors), which goes hand in hand with his interest in methodological individualism. Although we do not disagree (quite the contrary) with many of the points that Boudon makes, particularly in *La logique du social* (Paris: Hachette, 1979), we are inclined to adopt a somewhat different theoretical standpoint since our main interest is in the social interactions whereby the identity of the social actors is constructed and in the structure of the domain within which social relations are forged. We see our approach as a contribution to a sociology capable of taking account of both the relative autonomy of the actors and constraints imposed by the structures within which they must act.

154. Making rather free use of an idea proposed by Niklas Luhmann, for example, in "A General Theory of Organized Social Systems," in *European Contributions to Organization Theory,* ed. Geert Hofstede and Sami Kassem (1976), chap. 5. Luhmann defines position as the smallest element of analysis in the study of an organizational system.

155. For an analysis of mobility we refer readers to chapter 1. Worker mobility helps to shape the identity of the actors and thus the underlying logic of the system of authority.

156. Source: 1970 LEST study. The relatively high stability of skilled German workers is worth noting: their rate of social reproduction is 38.3 percent, compared with 24 percent in France.

157. For the period 1965–1970 (according to previously cited national studies).

158. Of the foremen, 21.5 percent were unskilled workers, and 19.8 percent skilled workers. In Germany the situation is the reverse: the figures are, respectively, 15 percent and 30 percent.

159. For an analysis of this phenomenon, see especially A. Touraine and O. Ragazzi, *Les ouvriers d'origine agricole* (Paris: Editions du Seuil, 1961).

160. Of skilled workers, 23.5 percent have a CEP, and 45.3 percent have a CAP. For the foremen, the figures are 29.1 percent and 40 percent, respectively. Based on 1970 nationwide survey.

161. Here and elsewhere, the notion of substitution, in the sense of functional substitute (crucial to functionalism) is not pertinent to our work because the firm in the example is an actor of quite another kind in relation to the educational system, which is also different. We use the term only by way of drawing a broad analogy.

162. Clearly we are proposing and avenue of research apparently neglected by both economists and sociologists. Cf. Charles Perrow, Random House, Inc. *Complex Organizations: A Critical Essay*, 2d (New York: Random House, Inc., 1979) pp. 237–247. Perrow gives succinct accounts of these approaches along with what he calls "ethno-Marxism," which he sees as perhaps pointing the way toward a revitalization of the sociology of organizations, though he does not make explicit what he has in mind.

163. Cf. Howard W. Aldrich, *Organization and Environments* (Englewood Cliffs, N. J.: Prentice-Hall, 1979), chap. 2 for another account of the ecological approach.

164. Traditionally this joint role has manifested itself in the chambers of commerce and industry and the Berufschule, as well as in the trilateral committees in which occupational training policies are discussed.

165. In the next chapter.

166. Here are some statistics regarding pay differences between workers and foremen in the two countries:

1970 national statistics for all industry:
Skilled workers (100)
Foremen (France): 138
Foremen (Germany): 127

LEST study (1977)
Petrochemical firms:

	France	Germany
Unskilled workers	100	100
Skilled workers	128	132
Foremen	196	168
Metals		
Unskilled workers	100	100
Skilled workers	138	120
Foremen	190	158

167. The variation due to technology does not seem to be closely related to these differences. The authority structure seems to vary with technology even less in French firms than in German firms.

168. By contrast, in Germany technical and professional values outweigh social-normative values.

169. Here we are borrowing an idea put forward by J.-D. Reynaud, "Conflit et régulation sociale: esquisse d'une théorie de la régulation conjointe," *Revue Française de sociologie* 20 (1979): 367–376.

170. The relative stability of the authority system is in fact related to the interaction of socialization, organization, and social relations.

171. Here we want to distinguish between middle and upper management. Collective bargaining agreements generally specify which employees are to be regarded as middle management.

172. The difference is even more pronounced if we look at large firms (employing more than 500 workers), where more than 55 percent of upper management personnel have college degrees, compared with only 25 percent in Germany.

173. Cf. Agnès Pitrou, "Un processus de récupération du statut social: le cas des cadres non diplômés," *Sociologie du travail* 1 (1977); see also Christian de Montliber, "L'éducation permanente et la promotion des classes moyennes," *Sociologie du travail* 3 (1977).

174. In this respect the system resembles the Japanese. In Japan firms hire many employees who have no training other than what they received in secondary school or college. They then socialize these employees with a complex system of internal training and performance-based promotions, winning employee loyalty by offering fairly good job security. Such a simplistic comparison ignores the many cultural, historical, and political differences between the two countries and obscures the significance of the features of each system. Still it does suggest that the economist's approach, which assumes that the market brings training, skills, and jobs into equilibrium, needs to be modifed to take account of cultural factors.

175. This relatively high figure is due to the fact that college graduates are generally accorded the status of Leitende Angestellte in German chemicals companies.

176. These remarks hold true for social mobility and educational mobility (mobility that takes place within the system of education and training), as well as occupational mobility.

177. A number of empirical studies have shown that French company presidents are older on the average than their German counterparts.

Chapter 3

1.

Share of personnel Costs in net value of production (%)

Sector	Germany	France
Foundry	68	68
Rubber-asbestos	60	57
Cement	36	35
Farm machinery	57	58
Plastics	53	53
Electrical construction	63	61
Clocks, optics, precision machine work	64	66

Source: P. Temple and J. J. Branchu, "Industries allemandes et françaises: Charges d'exploitation et productivités semblables." *Economie et statistiques* (1973): 7.

2. L. Seifert and H. Uebale, *Berufsbildung in Grossunternehmem* (Göttingen, 1974), p. 48.

3. H. Popitz, H. P. Bardt, E. A. Jures, and H. Kesting, *Das Gesellschaftsbild des Arbeiters* (Tübingen, 1957).

4. These remarks are borrowed from Michel Brossard, a Canadian student at LEST in 1974–1975, who took part in the study of French and German petrochemical plants. Readers may wish to consult his thesis, "La structure de l'organisation du travail dans l'entreprise et les pouvoirs dans le système de relations industrielles" (Faculté des Sciences Economiques, Universite d'Aix-Marseille II).

5. "Productivity has a pejorative connotation and is a term rarely used by personnel managers," according to A. Rosanvallon and J. F. Troussier, "Les primes dans le salaire ouvrier," *Revue française des affaires sociales* (July–September 1974).

6. On England see the thesis by François Reynaud, "Les différences franco-britanniques de salaires et de classifications" (Faculté des Sciences Economiques de l'Université d'Aix-Marseille II and LEST-ONRS, 1981).

7. E. Teschner, V. Mosler, and E. Schublich, "Aspekte betrieblicher Lohnpolitik," mimeographed (Frankfurt: Frankfurt Institut für Sozialforschung, Goethe Universität) pp. 12, 49, 58.

8. See our article, "La fonction de négociation dans la codécision 'simple' en Allemagne Fédérale," *Droit social* 11 (1972): 487ff.; and J. M. Luttringer, *La place du synidcat dans l'entreprise alllemande (RFA)* (Paris: Economica, 1979), p. 146.

9. Popitz et al., *Das Gesellschaftsbild.*

10. Cf. R. Boyer and J. Mistral, *Accumulation, Inflation, Crises* (Paris: Presses Universitaires de France, 1978), pp. 149, 240.

11. Douglas Miller, "Die betriebliche Präsenz von Gewerkschäften in der BDR," *Soziale Welt* 3 (1979): 340.

12. Since the time when France began to feel the effects of a high rate of inflation, labor accords have begun to indicate specific dates (generally quarterly) when wage increases are supposed to take effect or when the situation is supposed to be reexamined. But the basic principle is still that contracts are of unlimited duration.

13. Miller, "Die betriebliche Präsenz," pp. 336−342.

14. Cf. G. Hofmann, "Die Handschrift des Kanzlers," *Die Zeit*, 8 August 1980.

15. The following analysis is not vitiated by the spate of wildcat strikes that occurred in 1969 and again in 1978−1979 since the unions managed to regain control of the situation fairly quickly.

16. Imperfectly, given that there is a time lag in adjusting wages to price indexes.

17. H. Markmann, "Les grèves spontanées de l'automne 1969 dans la RFA," in G. S. Spitaels, *Les conflits sociaux en Europe; grèves sauvages, contestation, rajeunissement des structures* (Paris: Marabout, 1971), p. 14.

18. Notes of the Ministry of Labor, Employment, and Population, 27 March−2 April 1972, table 2, Ministry of Labor, Paris, 1972.

19. Personnel managers sometimes complain that they cannot obtain some of the information they should have.

20. In companies operating several plants, the central company council is known as the Gesamtbetriebsrat, or firm-wide council.

21. Except in the case where no election is held in a firm covered by the law.

22. See Luttringer, "La place," P. 196.

23. Cited by Miller, "Das betriebliche Präsenz," p. 335.

24. Not to be confused with comanagement (laws of 1951 and 1976); see below for further details.

25. Miller, "Das betriebliche Präsenz."

26. Luttringer, "La place," p. 149.

27. Cf. J. C. Javiller, *Droit du travail* (Paris, 1970). Note, however, that the situation may be improved by the terms of the contract.

28. Directives for the Vertrauensleute of the Chemical, Paper, and Ceramic Workers Union, issued by the union directorate on 29 September 1972. See I. G. Chemie-Papier-Keramic Sätzung 1972, p. 81.

29. Miller, "Das betriebliche Präsenz," p. 336.

30. F. Furstenberg, "Der Betriebsrat, Strukturanalyse einer Grensituation," *Kölner Zeitschrift fur Soziologie und Sozial Psychologie* (1958), pp. 418ff.

Chapter 4

1. The fact that every position in the organization, from the top to the bottom of the hierarchy, is assigned a coefficient is more than just a simple administrative tool; it reflects the presumption that there are no insuperable barriers to mobility, the notion that all careers are open to talent.

2. Our work is not concerned primarily with society as a whole but with industrial workers. Still, differences between the two countries with respect to work force stratification are inseparable from broader social differences.

3. We have not been interested primarily in the determinants of labor productivity, particularly since there is no striking difference between the two countries in this respect.

4. Particularly in chapter 1, section 1.3 and table 1.4, where we emphasized that wage inequalities in industry are markedly greater in France than in Germany, no matter what distinctions we make (manual versus nonmanual, skilled versus unskilled, supervisory versus nonsupervisory, and so forth).

5. Manual or nonmanual workers; office or production workers; differences between sectors of the economy; differences between large firms and subcontractors.

6. In regard to industrial organization, it is possible to conjecture that workplace relations are affected by the structure of industry. In Germany, for example, is it not the case that the distinctive characteristics of the skilled worker as we have described him have something to do with the fact that much of German industry is patterned after the machine tool sector? By contrast, the fact that in France the average worker is less skilled and the average manager or engineer more highly trained than his German counterpart may have something to do with the vitality of high technology industries in France coupled with the large, inert mass of labor-intensive traditional industries using relatively unskilled workers. In other words

French industry is polarized between two extreme models, whereas German industry clusters around a single center, machine tools. This argument is largely speculative, but still we can carry it one step further. It may be that multinational corporations, by pursuing their various strategies, do not contribute to bringing about industrial convergence as has been argued. Rather they may accentuate differences between different societies by using existing social resources as opportunities to be seized. In order to develop the comparison between the different German and French social patterns to the full, we would have to take account of complementary socioeconomic interchange between the two countries.

7. Although it is true that polyvalence is not widespread in either France or Germany, it does provide a good test case for comparing the different ways in which firms in the two countries view worker skill and qualifications.

8. The foreman's license explicitly recognizes his role as a trainer of other men. As part of his job he encourages the workers under him to sign up for courses organized by the company or in conjunction with the chambers of industry. A Meister's prestige dervies not only from his own training but also from the reputation of workers he trained.

9. The distinction is not altogether satisfactory, though it does suggest certain fundamental differences in methods of work force organization and management. We do not mean to imply that there is no professionalization of the French work force or that bureaucratic management techniques are not practiced in German firms. Our point is merely to suggest in a few words what otherwise would have required a long digression: professionalism in the workers is shaped by the firm's conception of what is rational.

10. Especially the recent reclassification of the metal trades. See F. Eyraud, "La fin des classifications Parodi," *Sociologie du travail* 3 (1978).

11. The recent (2 June 1980) renewal of Renault's labor contract incorporates a change that management considered essential. In order to provide for career advancement in the case of production agents (the new term for semiskilled assembly line workers), the most poorly paid of the company's employees, it was stipulated that they could be granted wage increases according to seniority. In other words, promotion by experience is now permitted, and this makes it possible for the company to raise a man's coefficient from 167 to 179 (the equivalent of an OP1) without changing his job. Doubtless this is an important innvoation, but it changes nothing in the logic of the system we have described. That it has been described as a crucial element of this accord shows clearly the limits of what has been acheived: the semiskilled worker's career is more an administrative convenience that a reflection of his broadened professional skills. The company rewards time spent on the job, regardless of whether that time has been used to acquire new skills.

12. This type of polyvalence recalls Georges Friedmann's analysis of the "pluri-specialized worker" (the semiskilled worker capable of performing a number of specialized tasks). According to Friedmann, this type of worker has increasingly been supplanting the traditional multiskilled professional craftsman, the true polyvalent. As Friedmann saw it, the pluri-specialized worker might well move from one job to another but without really acquiring new skills. If a worker's qualifications are to be upgraded, he not only has to learn a variety of jobs but also must acquire knowledge of new techniques. See Friedmann, *Le travail en miettes* (Paris, 1956). pp. 41–47.

13. Under the terms of the comanagement agreement, employee delegates have this right of control.

14. To borrow an expression from Michel Brossard, op. cit. pp. 361, 374. Brossard stresses what he calls the individualization of wages in Germany, where greater heed is paid than in France to the individual productive capacity of each worker.

15. There are grading and bonus systems that make it possible in theory to tailor each worker's pay to his productive contribution. But individual supplements of this kind tend to loss their effectiveness, either because they are awarded automatically or because unions are able to have the criteria for awarding them depersonalized. All workers receive the same bonus, or the bonus becomes a part of a worker's base pay. This is also a consequence of centralized personnel management, which leaves little or no autonomy to foremen, who are in the best position to evaluate each worker's individual contribution.

16. To borrow an expression of Brossard, op. cit., pp. 373–374.

17. In a number of the firms we looked at, including the Renault plant, foremen were assisted by so-called personnel assistants, whose job was to represent the personnel office at the shop level, following up individual and group performance and identifying workers with good potential for promotion.

18. Training then becomes an issue for the unions, which try to have training standards included in labor contracts. Their objective is to limit the employer's options by setting objective standards for promotion, as well as to champion training offered by the public schools in order to democratize access to teaching and keep employers from establishing a monopoly over the traning system. See Eyraud, "La fin des classifications Parodi," for an analysis of the recent negotiations over reforms in the classification system, which discusses the issues and the respective strategies of unions and management.

19. See Tresse, "La gestion des ressources humaines à la Régie Renault," p. 475: "Training offered by the company is geared to promotions and job assignments. The assignment generally determines the type of training offered. Training generally determines the type of training offered. Training generally follows a decision to move a man to new job.... Whether the change amounts merely to a shift to a

new position or to a genuine promotion, a mew job assignment is the main reason for sending a man to receive additional training."

20. In some firms skilled workers who hold a Meister's license are listed as eligible for promotion to Meister if a post should become available.

21. In Max Weber's view, bureaucracy, with its formalized rules and procedures, has a homogenizing effect that tends to foster equality, in the sense of reliance on impartial standards of selection and promotion. See Seymour Martin Lipset, *Political Man* (New York: Doubleday, 1960). In France, however, the introduction of such impartial standards in the name of a certain conception of democracy has resulted in a kind of pyrrhic victory, usually serving to make organizations and institutions more inflexible than they need to be.

22. In law a distinction is made between contractual qualification and personal qualification.

23. Strikes by semiskilled workers, particularly at Renault, are the best example of this.

24. See Eyraud, "La fin du système Parodi," p. 265.

25. For example, in France the dividing line between production and maintenance is more clearly drawn than in Germany.

26. This is undoubtedly an example of what Crozier has called a vicious circle, one of the causes of bureauratic inflexibility.

27. This is true in both Germany and France.

28. As we saw in chapter 2, the processes that help to shape the professional qualifications of the workers are relatively independent of technology.

29. This line of argument is developed by Joan Woodward in *Industrial organization: Behavior and Control* (Oxford: Oxford University Press, 1970), a book less well known than her 1965 work, *Industrial Organization: Theory and Practice.* (Oxford: Oxford University Press).

30. If the firm goes beyond those limits, it may be that it risks having an adverse effect on its performance.

31. The distinction is a crude one and is intended only to bring out certain important characteristics of each situation.

32. In this connection, we believe that the analysis we are developing here can help us to study history with an eye to discovering evidence of the kinds of structures that figure in our discussion.

33. This is reflected in the downgrading of b-c jobs and in the aspiration of young workers to find w-c employment as office employees, middle managers, civil servants, or even as craftsmen and small shopkeepers.

34. Although it is commonplace in France to here German unions accused of reformism, this does not translate into weakness.

35. Among supervisory personnel in line production firms, we find that 57 percent are foremen in France compared with only 34 percent in Germany, whereas only 16 percent are technicians in France compared with 26 percent in Germany.

36. The German word *technik* refers to production work in industry as well as to the associated knowledge and skills. See Peter Lawrence, *Managers and Management in West Germany*

37. A. L. Stinchcombe, "Social Structure and Organization," in James G. March, ed., *Handbook of Organizations* (New York: Rard McNally and Company, 1965), pp. 142–69, shows that, historically, the human resources available in different countries at different times had a large effect on the kinds of organizations that developed and on the ability of those organizations to survive social changes.

38. This kind of analysis has much in common with the work of Amitai Etzioni, *Modern Organizations* (New York: Free Press, 1964), pp. 68–70.

39. As a result workers tend to be autodidacts, and the employers' ideology stresses integration into the firm.

40. The factors that help to shape the collective identity of the workers are influenced by working-class solidarity and forms of collective action.

41. The bulk of these are not management personnel.

42. Gérard Sandoz, "Les organisations syndicales menacées par le lockout patronal," *Documents, revue des questions allemandes* 2 (1980): 9.

43. See René Lasserre, "Vers une co-gestion concertée de l'économie," *Revue des questions allemandes* 3 (1980): 110.

Appendix

1. Irving Fisher lays particular stress on this instantaneous definition of capital. See *The Nature of Capital and Income* (New York: Augvstvs M. Kelley Publishers, 1906).

2. Here we are thinking of Georges Gurvitch, who wrote that "every social class, every particular group, every element of a microsocial structure, in short, every We and every relation between Us and Others, every stratum of society, and even every social activity (whether religious, economic, technological, cognitive, moral, or educational) tends to move according to a time of its own.... The structure of time is affected by the social setting as much as the social setting is affected by the structure of time." See Gurvitch, *La vocation actuelle de la sociologie* (Paris: Presses universitaires de France, 1963), 2:325–327.

3. This does not mean that the temporality we have in mind here is not socially

constructed, for the market not only defines the value of time but determines its qualitative nature.

4. The most complete and systematic presentations of neoclassical theory lay special stress on the following important point: that the concept of economic behavior is inextricably intertwined with the notion of rational behavior. See, for example, Milton Friedman, *Theory of Prices* (1974) or E. Malinvaud, *Lecon de microeconomie* (Dunod: 1974). The principles of diminishing marginal utility, marginal efficiency, and income maximization can govern the behavior of an economic agent only to the extent that he is incorporated into the domain of capital.

5. Substitution of one form of investment for another is the concrete manifestation of this equivalence as well as a reflection of the unity of the concept capital.

6. For a more detailed analysis of these effects, see J. J. Silvestre, *Les inégalités de salaires* (Paris: Presses universitaires de France, 1978), p. 2, chap. 2.

7. See, for example, the following works: E. S. Phelps et al., *Microeconomic Foundations of Employment and Inflation Theory* (London: Macmillan, 1970); M. Spence, "Job Market Signaling," *Quarterly Journal of Economics* (1973); and G. Stiglitz, "Approaches of the Economics of Discrimination," *American Economic Review* (1973). Though fairly old, these works exemplify a type of theory that has been steadily refined over the past few years and has correspondingly gained increasing influence.

8. In the most recent formulations of the theory of consumer behavior, information plays a crucial role in capital formation. The consumer, according to L. Levy-Garboua, "must first perceive the qualities of objects, one after another, before he can evaluate them, before he can 'construct' an indirect estimate of their utility." See L. Levy-Garboua, "La nouvelle théorie du consommateur et la formation des choix," *Consommation* 3 (1976).

9. There are two aspects to the relationship of mobility, investment, and income. Mobility requires the worker to divert some of his income away from consumption and into investment, and it results in an increase not only in his employer's capital stock but in society's as well.

10. See Fritz Machlup, *Essais de sémantique économique* (Paris: Calmann-Lévy, 1971).

11. G. S. Becker, *Human Capital* (New York: Columbia University Press, 1964).

12. This can be done, for example, by introducing the notion of discriminatory preference into the theory of the labor market. See G. S. Becker, *The Economics of Discrimination* (Chicago: University of Chicago Press, 1971).

13. Karl Marx, *Capital* (New York: International Publishers: 1967), pp. 39, 73 (bk. I, sec. I).

14. The social relations to which Marxist theorists commonly attach so much importance are thus identified with market relations and have no autonomous existence.

15. J. P. de Gaudemar, "Mobilité du travail et accumulation du capital," *Economie et socialisme* 28 (1976).

16. Ibid., p. 125.

17. Ibid., p. 162. "In Marx's writing, the hypothetical possibility of perfect labor mobility is said to be a tendency inherent in the capitalist mode of production, nothing more."

18. Michel Aglietta, "Panorama sur les théories de l'emploi," *Revue economique* 19 (1978): 80–119.

19. "The production of use value," Marx says, "consists in the movement of useful labor. The labor process here appears under the aspect of quality."

20. Gaudemar, "Mobilité du travail," p. 135.

21. Michel Aglietta, *Régulation et crise du capitalisme: l'expérience des Etats Unis* (Paris: Calmann-Lévy, 1976).

22. Ibid., p. 35.

23. R. Edwards, D. Gordon, and M. Reich, "A Theory of the Labor Market," *American Economic Review* (May 1973).

24. Aglietta, "Panorama."

25. J. Mathiot, *Salaire et reproduction: reexamens de la théorie du salariat* (Lyon: Presses universitaires de Lyon, 1981).

26. P. Doeringer and M. Piore, *Internal Market and Manpower Analysis* (Lexington, Mass: D. C. Heath, 1971); M. Piore, "Notes for a Theory of Labor Market Stratification," working paper no. 95 (Cambridge: MIT, October 1972).

27. Looking at the question in this way leads to circular arguments. The supply of labor is said to be shaped by the demand. Wages are rigid and define rather than reward qualifications. Everything seems to be indeterminate, whereas other approaches show that there is a stable, coherent, and rational system.

28. Bernard Mottez, *La sociologie industrielle* (Paris: Presses universitaires de France, 1971), p. 74.

29. Ibid., p. 74.

30. *L'évolution du travail ouvrier aux Usines Renault* (Paris: Centre National de Recherche Scientifique, 1955).

31. What is called industrial sociology in Great Britain in part covers the same ground as the sociology of labor in France, Germany, and Italy. Cf. Lucien Karpik, "Trois concepts sociologiques: le projet de référence, le statut social et le bilan individuel," *Archives européennes de sociologie* 6 (1965): 115—128.

32. See John Goldthorpe et al., *The Affluent Workers: Industrial Attitudes and Behavior* (Cambridge: Cambridge University Press, 1968).

33. See Alain Touraine and Orietta Ragazzi, *Ouvriers d'origine agricole* (Paris: Editions du Seuil, 1961).

34. See Robert Blauner, *Alienation and Freedom: The Factory Worker and His Industry* (Chicago: University of Chicago Press, 1964). Blauner holds that some technologies and some industries are more alienating than others.

35. See David Silverman, *The Theory of Organizations* (London: Heinemann, 1972), pp. 184—185.

36. H. Hugues, *Men and Their Work* (Glencoe, Ill.: Free Press, 1958); H. S. Becker and J. W. Carper, "The Elements of Identification with an Occupation," *American Sociological Review* 21 (1956): 341—347; H. S. Becker and J. W. Carper, "The Development of Identification with an Occupation," *American Journal of Sociology* 61 (1956): 289—298.

37. Cf. Harold L. Wilenski, "The Professionalization of Everyone," *American Journal of Sociology* (1964): 137—158.

38. To use an expression of Silverman, *Theory of Organizations*, p. 213. This work contains a brief account of the work of the Chicago school in the sociology of labor.

39. Here we are using this notion broadly to refer to the relative stability or durability of a society's components, such as the state of social relations or the cultural system.

40. The main features of this line of analysis can be found in two reports to the Ministry of Labor prepared by Pierre Rolle and Pierre Tripier and their collaborators at the Université de Paris X: *Le mouvement des qualifications* (1979), and *Le mouvement des qualifications des informaticiens* (1980).

41. See especially *La vie de travail et ses problèmes* (Paris: Armand Colin, 1954) and *Essai sur la qualification du travail* (Paris: Rivière, 1956).

42. As Crozier and Friedberg do in *L' acteur et le système* (Paris: Editions du Seuil, 1977). An English translation of this book by the translator of the present work was published in 1981 by the University of Chicago Press as *Actors and Systems*. References here are to the French edition.

43. "Individus et organisations: évolution des conceptions et des modes d'analyse," *Sociologie du travail* 3 (1965).

44. See Crozier and Friedberg, *L'acteur et le système*, p. 84.

45. Although this school's representatives are found mainly in the English-speaking countries, France can claim Jean-Daniel Reynaud, though he is more inclined than his English and American colleagues to acknowledge that both parties to a conflict may be behaving rationally. See his "Conflits et negociation sociale; esquisse d'une théorie de la régulation conjointe," *Revue française de sociologie* (June 1979).

46. "Lecture actuelle de Durkheim," *Archives européennes de sociologie* (1963: 1–36, cited by Touraine, *La conscience ouvrière*, p. 55.

47. Ibid.

48. See Crozier and Friedberg, *L'acteur et le système*, chap. 4, for a critical account of this line of research, which has also been criticized by M. Maurice and M. Brossard, "Existe-t-il un modele universel des structures d'organisation?" *Sociologie du travail* 4 (1974).

49. This has been pointed out by S. B. Bacharach and E. J. Lawler, *Power and Politics in Organizations* (London: Jossey-Bass, 1980).

50. Peter M. Blau and Richard A. Schoenherr, *The Structure of Organizations* (New York: Basic Books, 1971), p. viii. Focusing primarily on structures, these authors explain their choice in this way: "The implicit assumption in this approach is that formal organizations, along with other social structures, manifest regularities which can be analyzed in themselves, apart from any knowledge of the behavior of their individual members.

51. According to which "technological requirements, via the performance constraint, determine organizational structures," to use Crozier and Friedberg's description in *L'acteur et le système*, p. 116.

52. Woodward, *Industrial Organization: Behavior and Control* (London: Oxford University Press, 1970).

53. Perrow, *Organizational Analysis*, p. 80.

54. A term used by the proponents of a structural approach to organization theory. Cf., among others, D. H. Hickson et al., "The Culture-Free Context of Organization Structure: A Trinational Comparison," *Sociology* 8 (1974): 59–81; and "Grounds for Comparative Organization Theory," in J. D. Hickson and C. J. Lammers, eds., *Organizations Alike and Unlike* (London: Routledge and Kegan Paul), 1979.

55. The notion of a societal effect is more heuristic than theoretical, though it is intended to indicate that our theoretical preference is to work from the specific toward the general.

56. "Organization: A Choice for Man," in John Child, ed., *Man and Organization* (London: Allen and Unwin, 1973).

57. Cf. J. Kenneth Benson, "Organizations: A Dialectical View," *Administrative Science Quarterly* 22 (1977): 1–21; see also Perrow, *Complex Organizations*.

58. A. L. Stinchcombe, "Social Structure and Organizations," in March, *Handbook of Organizations*, pp. 142–193.

59. Which has inspired, among others, Howard E. Aldrich, *Organizations and Environments* (Englewood Cliffs, N.J.: Prentice-Hall, 1979).

60. A fuller account of this theory may be found in M. Maurice, "For a Study of the Societal Effect: Universality and Specificity in Organization Research," in Lammers and Hickson, eds., *Organizations Alike and Unlike*, chap. 3.

61. Similar to Crozier and Friedberg's interpretation; see *L'acteur et le système*, p. 125.

62. Crozier, *Le phénomène bureaucratique*, p. 307.

63. Ibid., p. 308.

64. "Sentiments, organisations, et systèmes," *Revue francaise de sociologie* 11–12 (1970–1971): 149–150.

65. Crozier and Friedberg, *L'acteur et le système*, chap. 6.

66. Ibid., p. 191.

67. Ibid., p. 179.

68. Crozier, "Sentiments," p. 150.

69. Ibid., p. 150.

70. Crozier and Friedberg, *L'acteur et le système*, pp. 251–253.

71. Ibid., p. 9.

72. Epistemologically these notions tend to homogenize the domain of analysis by reducing the objects analyzed to their own terms.

73. Crozier and Friedberg, *L'acteur et le système*, p. 411.

74. Ibid., p. 406.

75. Boudon, *La logique du social*, p. 234.

76. Adam and Reynaud, *Conflits du travail et changement social*, p. 165.

77. Ibid., p. 236.

78. To borrow Boudon's title.

79. In this respect the works of Bourdieu and his followers represent a brand of sociology attractive to those hostile to structuralist Marxism who believe that

individuals enjoy some measure of autonomy and some capacity to make social innovations.

80. Our objective is not to provide an exegesis of this idea. Interested readers may refer to the critical accounts by François Bourricaud, "Contre le sociologisme: une critique et des propositions," *Revue francaise de sociologie* 16 (1975): 583–603, and more recently, Michel de Certeau, *L'Invention du quotidien* (Paris: Union générale de l'edition, 1980), vol. 1, chap. 4. See also Alain Caille, "La sociologie de l'intérêt est-elle intéressante?" *Sociologie du travail* 3 (1981): 257–274.

81. Certeau, *L'invention*, p. 118.

82. Bourdieu deliberately does not speak of actors. Rather he refers to individuals as socialized bodies in order to make clear that there is no sharp, dividing line between the individual and society. See *Questions de sociologie* (Paris: Editions de Minuit, 1981), p. 29.

83. In particular by Bourricaud, "Contre le sociologisme," p. 590.

84. Bourdieu, *Questions*, p. 135. Using an analogy with a computer program, Bourdieu suggests that the habitus is a sort of self-correcting program, capable of solving problems "in infinitely many ways not directly deducible from the conditions under which it was produced."

85. Ibid., p. 29.

86. In scholastic philosophy habitus is a form of property or capital; see ibid., p. 134.

87. Ibid., p. 135.

80. Ibid.

89. Ibid., p. 136.

90. Apart from differences of theoretical orientation, these authors may well be in substantial agreement when it comes to their theories of power. For Bourdieu power grows out of class relations, whereas Crozier holds that power is itself a kind of social relation. Accordingly Bourdieu envisions the possibility of turning economic capital into social capital, and vice, versa, whereas Crozier tries to subsume the diversity of social relations under the single head of power relations.

91. For Bourdieu opportunities are determined by class structures, whereas for Crozier and Friedberg they result from the essentially random and indeterminate character of human action.

92. This analysis points up the paradoxes implicit in the system, to borrow from the title of Yves Barel, *Le paradoxe et le système* (Grenoble: Presses universitaires de Grenoble, 1979). This stimulating book sets forth what may prove to be an interesting new approach to the social sciences (similar in some respects to Edgar Morin's recent work). For example, in regard to the relation of individual to

society, Barel has this to say: "An individual, like a society, has a potential universality which can only be conceptualized after the fact. The paradox, for society as well as the individual, is that the universal can only manifest itself in a singular form. This has two consequences: not only is there no universal expression of the universal, but what is expressed in a particular form need not be the expression of a particularity."

93. Pierre Laroque, *Les rapports entre patrons et ouvriers* (Paris, 1938).

94. Clark Kerr and Abraham Siegel, "The Interindustry Propensity to Strike: An International Comparison," in Kornhauser, Dubin, and Ross, eds., *Industrial Conflict* (New York: McGraw-Hill, 1954), chap. 14.

95. Clark Kerr and Abraham Siegel, "The Structuring of the Labor Force in Industrial Society: New Dimensions and New Questions," *Industrial and Labor Relations Review* (January 1955).

96. Much of the material in the next few pages has been taken from Kerr et al., *Industrialism and Industrial Man*, especially from the afterword to the 1973 Penguin reprint, pp. 279ff., esp. p. 292.

97. The authors repeatedly use the word we have italicized.

98. J. T. Dunlop, *Industrial Relations Systems* (Carbondale, Ill.: Southern Illinois University Press, 1958).

99. Touraine, *La conscience ouvrière*, p. 17.

100. D. Vidal, "Pouvoir et action syndicale," in G. Dion et al., eds., *Pouvoir et pouvoirs en relation du travail* (Quebec, 1971), pp. 127–38, reprinted in F. Sellier, *Relations industrielles: choix de textes commentés* (Paris: Presses Universitaires de France, 1976), pp. 100ff.

101. Marx, *Capital*, book 1, sec. 3.

102. Aglietta's remarks are taken from his book *Régulation et crises du capitalisme*, pp. 93ff.

103. A. Azouvi, "Théorie et pseudo-théorie: le dualisme du marché du travail" (mimeographed), p. 93.

104. Dunlop, *Industrial Relations Systems*.

105. Reynaud, "Conflits et négociation sociale," p. 371.

106. Reynaud, "Conflits du travail, classes sociales et contrôle social," *Sociologie du Travail* 1(1980): 103.

107. In the remainder of the text, citations are identified by initial, indicating either the title or the publisher.

108. Adam and Reynaud, *Conflits du travail*, pp. 237–238.

Index